SIRIS:

A CHAIN of

PHILOSOPHICAL REFLEXIONS

AND

INQUIRIES

Concerning the VIRTUES of

TAR WATER,

And divers other SUBJECTS connected together and arising one from another.

BY THE
Right Rev. Dr. GEORGE BERKELEY.
Lord Bishop of CLOYNE,
And Author of *The Minute Philosopher*.

As we have opportunity, let us do good unto all men. Gal. vi. 10.
Hoc opus, hoc studium, parvi properemus et ampli. Hor.

A NEW EDITION,
With ADDITIONS and EMENDATIONS.

DUBLIN Printed,
LONDON Re-printed,
For W. INNYS, and C. HITCH, in *Pater-noster-row*, and C. DAVIS in *Holbourn*. MDCCXLVII.
[Price Two Shillings.]

A Letter to T. P. *Esq. from the Author of* Siris.

AMONG the great numbers who drink Tar-water in Dublin, your letter informs me there are several, that make it too weak or too strong, or use it in an undue manner. To obviate these inconveniences, and render this water as generally useful as possible, you desire I would draw up some rules and remarks, in a small compass; which accordingly I here send you.

Norwegian tar being the most liquid, mixeth best with water. Put a gallon of cold water to a quart of this tar, stir and work them very strongly together, with a flat stick, for about four minutes. Let the vessel stand covered forty eight hours, that the tar may subside. Then pour off the clear water, and keep it close covered, or rather bottled, and well stopped, for use. This may do for a general rule; but as stomachs and constitutions are so various, for particular persons, their own experience is the best rule. The stronger the better; provided the stomach can bear it. Less water or more stirring makes it stronger; as more water, and less stirring makes it weaker. The same tar will not do quite so well a second time, but may serve for common uses.

Tar-water, when right, is not higher than French, nor deeper coloured, than Spanish white wine. If there be not a spirit very sensibly perceived on drinking, you may conclude, the tar water is not good. If you would have it good, see it made yourself. Those who begin with it, little and weak, may, by habit, come to drink more and stronger. According to the season of the year, or the humour of the patient, it may be taken, cold or warm.

As to the quantity, in chronical cases, one pint of tar-water a day may suffice, taken on an empty stomach, at two, or four times; to wit, night and morning; and about two hours after dinner and breakfast. Alteratives, in general, taken little and often, mix best with the blood. How oft, or how strong, each stomach can bear, experience will shew: nor is there any danger in making the experiment. Those who labour under old habitual illnesses, must have great patience and perseverance in the use of this, as well as in all other medicines; which, if sure and safe, must yet be slow in chronical disorders; which, if grievous or inveterate, may require a full quart every day to be taken, at six doses, one third of a pint in each, with a regular diet. In acute cases, as fevers, of all kinds, it must be drank warm in bed, and in great quantity; perhaps a pint every hour, till the patient be relieved; which I have known to work surprizing cures.

My experiments have indeed been made within a narrow compass; but as this water is now grown into publick use (though it seems not without that opposition which is wont to attend novelty) I make no doubt, its virtues will be more fully discovered. Mean while, I must own myself persuaded, from what I have already seen and tryed, that tar water may be drunk with great safety and success, in the cure or relief of most if not all diseases, in ulcers, eruptions, and all foul cases; scurvies of all kinds, disorders of the lungs, stomach, and bowels; in nervous cases, in all inflammatory distempers; in decays, and other maladies: Nor is it of use only in the cure of sickness; it is also used to preserve health, and a guard against infection and old age; as it gives lasting spirits, and invigorates the blood. I am even induced, by the nature and analogy of things, and its wonderful success in all kinds of fevers, to think, that tar water may be very useful in the plague, both as a cure and preservative.

But, I doubt no medicine can withstand that execrable plague of distilled spirits, which operate as a slow poison, preying on the vitals, and wasting the health and strength of the body and soul; which pest of human kind, is, I am told, by the attempts of our * Whisky patriots, gaining ground in this wretched country, already too thin of inhabitants. I am, &c.

* Whisky *is a spirit distilled from malt, the making of which poison, cheap and plenty, as being of our growth, is esteemed, by some unlucky patriots, a benefit to their country*

SIRIS:

A CHAIN of PHILOSOPHICAL REFLEXIONS AND INQUIRIES, &c.

FOR INTRODUCTION to the following piece I assure the reader, that nothing could, in my present situation, have induced me to be at the pains of writing it, but a firm belief that it would prove a valuable present to the public. What entertainment soever the reasoning or notional part may afford the mind, I will venture to say, the other part seemeth so surely calculated to do good to the body, that both must be gainers. For if the lute be not well tuned, the musician fails of his harmony. And in our present state, the operations of the mind, so far depend on the right tone or good condition of it's instrument, that any thing which greatly contributes to preserve or recover the health of the body, is well worth the attention of the mind. These considerations have moved me to communicate to the public the salutary virtues of tar-water; to which I thought myself indispensably obliged, by the duty every man owes to mankind. And, as effects are linked with their causes, my thoughts on this low, but useful theme, led to farther inquiries, and those on to others, remote perhaps, and speculative, but, I hope, not altogether useless or unentertaining.

1. In

1. IN certain parts of America, tar-water is made by putting a quart of cold water to a quart of tar, and stirring them well together in a vessel, which is left standing till the tar sinks to the bottom. A glass of clear water being poured off for a draught is replaced by the same quantity of fresh water, the vessel being shaken and left to stand as before. And this is repeated for every glass, so long as the tar continues to impregnate the water sufficiently, which will appear by the smell and taste. But as this method produceth tar-water of different degrees of strength, I chuse to make it in the following manner: Pour a gallon of cold water on a quart of tar, and stir and mix them thoroughly with a ladle or flat stick for the space of three or four minutes, after which the vessel must stand eight and forty hours that the tar may have time to subside, when the clear water is to be poured off and kept covered for use, no more being made from the same tar, which may still serve for common purposes.

2. The cold infusion of tar hath been used in some of our colonies, as a preservative or preparative against the small-pox, which foreign practice induced me to try it in my own neighbourhood, when the small-pox raged with great violence. And the trial fully answered my expectation: all those, within my knowledge, who took the tar-water, having either escaped that distemper, or had it very favourably. In one family there was a remarkable instance of seven children, who came all very well through the small-pox, except one young child which could not be brought to drink tar-water as the rest had done.

3. Several were preserved from taking the small-pox by the use of this liquor: others had it in the mildest

mildest manner, and others, that they might be able to take the infection, were obliged to intermit drinking the tar-water. I have found it may be drunk with great safety and success for any length of time, and this not only before, but also during the distemper. The general rule for taking it is, about half a pint night and morning on an empty stomach, which quantity may be varied, according to the case and age of the patient, provided it be always taken on an empty stomach, and about two hours before or after a meal. For children and squeamish persons it may be made weaker, and given little and often. More cold water, or less stirring, makes it weaker; as less water, or more stirring, makes it stronger. It should not be lighter than French, nor deeper coloured than Spanish white wine. If a spirit be not very sensibly perceiv'd on drinking, either the tar must have been bad, or already us'd, or the tar-water carelessly made.

4. It seemed probable, that a medicine of such efficacy in a distemper attended with so many purulent ulcers, might be also useful in other foulnesses of the blood; accordingly I tried it on several persons infected with cutaneous eruptions and ulcers, who were soon relieved, and soon after cured. Encouraged by these successes I ventured to advise it in the foulest distempers, wherein it proved much more successful than salivations and wood-drinks had done.

5. Having tried it in a great variety of cases, I found it succeed beyond my hopes; in a tedious and painful ulceration of the bowels, in a consumptive cough and (as appeared by expectorated pus) an ulcer in the lungs; in a pleurisy and peripneumony. And when a person, who for some years had been subject to erysipelatous fevers, perceived the usual fore-running symptoms to come on, I advised her

to

to drink tar-water which prevented the eryſipelas.

6. I never knew any thing ſo good for the ſtomach as tar-water: it cures indigeſtion and gives a good appetite. It is an excellent medicine in an aſthma. It imparts a kindly warmth and quick circulation to the juices, without heating, and is therefore uſeful, not only as a pectoral and balſamic; but alſo as a powerful and ſafe deobſtruent in cachectic and hyſteric caſes. As it is both healing and diuretic, it is very good for the gravel. I believe it to be of great uſe in a dropſy, having known it cure a very bad anaſarca in a perſon whoſe thirſt, though very extraordinary, was in a ſhort time removed by the drinking of tar-water.

7. The uſefulneſs of this medicine in inflammatory caſes is evident, from what has been already obſerved (*a*). And yet ſome perhaps may ſuſpect that, as the tar itſelf is ſulphureous, tar-water muſt be of a hot and inflaming nature. But it is to be noted, that all balſams contain an acid ſpirit, which is in truth a volatile ſalt. Water is a menſtruum that diſſolves all ſorts of ſalts, and draws them from their ſubjects. Tar, therefore, being a balſam, it's ſalutary acid is extracted by water, which yet is incapable of diſſolving it's groſs reſinous parts, whoſe proper menſtruum is ſpirit of wine. Therefore tar-water, not being impregnated with reſin, may be ſafely uſed in inflammatory caſes: and in fact it hath been found an admirable febrifuge, at once the ſafeſt cooler and cordial.

8. The volatile ſalts ſeparated by infuſion from tar, may be ſuppoſed to contain it's ſpecific virtues. Mr. Boyle, and other later chemiſts, are agreed, that fixed ſalts are much the ſame in all bodies. But it is well known that volatile ſalts do greatly differ, and the eaſier they are ſeparated

(*a*) Sect. 5

from

from the subject, the more do they possess of it's specific qualities. Now the most easy separation is by infusion of tar in cold water, which to smell and taste shewing it self well impregnated, may be presumed to extract and retain the most pure volatile and active particles of that vegetable balsam.

9. Tar was by the ancients esteemed good against poisons, ulcers, the bites of venomous creatures, also for pthisical, scrophulous, paralytic and asthmatic persons. But the method of rendering it an inoffensive medicine and agreeable to the stomach, by extracting it's virtues in cold water, was unknown to them. The leaves and tender tops of pine and fir are in our times used for diet-drinks, and allowed to be antiscorbutic and diuretic. But the most elaborate juice, salt, and spirit of those evergreens are to be found in tar; whose virtues extend not to animals alone, but also to vegetables. Mr. Evelyn, in his treatise on Forest trees, observes with wonder, that stems of trees, smeared over with tar, are preserved thereby from being hurt by the invenomed teeth of goats and other injuries, while every other thing of an unctuous nature is highly prejudicial to them.

10. It seems that tar and turpentine may be had more or less, from all sorts of pines and firs whatsoever; and that the native spirits and essential salts of those vegetables are the same in turpentine and common tar. In effect this vulgar tar, which cheapness and plenty may have rendered contemptible, appears to be an excellent balsam, containing the virtues of most other balsams, which it easily imparts to water, and by that means readily and inoffensively insinuates them into the habit of the body.

11. The resinous exsudations of pines and firs are an important branch of the materia medica,

and

and not only useful in the prescriptions of physicians, but have been also thought otherwise conducive to health. Pliny tells us, that wines in the time of the old Romans were medicated with pitch and resin; and Jonstonus, in his Dendrographia, observes, that it is wholesome to walk in groves of pine trees, which impregnate the air with balsamic particles. That all turpentines and resins are good for the lungs, against gravel also and obstructions, is no secret. And that the medicinal properties of those drugs are found in tar-water, without heating the blood, or disordering the stomach, is confirmed by experience: and particularly that pthisical and asthmatic persons receive speedy and great relief from the use of it.

12. Balsams, as all unctuous and oily medicines, create a nauseating in the stomach. They cannot therefore be taken in substance, so much or so long, as to produce all those salutary effects, which, if thoroughly mixed with the blood and juices, they would be capable of producing. It must therefore be a thing of great benefit, to be able to introduce any requisite quantity of their volatile parts into the finest ducts and capillaries, so as not to offend the stomach, but, on the contrary, to comfort and strengthen it in a great degree.

13. According to Pliny, liquid pitch (as he calls it) or tar, was obtained by setting fire to billets of old fat pines or firs. The first running was tar, the latter or thicker running was pitch. Theophrastus is more particular: he tells us the Macedonians made huge heaps of the cloven trunks of those trees, wherein the billets were placed erect beside each other. That such heaps or piles of wood were sometimes a hundred and eighty cubits round, and sixty or even a hundred high: and that having covered them with sods of earth to

prevent the flame from bursting forth (in which case the tar was lost) they set on fire those huge heaps of pine or fir, letting the tar and pitch run out in a channel.

14. Pliny saith, it was customary for the ancients, to hold fleeces of wool over the steam of boiling tar, and squeeze the moisture from them, which watery substance was called pissinum. Ray will have this to be the same with the pisselæum of the ancients; but Hardouin in his notes on Pliny, thinks the pisselæum to have been produced from the cones of cedars. What use they made of these liquors anciently I know not: but it may be presumed they were used in medicine, though at present, for ought I can find, they are not used at all.

15. From the manner of procuring tar (*a*) it plainly appears to be a natural production, lodged in the vessels of the tree, whence it is only freed and let loose (not made) by burning. If we may believe Pliny, the first running or tar was called cedrium, and was of such efficacy to preserve from putrefaction, that in Egypt they embalmed dead bodies with it. And to this he ascribes their mummies continuing uncorrupted for so many ages.

16. Some modern writers inform us that tar flows from the trunks of pines and firs, when they are very old, through incisions made in the bark near the root; that pitch is tar inspissated; and both are the oil of the tree grown thick and ripened with age and sun. The trees, like old men, being unable to perspire, and their secretory ducts obstructed, they are, as one may say, choaked and stuffed with their own juice.

17. The method used by our colonies in America, for making tar and pitch, is in effect the same with that of the ancient Macedonians; as

(*a*) Sect. 13.

appears from the account given in the Philoſophical Tranſactions. And the relation of Leo Africanus, who deſcribes, as an eye witneſs, the making of tar on mount Atlas, agrees in ſubſtance with the methods uſed by the Macedonians of old, and the people of New England at this day.

18. Johnſtonus in his Dendrographia, is of opinion, that pitch was anciently made of cedar, as well as of the pine and fir grown old and oily. It ſhould ſeem indeed that one and the ſame word was uſed by the ancients in a large ſenſe, ſo as to comprehend the juices iſſuing from all thoſe trees. Tar and all ſorts of exſudations from evergreens are, in a general acceptation, included under the name reſin. Hard coarſe reſin or dry pitch is made from tar, by letting it blaze till the moiſture is ſpent. Liquid reſin is properly an oily viſcid juice, oozing from the bar of evergreen trees, either ſpontaneouſly or by inciſion. It is thought to be the oil of the bark inſpiſſated by the ſun. As it iſſues from the tree it is liquid, but becomes dry and hard being condenſed by the ſun or by fire.

19. According to Theophraſtus, reſin was obtained by ſtripping off the bark from pines, and by inciſions made in the ſilver fir and the pitch pine. The inhabitants of mount Ida, he tells us, ſtripped the trunk of the pine on the ſunny ſide two or three cubits from the ground. He obſerves that a good pine might be made to yield reſin every year; and indifferent every other year; and the weaker trees once in three years; and that three runnings were as much as a tree could bear. It is remarked by the ſame author, that a pine doth not at once produce fruit and reſin, but the former only in its youth, the latter in its old age.

20. Turpentine is a fine reſin. Four kinds of this are in uſe. The turpentine of Chios or Cy-

prus

prus which flows from the turpentine tree; the Venice turpentine which is got by piercing the Larch tree; the Strasburgh Turpentine which Mr. Ray informs us is procured from the knots of the silver fir; it is fragrant and grows yellow with age: The fourth kind is common turpentine, neither transparent, nor so liquid as the former; and this Mr. Ray taketh to flow from the mountain pine. All these turpentines are useful in the same intentions. Theophrastus saith the best resin or turpentine is got from the Terebinthus growing in Syria and some of the Greek islands. The next best from the silver fir and pitch pine.

21. Turpentine is on all hands allowed to have great medicinal virtues. Tar and it's infusion contain those virtues. Tar-water is extremely pectoral and restorative, and, if I may judge from what experience I have had, it possesseth the most valuable qualities ascribed to the several balsams of Peru, of Tolu, of Capivi, and even to the balm of Gilead; such is it's virtue in asthmas and pleurisies, in obstructions and ulcerous erosions of the inward parts. Tar in substance, mix'd with honey, I have found an excellent medicine for coughs. Balsams, as hath been already observed, are apt to offend the stomach. But tar-water may be taken without offending the stomach: For the strengthening whereof it is the best medicine I have ever tried.

22. The folly of man rateth things by their scarceness, but Providence hath made the most useful things most common. Among those liquid oily extracts from trees and shrubs which are termed balsams, and valued for medicinal virtues, tar may hold it's place as a most valuable balsam. It's fragancy sheweth, that it is possessed of active qualities, and it's oiliness, that it is fitted to retain them. This excellent balsam may be pur-

chaſed for a penny a pound, whereas the balſam of Judæa, when moſt plenty, was ſold on the very ſpot that produced it, for double it's weight in ſilver, if we may credit Pliny; who alſo informs us that the beſt balſam of Judæa flowed only from the bark, and that it was adulterated with reſin and oil of turpentine. Now comparing the virtues I have experienced in tar, with thoſe I find aſcribed to the precious balm of Judæa, of Gilead, or of Mecha (as it is diverſly called) I am of opinion, that the latter is not a medicine of more value or efficacy than the former.

23. Pliny ſuppoſed amber to be a reſin, and to diſtil from ſome ſpecies of pine, which he gathered from it's ſmell. Neverthelesſ it's being dug out of the earth ſhews it to be a foſſil, though of a very different kind from other foſſils. But thus much is certain, that the medicinal virtues of amber are to be found in the balſamic juices of pines and firs. Particularly the virtues of the moſt valuable preparation, I mean ſalt of amber, are in a great degree anſwered by tar-water, as a detergent, diaphoretic, and diuretic.

24. There is, as hath been already obſerved, more or leſs oil and balſam in all evergreen trees, which retains the acid ſpirit, that principle of life and verdure; the not retaining whereof in ſufficient quantity, cauſeth other plants to droop and wither. Of theſe evergreen trees productive of reſin, pitch, and tar, Pliny enumerates ſix kinds in Europe; Johnſtonus reckons up thrice that number of the pine and fir family. And indeed, their number, their variety, and their likeneſs makes it difficult to be exact.

25. It is remarked both by Theophraſtus and Johnſtonus, that trees growing in low and ſhady places do not yield ſo good tar, as thoſe which

grow

grow in higher and more exposed situations. And Theophrastus further observes, that the inhabitants of mount Ida in Asia, who distinguish the Idæan pine from the maritime, affirm, that the tar flowing from the former is in greater plenty, as well as more fragrant than the other. Hence it should seem, the pines or firs in the mountains of Scotland might be employed that way, and rendered valuable; even where the timber, by it's remoteness from water-carriage, is of small value. What we call the Scotch fir is falsly so called, being in truth a wild forest pine, and (as Mr. Ray informs us) agreeing much with the description of a pine growing on mount Olympus in Phrygia, probably the only place where it is found out of these islands; in which of late years it is so much planted and cultivated with so little advantage, while the cedar of Lebanon might perhaps be raised, with little more trouble, and much more profit and ornament.

26. The pines which differ from the firs in the length and disposition of their leaves and hardness of the wood, do not, in Pliny's account, yield so much resin as the fir trees. Several species of both are accurately described and delineated by the naturalists. But they all agree so far as to seem related. Theophrastus gives the preference to that resin which is got from the silver fir and pitch tree (ἐλάτη and πίτυς) before that yielded by the pine, which yet, he saith, is in greater plenty. Pliny, on the contrary, affirms, that the pine produceth the smallest quantity. It should seem therefore that the interpreter of Theophrastus might have been mistaken, in rendering πεύκη by pinus, as well as Johnstonus, who likewise takes the pine for the πεύκη of Theophrastus. Hardouin will have the pinus of Pliny to have been by others called πεύκη, but by Theophrastus πίτυς. Ray thinks the common

fir,

fir, or picea of the Latins, to be the male fir of Theophraſtus. This was probably the ſpruce fir; for the picea, according to Pliny, yields much reſin, loves a cold and mountainous ſituation, and is diſtinguiſhed, tonſili facilitate, by it's fitneſs to be ſhorn, which agrees with the ſpruce fir, whereof I have ſeen cloſe ſhorn hedges.

27. There ſeems to have been ſome confuſion in the naming of theſe trees, as well among the ancients as the moderns. The ancient Greek and Latin names are by later authors applied very differently. Pliny himſelf acknowledgeth, it is not eaſy even for the ſkilful to diſtinguiſh the trees by their leaves, and know their ſexes and kinds: and that difficulty is ſince much encreaſed, by the diſcovery of many new ſpecies of that evergreen tribe, growing in various parts of the globe. But deſcriptions are not ſo eaſily miſapplied as names. Theophraſtus tells us, that πίτυς differeth from πεύκη, among other things, in that it is neither ſo tall nor ſo ſtraight, nor hath ſo large a leaf. The fir he diſtinguiſheth into male and female: the latter is ſofter timber than the male, it is alſo a taller and fairer tree, and this is probably the ſilver fir.

28. To ſay no more on this obſcure buſineſs, which I leave to the critics, I ſhall obſerve, that according to Theophraſtus, not only the turpentine trees, the pines, and the firs yield reſin or tar, but alſo the cedars and palm trees; and the words pix and reſina are taken by Pliny in ſo large a ſenſe as to include the weepings of the lentiſcus and cypreſs, and the balms of Arabia and Judæa; all which perhaps are near of kin, and in their moſt uſeful qualities concur with common tar, eſpecially the Norvegian, which is the moſt liquid and beſt for medicinal uſes of any that I have experienced. Thoſe trees that grow on mountains, expoſed to the

the ſun or the north wind, are reckoned by Theophraſtus to produce the beſt and pureſt tar: And the Idæan pines were diſtinguiſhed from thoſe growing on the plain, as yielding a thinner, ſweeter, and better ſcented tar, all which differences I think I have obſerved, between the tar that comes from Norway, and that which comes from low and ſwampy countries.

29. Agreeably to the old obſervation of the Peripatetics, that heat gathereth homogeneous things and diſperſeth ſuch as are heterogeneous, we find chemiſtry is fitted for the analyſis of bodies. But the chemiſtry of nature is much more perfect than that of human art, inaſmuch as it joineth to the power of heat that of the moſt exquiſite mechaniſm. Thoſe who have examined the ſtructure of trees and plants by microſcopes, have diſcovered an admirable variety of fine capillary tubes and veſſels, fitted for ſeveral purpoſes, as the imbibing or attracting of proper nouriſhment, the diſtributing thereof through all parts of the vegetable, the diſcharge of ſuperfluities, the ſecretion of particular juices. They are found to have ducts anſwering to the trachæ in animals, for the conveying of air; they have others anſwering to lacteals, arteries, and veins. They feed, digeſt, reſpire, perſpire, and generate their kind, and are provided with organs nicely fitted for all thoſe uſes.

30. The ſap veſſels are obſerved to be fine tubes running up through the trunk from the root. Secretory veſſels are found in the bark, buds, leaves, and flowers. Exhaling veſſels for carrying off excrementitious parts, are diſcovered throughout the whole ſurface of the vegetable. And (though this point be not ſo well agreed) Doctor Grew in his Anatomy of plants, thinks there appears

a cir-

circulation of the ſap, moving downwards in the root, and feeding the trunk upwards.

31. Some difference indeed there is between learned men, concerning the proper uſe of certain parts of vegetables. But whether the diſcoverers have rightly gueſſed at all their uſes or no, thus much is certain, that there are innumerable fine and curious parts in a vegetable body, and a wonderful ſimilitude or analogy between the mechaniſm of plants and animals. And perhaps ſome will think it not unreaſonable to ſuppoſe the mechaniſm of plants more curious than even that of animals, if we conſider not only the ſeveral juices ſecreted by different parts of the ſame plant, but alſo the endleſs variety of juices drawn and formed out of the ſame ſoil, by various ſpecies of vegetables; which muſt therefore differ in an endleſs variety, as to the texture of their abſorbent veſſels and ſecretory ducts.

32. A body, therefore, either animal or vegetable, may be conſidered as an organiſed ſyſtem of tubes and veſſels, containing ſeveral ſorts of fluids. And as fluids are moved through the veſſels of animal bodies, by the ſyſtole and diaſtole of the heart, the alternate expanſion and condenſation of the air, and the oſcillations in the membranes and tunicks of the veſſels; even ſo by means of air expanded and contracted in the trachæ or veſſels made up of elaſtic fibres, the ſap is propelled through the arterial tubes of a plant, and the vegetable juices, as they are rarefied by heat or condenſed by cold, will either aſcend and evaporate into air, or deſcend in the form of a groſs liquor.

33. Juices therefore, firſt purified by ſtraining through the fine pores of the root, are afterwards exalted by the action of the air and the veſſels of the plant, but, above all, by the action of the ſun's

 light;

light; which at the ſame time that it heats, doth wonderfully rarefy and raiſe the ſap; till it perſpires and forms an atmoſphere, like the effluvia of animal bodies. And though the leaves are ſuppoſed to perform principally the office of lungs, breathing out excrementitious vapours, and drawing in alimentary; yet it ſeems probable, that the reciprocal actions of repulſion and attraction are performed all over the ſurface of vegetables, as well as animals. In which reciprocation, Hippocrates ſuppoſeth the manner of nature's acting, for the nouriſhment and health of animal bodies, chiefly to conſiſt. And, indeed, what ſhare of a plant's nouriſhment is drawn through the leaves and bark, from that ambient heterogeneous fluid called air, is not eaſy to ſay. It ſeems very conſiderable and altogether neceſſary, as well to vegetable as animal life.

34. It is an opinion received by many, that the ſap circulates in plants as the blood in animals: that it aſcends through capillary arteries in the trunk, into which are inoſculated other veſſels of the bark anſwering to veins, which bring back to the root the remainder of the ſap, over and above what had been depoſited, during its aſcent by the arterial veſſels, and ſecreted for the ſeveral uſes of the vegetable throughout all its parts, ſtem, branches, leaves, flowers, and fruit. Others deny this circulation, and affirm that the ſap doth not return through the bark veſſels. It is nevertheleſs agreed by all, that there are aſcending and deſcending juices; while ſome will have the aſcent and deſcent to be a circulation of the ſame juices through different veſſels: others will have the aſcending juice to be one ſort attracted by the root, and the deſcending another imbibed by the leaves, or extremities of the branches: laſtly, others think that

the ſame juice, as it is rarefied or condenſed by heat or cold, riſes and ſubſides in the ſame tube. I ſhall not take upon me to decide this controverſy. Only I cannot help obſerving, that the vulgar argument from analogy between plants and animals loſeth much of its force, if it be conſidered, that the ſuppoſed circulating of the ſap, from the root or lacteals through the arteries, and thence returning, by inoſculations, through the veins or bark veſſels to the root or lacteals again, is in no ſort conformable or analogous to the circulation of the blood.

35. It is ſufficient to obſerve, what all muſt acknowledge, that a plant or tree is a very nice and complicated machine (*a*); by the ſeveral parts and motions whereof, the crude juices admitted through the abſorbent veſſels, whether of the root, trunk, or branches, are variouſly mixed, ſeparated, altered, digeſted, and exalted in a very wonderful manner. The juice as it paſſeth in and out, up and down, through tubes of different textures, ſhapes, and ſizes, and is affected by the alternate compreſſion and expanſion of elaſtic veſſels, by the viciſſitudes of ſeaſons, the changes of weather, and the various action of the ſolar light, grows ſtill more and more elaborate.

36. There is therefore no chemiſtry like that of nature, which addeth to the force of fire, the moſt delicate, various, and artificial percolation (*b*). The inceſſant action of the ſun upon the elements of air, earth, and water, and on all ſorts of mixed bodies, animal, vegetable and foſſil, is ſuppoſed to perform all ſorts of chemical operations. Whence it ſhould follow, that the air contains all ſorts of chemic productions, the vapours, fumes, oils, ſalts,

(*a*) 30, 31. (*b*) 29.

and ſpirits of all the bodies we know: from which general aggregate or maſs, thoſe that are proper being drawn in, through the fine veſſels of the leaves, branches, and ſtem of the tree, undergo, in its various organs, new alterations, ſecretions, and digeſtions, till ſuch time as they aſſume the moſt elaborate form.

37. Nor is it to be wondered, that the peculiar texture of each plant or tree, co-operating with the ſolar fire and pre-exiſting juices, ſhould ſo alter the fine nouriſhment drawn from earth and air (*a*), as to produce various ſpecific qualities of great efficacy in medicine: eſpecially if it be conſidered that in the opinion of learned men, there is an influence on plants derived from the ſun, beſides its mere heat. Certainly doctor Grew, that curious anatomiſt of plants, holds the ſolar influence to differ from that of a mere culinary fire, otherwiſe than by being only a more temperate and equal heat.

38. The alimentary juice taken into the lacteals, if I may ſo ſay, of animals or vegetables, conſiſts of oily, aqueous, and ſaline particles, which being diſſolved, volatiliſed, and diverſly agitated, part thereof is ſpent and exhaled into the air; and that part which remains is by the œconomy of the plant, and action of the ſun, ſtrained, purified, concocted, and ripened into an inſpiſſated oil or balſam, and depoſited in certain cells placed chiefly in the bark, which is thought to anſwer the panniculus adipoſus in animals, defending trees from the weather, and, when in ſufficient quantity, rendering them evergreen. This balſam, weeping or ſweating through the bark, hardens into reſin; and this moſt copiouſly in the ſeveral ſpecies of pines and

(*a*) 33.

firs, whose oil being in greater quantity, and more tenacious of the acid spirit or vegetable soul (as perhaps it may not improperly be called) abides the action of the sun, and attracting the sun beams, is thereby exalted and enriched, so as to become a most noble medicine; such is the last product of a tree, perfectly maturated by time and sun.

39. It is remarked by Theophrastus, that all plants and trees, while they put forth, have most humour, but when they have ceased to germinate and bear, then the humour is strongest and most sheweth the nature of the plant, and that, therefore, trees yielding resin should be cut after germination. It seems also very reasonable to suppose the juice of old trees, whose organs bring no new sap, should be better ripened than that of others.

40. The aromatic flavours of vegetables seem to depend upon the sun's light, as much as colours. As in the production of the latter, the reflecting powers of the object, so in that of the former, the attractive and organical powers of the plant co-operate with the sun (*a*). And as from Sir Isaac Newton's experiments it appears, that all colours are virtually in the white light of the sun, and shew themselves when the rays are separated by the attracting and repelling powers of objects, even so the specific qualities of the elaborate juices of plants, seem to be virtually or eminently contained in the solar light, and are actually exhibited upon the separation of the rays, by the peculiar powers of the capillary organs in vegetables, attracting and imbibing certain rays, which produce certain flavours and qualities, in like manner as certain rays, being reflected, produce certain colours.

(*a*) 36, 37.

41. It hath been obſerved by ſome curious anatomiſts, that the ſecretory veſſels in the glands of animal bodies are lined with a fine down, which in different glands is of different colours. And it is thought, that each particular down, being originally imbued with its own proper juice, attracts none but that ſort; by which means ſo many various juices are ſecreted in different parts of the body. And perhaps there may be ſomething analogous to this, in the fine abſorbent veſſels of plants, which may co-operate towards producing that endleſs variety of juices, elaborated in plants from the ſame earth and air.

42. The balſam or eſſential oil of vegetables contains a ſpirit, wherein conſiſt the ſpecific qualities, the ſmell and taſte of the plant. Boerhaave holds the native preſiding ſpirit to be neither oil, ſalt, earth, or water; but ſomewhat too fine and ſubtile to be caught alone and rendered viſible to the eye. This, when ſuffered to fly off, for inſtance, from the oil of roſemary, leaves it deſtitute of all flavour. This ſpark of life, this ſpirit or ſoul, if we may ſo ſay, of the vegetable, departs without any ſenſible diminution of the oil or water wherein it was lodged.

43. It ſhould ſeem that the forms, ſouls, or principles of vegetable life, ſubſiſt in the light or ſolar emanation (*a*), which in reſpect of the macrocoſm is what the animal ſpirit is to the macrocoſm; the interior tegument, the ſubtile inſtrument and vehicle of power. No wonder then that the ens primum, or ſcintilla ſpirituoſa, as it is called, of plants ſhould be a thing ſo fine and fugacious as to eſcape our niceſt ſearch. It is evident that nature at the ſun's approach vegetates; and

(*a*) 40.

languiſhes

languishes at his recess; this terrestrial globe seeming only a matrix disposed and prepared to receive life from his light; whence Homer in his hymns stileth earth the wife of heaven, ἄλοχ' οὐρανοῦ ἀστερόεντος.

44. The luminous spirit which is the form or life of a plant, from whence its differences and properties flow, is somewhat extremely volatile. It is not the oil, but a thing more subtile, whereof oil is the vehicle, which retains it from flying off, and is lodged in several parts of the plant, particularly in the cells of the bark and in the seeds. This oil purified and exalted by the organical powers of the plant, and agitated by warmth, becomes a proper receptacle of the spirit; part of which spirit exhales through the leaves and flowers, and part is arrested by this unctuous humour that detains it in the plant. It is to be noted, this essential oil animated, as one may say, with the flavour of the plant, is very different from any spirit that can be procured from the same plant by fermentation.

45. Light impregnates air (*a*), air impregnates vapour; and this becomes a watery juice by distillation, having risen first in the cold still with a kindly gentle heat. This fragrant vegetable water is possessed of the specific odour and taste of the plant. It is remarked, that distilled oils added to water for counterfeiting the vegetable water, can never equal it, artificial chemistry falling short of the natural.

46. The less violence is used to nature the better its produce. The juice of olives or grapes issuing by the lightest pressure is best. Resins that drop from the branches spontaneously, or ooze upon the slightest incision, are the finest and most

(*a*) 37. 43.

fragrant,

fragrant. And infusions are observed to act more strongly than decoctions of plants, the more subtile and volatile salts and spirits, which might be lost or corrupted by the latter, being obtained in their natural state by the former. It is also observed, that the finest, purest, and most volatile part is that which first ascends in distillation. And, indeed, it should seem the lightest and most active particles required least force to disengage them from the subject.

47. The salts, therefore, and more active spirits of the tar are got by infusion in cold water: but the resinous part is not to be dissolved thereby (*a*). Hence the prejudice which some perhaps may entertain against Tar-water, as a medicine, the use whereof might inflame the blood by its sulphur and resin, appears to be not well grounded; it being indeed impregnated with a fine acid spirit, balsamic, cooling, diuretic, and possessed of many other virtues (*b*). Spirits are supposed to consist of salts and phlegm, probably too somewhat of a fine oily nature, differing from oil in that it mixeth with water, and agreeing with oil, in that it runneth in rivulets by distillation. Thus much is allowed, that the water, earth, and fixed salt are the same in all plants: that, therefore, which differenceth a plant or makes it what it is, the native spark or form, in the language of the chemists or schools, is none of those things, nor yet the finest oil, which seemeth only its receptacle or vehicle. It is observed by chemists, that all sorts of balsamic wood afford an acid spirit, which is the volatile oily salt of the vegetable: Herein are chiefly contained their medicinal virtues, and by the trials I have made, it appears, that the

(*a*) Sect. 7. (*b*) Sect. 42, 44.

acid

acid ſpirit in tar-water poſſeſſeth the virtues, in an eminent degree, of that of guaiacum, and other medicinal woods.

48. Qualities in a degree too ſtrong for human nature to ſubdue, and aſſimilate to itſelf, muſt hurt the conſtitution. All acids, therefore, may not be uſeful or innocent. But this ſeemeth an acid ſo thoroughly concocted, ſo gentle, bland, and temperate, and withal a ſpirit ſo fine and volatile, as readily to enter the ſmalleſt veſſels, and be aſſimilated with the utmoſt eaſe.

49. If any one were minded to diſſolve ſome of the reſin, together with the ſalt or ſpirit, he need only mix ſome ſpirit of wine with the water. But ſuch an intire ſolution of reſins and gums, as to qualify them for entering and pervading the animal ſyſtem, like the fine acid ſpirit that firſt flies off from the ſubject, is perhaps impoſſible to obtain. It is an apophthegm of the chemiſts, derived from Helmont, that whoever can make myrrh ſoluble by the human body, has the ſecret of prolonging his days: and Boerhaave owns that there ſeems to be truth in this, from its reſiſting putrefaction. Now this quality is as remarkable in tar, with which the ancients embalmed and preſerved dead bodies. And though Boerhaave himſelf, and other chemiſts before him, have given methods for making ſolutions of myrrh, yet it is by means of alcohol, which extracts only the inflammable parts. And it doth not ſeem that any ſolution of myrrh is impregnated with its ſalt or acid ſpirit. It may not, therefore, ſeem ſtrange if this water ſhould be found more beneficial for procuring health and long life, than any ſolution of myrrh whatſoever.

50. Certainly divers reſins and gums may have virtues, and yet not be able for their groſſneſs to

paſs

paſs the lacteals and other finer veſſels, nor yet, perhaps, readily impart thoſe virtues to a menſtruum, that may with ſafety and ſpeed convey them throughout the human body. Upon all which accounts, I believe tar-water will be found to have ſingular advantages. It is obſerved that acid ſpirits prove the ſtronger, by how much the greater degree of heat is required to raiſe them. And indeed, there ſeemeth to be no acid more gentle than this, obtained by the ſimple affuſion of cold water; which carries off from the ſubject the moſt light and ſubtile parts, and, if one may ſo ſpeak, the very flower of it's ſpecific qualities. And here it is to be noted, that the volatile ſalt and ſpirit of vegetables do, by gently ſtimulating the ſolids, attenuate the fluids contained in them, and promote ſecretions, and that they are penetrating and active, contrary to the general nature of other acids.

51. It is a great maxim for health, that the juices of the body be kept fluid in a due proportion. Therefore, the acid volatile ſpirit in tar-water, at once attenuating and cooling in a moderate degree, muſt greatly conduce to health, as a mild ſalutary deobſtruent, quickening the circulation of the fluids without wounding the ſolids, thereby gently removing or preventing thoſe obſtructions, which are the great and general cauſe of moſt chronical diſeaſes; in this manner anſwering to the antihyſterics, aſſa fœtida, galbanum, myrrh, amber, and, in general, to all the reſins and gums of trees or ſhrubs uſeful in nervous caſes.

52. Warm water is it ſelf a deobſtruent. Therefore the infuſion of tar drunk warm, is eaſier inſinuated into all the nice capillary veſſels, and acts not only by virtue of the balſam, but alſo by that

of the vehicle. It's taste, it's diuretic quality, it's being so great a cordial, shew the activity of this medicine. And at the same time that it quickens the sluggish blood of the hysterical, it's balsamic oily nature abates the too rapid motion of the sharp thin blood in those who are hectic. There is a lentour and smoothness in the blood of healthy strong people; on the contrary, there is often an acrimony and solution in that of weakly morbid persons. The fine particles of tar are not only warm and active, they are also balsamic and emollient; softening and enriching the sharp and vapid blood, and healing the erosions occasioned thereby in the blood-vessels and glands.

53. Tar-water possesseth the stomachic and cardiac qualities of Elixir proprietatis, Stoughton's drops, and many such tinctures and extracts, with this difference, that it worketh it's effect more safely, as it hath nothing of that spirit of wine; which, however mixed and disguised, may yet be well accounted a poison in some degree.

54. Such medicines are supposed to be diaphoretic, which, being of an active and subtile nature, pass through the whole system, and work their effect in the finest capillaries and perspiratory ducts, which they gently cleanse and open. Tar-water is extremely well fitted to work by such an insensible diaphoresis, by the fineness and activity of it's acid volatile spirit. And surely those parts ought to be very fine, which can scour the perspiratory ducts, under the scarf skin or cuticle, if it be true that one grain of sand would cover the mouths of more than a hundred thousand.

55. Another way wherein tar-water operates, is by urine, than which perhaps none is more safe and effectual, for cleansing the blood and carrying

off

off it's salts. But it seems to produce it's principal effect as an alterative, sure and easy, much safer than those vehement purgative, emetic, and salivating medicines, which do violence to nature.

56. An obstruction of some vessels causeth the blood to move more swiftly in other vessels, which are not obstructed. Hence manifold disorders. A liquor that dilutes and attenuates, resolves the concretions which obstruct. Tar-water is such a liquor. It may be said, indeed, of common water, that it attenuates, also of mercurial preparations that they attenuate. But it should be considered that mere water only distends the vessels and thereby weakens their tone; and that mercury, by it's great momentum, may justly be suspected of hurting the fine capillaries, which two deobstruents therefore might easily over-act their parts, and (by lessening the force of the elastic vessels) remotely produce those concretions they are intended to remove.

57. Weak and rigid fibres are looked on by the most able physicians, as sources of two different classes of distempers: a sluggish motion of the liquids occasions weak fibres: therefore tar-water is good to strengthen them as it gently accelerates their contents. On the other hand, being an unctuous bland fluid, it moistens and softens the dry and stiff fibres: and so proves a remedy for both extremes.

58. Common soaps are compositions of lixivial salt and oil. The corrosive acrimony of the saline particles being softened by the mixture of an unctuous substance they insinuate themselves into the small ducts with less difficulty and danger. The combination of these different substances makes up a very subtile and active medicine, fitted for mixing with all humours, and resolving

all obſtructions. Soap therefore is juſtly eſteemed a moſt efficacious medicine in many diſtempers. Alcaline ſoap is allowed to be cleanſing, attenuating, opening, reſolving, ſweetening; it is pectoral, vulnerary, diuretic, and hath other good qualities, which are alſo to be found in tar-water. It is granted, that oil and acid ſalts combined together exiſt in vegetables, and that conſequently there are acid ſoaps as well as alcaline. And the ſaponaceous nature of the acid vegetable ſpirits, is what renders them ſo diuretic, ſudorific, penetrating, abſterſive and reſolving. Such, for inſtance, is the acid ſpirit of Guaiacum. And all theſe ſame virtues ſeem to be in tar-water in a mild and ſalutary degree.

59. It is the general opinion that all acids coagulate the blood. Boerhaave excepts vinegar, which he holds to be a ſoap, inaſmuch as it is found to contain an oil as well as an acid ſpirit. Hence it is both unctuous and penetrating, a powerful antiphlogiſtic, and preſervative againſt corruption and infection. Now it ſeems evident that tar-water is a ſoap as well as vinegar. For though it be the character of reſin, which is an inſpiſſated groſs oil, not to diſſolve in water (*a*), yet the ſalts attract ſome fine particles of eſſential oil: which fine oil ſerves as a vehicle for the acid ſalts, and ſhews itſelf in the colour of the tar-water; for all pure ſalts are colourleſs. And though the reſin will not diſſolve in water, yet the ſubtile oil, in which the vegetable ſalts are lodged, may as well mix with water as vinegar doth, which contains both oil and ſalt. And as the oil in tar-water diſcovers itſelf to the eye, ſo the acid ſalts do manifeſt

(*a*) Sect. 47.

themſelves to the taſte. Tar-water therefore is a ſoap, and as ſuch hath the medicinal qualities of ſoaps.

60. It operates more gently as the acid ſalts loſe their acrimony being ſheathed in oil, and thereby approaching the nature of neutral ſalts, are more benign and friendly to the animal ſyſtem: and more effectually, as, by the help of a volatile ſmooth inſinuating oil, thoſe ſame ſalts are more eaſily introduced into the capillary ducts. Therefore in fevers and epidemical diſtempers it is (and I have found it ſo) as well as in chronical diſeaſes, a moſt ſafe and efficacious medicine, being good againſt too great fluidity as a balſamic, and good againſt viſcidity as a ſoap. There is ſomething in the fiery corroſive nature of lixivial ſalts, which makes alcaline ſoap a dangerous remedy in all caſes where an inflammation is apprehended. And as inflammations are often occaſioned by obſtructions, it ſhould ſeem an acid ſoap was much the ſafer deobſtruent.

61. Even the beſt turpentines, however famous for their vulnerary and detergent qualities, have yet been obſerved by their warmth to diſpoſe to inflammatory tumours. But the acid ſpirit (*a*) being in ſo great proportion in tar-water renders it a cooler and ſafer medicine. And the ætherial oil of turpentine, though an admirable drier, healer, and anodyne, when outwardly applied to wounds and ulcers, and not leſs uſeful in cleanſing the urinary paſſages and healing their ulcerations, yet is known to be of a nature ſo very relaxing as ſometimes to do much miſchief, when taken inwardly. Tar-water is not attended with the ſame ill effects, which I believe are owing in a great meaſure to the ætherial

(*a*) Sect. 7, 8.

oil's

oil's being deprived of the acid spirit in distillation, which vellicating and contracting as a stimulus might have proved a counterpoise to the excessive lubricating and relaxing qualities of the oil.

62. Woods in decoction do not seem to yield so ripe and elaborate a juice, as that which is deposited in the cells or loculi terebinthiaci, and spontaneously oozes from them. And indeed though the balsam of Peru, obtained by boiling wood and scumming the decoction, be a very valuable medicine and of great account in divers cases, particularly asthmas, nephritic pains, nervous colics, and obstructions, yet I do verily think (and I do not say this without experience) that tar-water is a more efficacious remedy in all those cases than even that costly drug.

63. It hath been already observed, that the restorative pectoral antihysterical virtues of the most precious balsams and gums are possessed in a high degree by tar-water (*a*). And I do not know any purpose answered by the wood drinks, for which tar-water may not be used with at least equal success. It contains the virtues even of Guaiacum which seems the most efficacious of all the woods, warming and sweetening the humours, diaphoretic and useful in gouts, dropsies and rheums, as well as in the foul disease. Nor should it seem strange, if the virtues obtained by boiling an old dry wood prove inferior to those extracted from a balsam.

64. There is a fine volatile spirit in the waters of Geronster, the most esteemed of all the fountains about Spa, but whose waters do not bear transporting. The stomachic, cardiac, and diuretic qualities of this fountain somewhat resemble those of tar-water, which, if I am not greatly mistaken, con-

(*a*) Sect. 9, 21, 22, 23.

tains

tains the virtues of the best chalybeat and sulphureous waters; with this difference, that those waters are apt to affect the head in taking, which tar-water is not. Besides, there is a regimen of diet to be observed, especially with chalybeat waters, which I never found necessary with this. Tar-water layeth under no restraint either as to diet, hours, or employment. A man may study, or exercise, or repose, keep his own hours, pass his time either within or without, and take wholesome nourishment of any kind.

65. The use of chalybeat waters, however excellent for the nerves and stomach, is often suspended by colds and inflammatory disorders; in which they are acknowledged to be very dangerous. Whereas tar-water is so far from hurting in those cases, or being discontinued on that account, that it greatly contributes to their cure (*a*).

66. Cordials, vulgarly so called, act immediately on the stomach, and by consent of nerves on the head. But medicines of an operation too fine and light to produce a sensible effect in the primæ viæ, may, nevertheless, in their passage through the capillaries, operate on the sides of those small vessels, in such manner as to quicken their oscillations, and consequently the motion of their contents, producing, in issue and effect, all the benefits of a cordial much more lasting and salutary than those of distilled spirits, which by their caustic and coagulating qualities do incomparably more mischief than good. Such a cardiac medicine is tar-water. The transient fits of mirth, produced from fermented liquors and distilled spirits, are attended with proportionable depressions of spirits in their intervals. But the calm chearfulness arising from

(*a*) Sect. 7.

this

this water of health (as it may be juſtly called) is permanent. In which is emulates the virtues of that famous plant Gen Seng, ſo much valued in China as the only cordial that raiſeth the ſpirits without depreſſing them. Tar-water is ſo far from hurting the nerves as common cordials do, that it is highly uſeful in cramps, ſpaſms of the viſcera, and paralytic numbneſs.

67. Emetics are on certain occaſions adminiſtred with great ſucceſs. But the overſtraining and weakening of nature may be very juſtly apprehended from a courſe of emetics. They are nevertheleſs preſcribed and ſubſtituted for exerciſe. But it is well remarked in Plato's Timæus, that vomits and purges are the worſt exerciſe in the world. There is ſomething in the mild operation of tar-water, that ſeems more friendly to the œconomy, and forwards the digeſtions and ſecretions in a way more natural and benign, the mildneſs of this medicine being ſuch that I have known children take it, for above ſix months together, with great benefit, and without any inconvenience, and after long and repeated experience I do eſteem it a moſt excellent diet-drink, fitted to all ſeaſons and ages.

68. It is, I think, allowed that the origin of the gout lies in a faulty digeſtion. And it is remarked by the ableſt phyſicians, that the gout is ſo difficult to cure, becauſe heating medicines aggravate it's immediate, and cooling it's remote cauſe. But tar-water, although it contain active principles that ſtrengthen the digeſtion beyond any thing I know, and conſequently muſt be highly uſeful, either to prevent or leſſen the following fit, or by invigorating the blood to caſt it upon the extremities, yet it is not of ſo heating a nature as to do harm even in the fit. Nothing is

more

more difficult or disagreeable than to argue men out of their prejudices; I shall not therefore enter into controversies on this subject, but, if men dispute and object, shall leave the decision to time and trial.

69. In the modern practice, soap, opium, and mercury bid fairest for universal medicines. The first of these is highly spoken of. But then those who magnify it most, except against the use of it in such cases where the obstruction is attended with a putrefactive alkali, or where an inflammatory disposition appears. It is acknowledged to be very dangerous in a phthisis, fever, and some other cases, in which tar-water is not only safe but useful.

70. Opium, though a medicine of great extent and efficacy, yet is frequently known to produce grievous disorders in hysterical or hypochondriacal persons, who make a great part, perhaps the greatest of those who lead sedentary lives in these islands. Besides, upon all constitutions dangerous errors may be committed in the use of opium.

71. Mercury hath of late years become a medicine of very general use. The extreme minuteness, mobility, and momentum of it's parts, rendering it a most powerful cleanser of all obstructions, even in the most minute capillaries. But then we should be cautious in the use of it, if we consider, that the very thing which gives it power of doing good above other deobstruents, doth also dispose it to do mischief. I mean it's great momentum, the weight of it being about ten times that of blood, and the momentum being the joint product of the weight and velocity, it must needs operate with great force; and may it not be justly feared, that so great a force entering the minutest

vessels, and breaking the obstructed matter, might also break or wound the fine tender coats of those small vessels, and so bring on the untimely effects of old age, producing more perhaps, and worse obstructions than those it removed? Similar consequences may justly be apprehended from other mineral and ponderous medicines. Therefore upon the whole, there will not perhaps be found any medicine, more general in it's use, or more salutary in it's effects than tar-water.

72. To suppose that all distempers arising from very different, and, it may be, from contrary causes, can be cured by one and the same medicine, must seem chimerical. But it may with truth be affirmed, that the virtue of tar-water extends to a surprizing variety of cases very distant and unlike (*a*). This I have experienced in my neighbours, my family, and myself. And as I live in a remote corner among poor neighbours, who for want of a regular physician have often recourse to me, I have had frequent opportunities of trial, which convince me it is of so just a temperament as to be an enemy to all extremes. I have known it do great good in a cold watery constitution, as a cardiac and stomachic; and at the same time allay heat and feverish thirst in another. I have known it correct costive habits in some, and the contrary habit in others. Nor will this seem incredible, if it be considered that middle qualities naturally reduce the extreme. Warm water, for instance, mixed with hot and cold will lessen the heat in that, and the cold in this.

73. They who know the great virtues of common soap, whose coarse lixivial salts are the pro-

(*a*) Sect. 3, 4, 5, 6, 21. &c.

duct of culinary fire, will not think it incredible that virtues of mighty force and extent should be found in a fine acid soap (*a*), the salts and oil whereof are a most elaborate product of nature and the solar light.

74. It is certain tar-water warms, and therefore some may perhaps still think it cannot cool. The more effectually to remove this prejudice, let it be farther considered, that, as on the one hand, opposite causes do sometimes produce the same effect, for instance, heat by rarefaction and cold by condensation do both increase the air's elasticity: so, on the other hand, the same cause shall sometime produce opposite effects: heat, for instance, thins, and again, heat coagulates the blood. It is not therefore strange that tar-water should warm one habit, and cool another, have one good effect on a cold constitution, and another good effect on an inflamed one; nor, if this be so, that it should cure opposite disorders. All which justifies to reason, what I have often found true in fact. The salts, the spirits, the heat of tar-water are of a temperature congenial to the constitution of a man, which receives from it a kindly warmth, but no inflaming heat. It was remarkable that two children in my neighbourhood, being in a course of tar-water, upon an intermission of it, never failed to have their issues inflamed by an humour much more hot and sharp than at other times. But it's great use in the small pox, pleurisies, and fevers, is a sufficient proof that tar-water is not of an inflaming nature.

75. I have dwelt the longer on this head, because some gentlemen of the faculty have thought fit to

(*a*) 58.

declare that tar-water must inflame, and that they would never visit any patient in a fever, who had been a drinker of it. But I will venture to affirm, that it is so far from increasing a feverish inflammation, that it is, on the contrary, a most ready means to allay and extinguish it. It is of admirable use in fevers, being at the same time the surest, safest and most effectual both paregoric and cordial; for the truth of which, I appeal to any person's experience, who shall take a large draught of it milk warm in the paroxysm of a fever, even when plain water or herb teas shall be found to have little or no effect. To me it seems that it's singular and surprizing use in fevers of all kinds, were there nothing else, would be alone sufficient to recommend it to the public.

76. The best physicians make the idea of a fever to consist in a too great velocity of the heart's motion, and too great resistance at the capillaries. Tar-water, as it softens and gently stimulates those nice vessels, helps to propel their contents, and so contributes to remove the latter part of the disorder. And for the former, the irritating acrimony which accelerates the motion of the heart is diluted by watery, corrected by acid, and softened by balsamic remedies, all which intentions are answered by this aqueous acid balsamic medicine. Besides the viscid juices coagulated by the febrile heat are resolved by tar-water as a soap, and not too far resolved, as it is a gentle acid soap; to which we may add, that the peccant humours and salts are carried off by it's diaphoretic and diuretic qualities.

77. I found all this confirmed by my own experience in the late sickly season of the year one thousand seven hundred and forty one, having had twenty-

twenty-five fevers in my own family cured by this medicinal water, drunk copiously. The same method was practised on several of my poor neighbours with equal success. It suddenly calmed the feverish anxieties, and seemed every glass to refresh, and infuse life and spirit into the patient. At first some of those patients had been vomited; but afterwards I found that without vomiting, bleeding, blistering, or any other evacuation or medicine whatever, very bad fevers could be cured by the sole drinking of tar-water, milk warm, and in good quantity, perhaps a large glass every hour, or oftener, taken in bed. And it was remarkable, that such as were cured by this comfortable cordial, recovered health and spirits at once, while those who had been cured by evacuations often languished long, even after the fever had left them, before they could recover of their medicines and regain their strength.

78. In peripneumonies and pleurisies I have observed tar-water to be excellent, having known some pleuritic persons cured without bleeding, by a blister early applied to the stitch, and the copious drinking of tar-water, four or five quarts, or even more in four and twenty hours. And I do recommend it to farther trial, whether in all cases of a pleurisy, one moderate bleeding, a blister on the spot, and plenty of tepid tar-water may not suffice, without those repeated and immoderate bleedings, the bad effects of which are perhaps never got over. I do even suspect, that a pleuritic patient betaking himself to bed betimes, and drinking very copiously of tar-water, may be cured by that alone without bleeding, blistering, or any other medicine whatever: certainly I have found this succeed at a glass every half hour.

79. I have known a bloody flux of long continuance, after divers medicines had been tried in vain, cured by tar-water. But that which I take to be the most speedy and effectual remedy in a bloody flux, is a clyster of an ounce of common brown rosin dissolved over a fire in two ounces of oil, and added to a pint of broth; which not long since I had frequent occasion of trying, when that distemper was epidemical. Nor can I say that any to whom I advised it miscarried. This experiment I was led to make by the opinion I had of tar as a balsamic: and rosin is only tar inspissated.

80. Nothing that I know corroborates the stomach so much as tar-water (a). Whence it follows, that it must be of singular use to persons afflicted with the gout. And from what I have observed in five or six instances, I do verily believe it the best and safest medicine either to prevent the gout, or so to strengthen nature against the fit, as to drive it from the vitals; or, at other times to change a worse illness into the gout, and so get rid of it; Doctor Sydenham, in his treatise of the gout, declares, that whoever finds a medicine the most efficacious for strengthening digestion, will do more service in the cure of that and other chronical distempers, than he can even form a notion of. And I leave it to trial, whether tar-water be not that medicine, as I myself am persuaded it is, by all the experiments I could make. But in all trials I would recommend discretion; for instance, a man with the gout in his stomach ought not to drink cold tar-water. This essay leaves room for future experiment in every part of it, not pretending to be a complete treatise.

81. It is evident to sense, that blood, urine, and other animal juices, being let to stand, soon

(a) Sect. 68.

contract a great acrimony. Juices, therefore, from a bad digestion retained and stagnating in the body, grow sharp and putrid. Hence a fermenting heat, the immediate cause of the gout. The curing this by cooling medicines, as they would increase the antecedent cause, must be a vain attempt. On the other hand, spices and spirituous liquors, while they contribute to remove the antecedent cause, or bad digestion, would, by inflaming the blood, increase the proximate or immediate cause of the gout, to wit, the fermenting heat. The scope therefore must be, to find a medicine that shall corroborate, but not inflame. Bitter herbs are recommended; but they are weak in comparison of tar-war.

82. The great force of tar-water, to correct the acrimony of the blood, appears in nothing more than in the cure of a gangrene, from an internal cause; which was performed on a servant of my own, by prescribing the copious and constant use of tar-water for a few weeks. From my representing tar-water as good for so many things, some perhaps may conclude it is good for nothing. But charity obligeth me to say what I know, and what I think, howsoever it may be taken. Men may censure and object as they please, but I appeal to time and experiment. Effects misimputed, cases wrong told, circumstances overlooked, perhaps too, prejudices and partialities against truth, may for a time prevail and keep her at the bottom of her well, from whence nevertheless she emergeth sooner or later, and strikes the eyes of all who do not keep them shut.

83. Boerhaave thinks a specific may be found, for that peculiar venom, which infects the blood in the small pox, and that the prospect of so great a public benefit should stir up men to search for it.

It's

It's wonderful ſucceſs, in preventing and mitigating that diſtemper (*a*), would incline one to ſuſpect that tar-water is ſuch a ſpecific, eſpecially ſince I have found it of ſovereign uſe, as well during the ſmall pox, as before it. Some think an Eryſipelas and the Plague differ only in degree. If ſo, tar-water ſhould be uſeful in the Plague, for I have known it cure an Eryſipelas.

84. Tar-water, as cleanſing, healing, and balſamic, is good in all diſorders of the urinary paſſages, whether obſtructed or ulcerated. Doctor Liſter ſuppoſeth, indeed, that turpentines act by a cauſtic quality, which irritates the coats of the urinary ducts to expel ſand or gravel. But, it ſhould ſeem, this expelling diuretic virtue conſiſted rather in the ſalts than the reſin, and conſequently reſides in the tar-water, gently ſtimulating by it's ſalts, without the dangerous force of a cauſtic. The violent operation of Ipecacuanha lies in it's reſin, but the ſaline extract is a gentle purge and diuretic, by the ſtimulus of it's ſalts.

85. That which acts as a mild cordial (*b*), neither hurting the capillary veſſels as a cauſtic, nor affecting the nerves, nor coagulating the juices, muſt in all caſes be a friend to nature, and aſſiſt the vis vitæ in it's ſtruggle againſt all kinds of contagion. And from what I have obſerved, tar-water appears to me an uſeful preſervative in all epidemical diſorders, and againſt all other infection whatſoever, as well as that of the ſmall-pox. What effects the animi pathemata have in human maladies, is well known, and conſequently the general benefit of ſuch a cardiac may be reaſonably ſuppoſed.

86. As the body is ſaid to clothe the ſoul, ſo the nerves may be ſaid to conſtitute her inner garment. And as the ſoul animates the whole, what

(*a*) 2, 3. (*b*) 66.

nearly touches the soul relates to all. Therefore the asperity of tartarous salts, and the fiery acrimony of alcaline salts, irritating and wounding the nerves, produce nascent passions and anxieties in the soul; which both aggravate distempers, and render mens lives restless and wretched, even when they are afflicted with no apparent distemper. This is the latent spring of much woe, spleen, and tædium vitæ. Small imperceptible irritations of the minutest fibres or filaments, caused by the pungent salts of wines and sauces, do so shake and disturb the microcosms of high livers, as often to raise tempests in courts and senates. Whereas the gentle vibrations that are raised in the nerves, by a fine subtile acid, sheathed in a smooth volatile oil (*a*), softly stimulating and bracing the nervous vessels and fibres, promotes a due circulation and secretion of the animal juices, and creates a calm satisfied sense of health. And accordingly I have often known tar-water procure sleep and compose the spirits in cruel vigils, occasioned either by sickness or by too intense application of mind.

87. In diseases sometimes accidents happen from without by mismanagement, sometimes latent causes operate within, jointly with the specific taint or peculiar cause of the malady. The causes of distempers are often complicated, and there may be something in the idiosyncrasy of the patient that puzzles the physician. It may therefore be presumed that no medicine is infallible, not even in any one disorder. But as tar-water possesseth the virtues of fortifying the stomach, as well as purifying and invigorating the blood, beyond any medicine that I know, it may be presumed of great

(*a*) 59, 61.

and general efficacy in all those numerous illnesses, which take their rise from foul or vapid blood, or from a bad digestion. The animal spirits are elaborated from the blood. Such therefore as the blood is, such will be the animal spirit, more or less, weaker or stronger. This sheweth the usefulness of tar-water in all hysteric and hypochondriac cases; which together with the maladies from indigestion comprise almost the whole tribe of chronical diseases.

88. The scurvy may be reckoned in these climates an universal malady, as people in general are subject to it, and as it mixes more or less in almost all diseases. Whether this proceeds from want of elasticity in our air, upon which the tone of the vessels depends, and upon that the several secretions; or whether it proceeds from the moisture of our climate, or the grossness of our food, or the salts in our atmosphere, or from all these together; thus much at least seems not absurd to suppose, that, as physicians in Spain and Italy are apt to suspect the venereal taint to be a latent principle, and bear a part in every illness, so, for as good reason, the scurvy should be considered by our physicians, as having some share in most disorders and constitutions that fall in their way. It is certain our perspiration is not so free as in clearer air and warmer climates. Perspirable humours not discharged will stagnate and putrify. A diet of animal food will be apt to render the juices of our bodies alcalescent. Hence ichorous and corrosive humours and many disorders. Moist air makes viscid blood; and saline air inflames this viscid blood. Hence broken capillaries, extravasated blood, spots, and ulcers, and other scorbutic symptoms. The body of a man attracts and imbibes the moisture and salts of the air, and what-

ever floats in the atmosphere, which, as it is common to all, so it affects all more or less.

89. Doctor Musgrave thinks the Devonshire scurvy a relicque of the leprosy, and that it is not owing to the qualities of the air. But as these insulars in general live in a gross saline air, and their vessels being less elastic, are consequently less able to subdue and cast off what their bodies, as sponges, draw in, one would be tempted to suspect the air not a little concerned, especially in such a situation as that of Devonshire. In all these British islands we enjoy a great mediocrity of climate, the effect whereof is, that we have neither heat enough to exalt and dissipate the gross vapours, as in Italy, nor cold enough to condense and precipitate them, as in Sweden. So they are left floating in the air, which we constantly breath, and imbibe through the whole surface of our bodies. And this, together with exhalations from coal fires, and the various fossils wherein we abound, doth greatly contribute to render us scorbutic and hypochondriac.

90. There are some who derive all diseases from the scurvy, which indeed must be allowed to create or mimic most other maladies. Boerhaave tells us, it produceth pleuritic, colic, nephritic, hepatic pains, various fevers, hot, malignant, intermitting, dysenteries, faintings, anxieties, dropsies, consumptions, convulsions, palsies, fluxes of blood. In a word, it may be said to contain the seeds and origin of almost all distempers. Insomuch that a medicine which cures all sorts of scurvy, may be presumed good for most other maladies.

91. The scurvy doth not only in variety of symptoms imitate most distempers, but also when come to a height, in degree of virulence equal the most malignant. Of this we have a remarkable proof, in that horrible description of the scorbutic

 patients

patients in the hospitals of Paris, given by monsieur Poupart, in the Memoirs of the royal academy of sciences, for the year one thousand six hundred and ninety-nine. That author thinks he saw some resemblance in it to the plague of Athens. It is hard to imagine any thing more dreadful than the case of those men, rotting alive by the scurvy in its supreme degree. To obviate such putrefaction, I believe the most effectual method would be, to embalm (if one may so say) the living body with tar-water copiously drunk; and this belief is not without experience.

92. It is the received opinion that the animal salts of a sound body are of a neutral, bland and benign nature: that is, the salts in the juices past the primæ viæ, are neither acid nor alcaline, having been subdued by the constitution, and changed into a third nature. Where the constitution wants force to do this, the aliment is not duly assimilated; and so far as the salts retain their pristine qualities, sickly symptoms ensue, acids and alkalies, not perfectly subdued, producing weak ferments in the juices. Hence scurvy, cachexy, and a long train of ills.

93. A cachexy or ill habit is much of the same kind with the scurvy, proceeds from the same causes, and is attended with like symptoms, which are so manifold and various, that the scurvy may well be looked on as a general cachexy, infecting the whole habit, and vitiating all the digestions. Some have reckoned as many sorts of the scurvy, as there are different taints of the blood. Others have supposed it a collection of all illnesses together. Some suppose it an accumulation of several diseases in fieri. Others take it for an assemblage of the reliques of old distempers.

94. But

94. But thus much is certain, the cure of the scurvy is no more to be attempted by strongly active medicines than (to use the similitude of an ingenious writer) a thorn in the flesh, or pitch on silk to be removed by force. The viscid humour must be gently resolved and diluted, the tone of the vessels recovered by a moderate stimulation, and the tender fibres and capillary vessels gradually cleared from the concreted stuff, that adheres and obstructs them. All which is in the aptest manner performed by a watery diluent, containing a fine vegetable soap. And although a complete cure by alteratives, operating on the small capillaries, and by insensible discharges, must require length of time, yet the good effect of this medicine on cachectic and scorbutic persons, is soon perceived, by the change it produceth in their pale discoloured looks, giving a florid healthy countenance in less time than perhaps any other medicine.

95. It is supposed by physicians, that the immediate cause of the scurvy lies in the blood, the fibrous part of which is too thick and the serum too thin and sharp: and that hence ariseth the great difficulty in the cure, because in the correcting of one part, regard must be had to the other. It is well known how extremely difficult it is to cure an inveterate scurvy: how many scorbutic patients have grown worse by an injudicious course of evacuations: how many are even rendered incurable by the treatment of inconsiderate physicians: and how difficult, tedious and uncertain the cure is in the hands even of the best, who are obliged to use such variety and change of medicines, in the different stages of that malady: which nevertheless may be cured (if I may judge by what I have experienced) by the sole, regular, constant, copious use of tar-water.

96. Tar-

96. Tar-water moderately inspissates with its balsamic virtue, and renders mild the thin and sharp part of the blood. The same, as a soapy medicine, dissolves the grumous concretions of the fibrous part. As a balsam it destroys the ulcerous acrimony of the humours, and as a deobstruent it opens and cleans the vessels, restores their tone, and strengthens the digestion, whose defects are the principal cause of scurvy and cachexy.

97. In the cure of the scurvy, the principal aim is to subdue the acrimony of the blood and juices. But as this acrimony proceeds from different causes, or even opposite, as acid and alkaline, what is good in one sort of scurvy proves dangerous, or even mortal, in another. It is well known, that hot antiscorbutics, where the juices of the body are alcalescent, increase the disease. And sour fruits and vegetables produce a like effect in the scurvy, caused by an acid acrimony. Hence fatal blunders are committed by unwary practitioners, who, not distinguishing the nature of the disease, do frequently aggravate, instead of curing it. If I may trust what trials I have been able to make, this water is good in the several kinds of scurvy, acid, alcaline, and muriatic, and I believe it the only medicine that cures them all without doing hurt in any. As it contains a volatile acid (a) with a fine volatile oil, why may not a medicine cool in one part and warm in another, be a remedy to either extreme (b)? I have observed it to produce a kindly genial warmth without heat, a thing to be aimed at in all sorts of scurvy. Besides, the balsam in tar-water sheaths all scorbutic salts alike: and its great virtues as a digester and deob-

(a) 7. (b) 72.

ſtruent are of general uſe in all ſcorbutic, and, I may add, in all chronical caſes whatſoever.

98. I cannot be ſure that I have tried it in a ſcrophulous caſe, though I have tried it ſucceſsfully in one that I ſuſpected to be ſo. And I apprehend it would be very ſerviceable in ſuch diſorders. For although Doctor Gibbs, in his treatiſe of the King's Evil, derives that diſeaſe from a coagulating acid, which is alſo agreeable to the opinion of ſome other phyſicians, and although tar-water contains an acid, yet as it is a ſoap (*a*), it reſolves inſtead of coagulating the juices of the body.

99. For hyſterical and hypochondriacal diſorders ſo frequent among us, it is commonly ſuppoſed that all acids are bad. But I will venture to except the acid ſoap of tar-water, having found, by my own experience, and that of many others, that it raiſeth the ſpirits, and is an excellent antihyſteric, nor leſs innocent than potent, which cannot be ſaid of thoſe others in common uſe, that often leave people worſe than they found them.

100. In a high degree of ſcurvy a mercurial ſalivation is looked on by many as the only cure. Which, by the vehement ſhock it gives the whole frame, and the ſenſible ſecretion it produceth, may be thought to be more adequate to ſuch an effect. But the diſorder occaſioned by that violent proceſs, it is to be feared, may never be got over. The immediate danger, the frequent bad effects, the extreme trouble and nice care attending ſuch a courſe do very deſervedly make people afraid of it. And though the ſenſible ſecretion therein be ſo great, yet in a longer tract of time the uſe of tar-water may produce as great

(*a*) 58.

a diſa discharge of scorbutic salts by urine and by perspiration, the effect of which last, though not so sensible, may yet be greater than that of salivation; especially if it be true, that in common life insensible perspiration is to nutrition, and all sensible excretions, as five to three.

101. Many hysteric and scorbutic ailments, many taints contracted by themselves, or inherited from their ancestors, afflict the people of condition in these islands, often rendering them, upon the whole, much more unhappy than those whom poverty and labour have ranked in the lowest lot of life; which ailments might be safely removed or relieved by the sole use of tar-water; and those lives, which seem hardly worth living, for bad appetite, low spirits, restless nights, wasting pains and anxieties, be rendered easy and comfortable.

102. As the nerves are instruments of sensation, it follows that spasms in the nerves may produce all symptoms, and therefore a disorder in the nervous system shall imitate all distempers, and occasion, in appearance, an asthma for instance, a pleurisy, or a fit of the stone. Now whatever is good for the nerves in general, is good against all such symptoms. But tar-water, as it includes in an eminent degree the virtues of warm gums and resins, is of great use for comforting and strengthening the nerves *(a)*, curing twitches in the nervous fibres, cramps also, and numbness in the limbs, removing anxieties and promoting sleep, in all which cases I have known it very successful.

103. This safe and cheap medicine suits all circumstances and all constitutions, operating easily, curing without disturbing, raising the spirits without depressing them, a circumstance that deserves

(a) 86.

repeated

repeated attention, especially in these climates where strong liquors so fatally and so frequently produce those very distresses they are designed to remedy; and, if I am not misinformed, even among the ladies themselves, who are truly much to be pitied. Their condition of life makes them a prey to imaginary woes, which never fail to grow up in minds unexercised and unemployed. To get rid of these, it is said, there are who betake themselves to distilled spirits. And it is not improbable they are led gradually to the use of those poisons by a certain complaisant pharmacy, too much used in the modern practice, palsy drops, poppy cordial, plague water, and such like, which being in truth nothing but drams disguised, yet coming from the apothecaries, are considered only as medicines.

104. The soul of man was supposed by many ancient sages, to be thrust into the human body as into a prison, for punishment of past offences. But the worst prison is the body of an indolent Epicure, whose blood is inflamed by fermented liquors (*a*) and high sauces, or render'd putrid, sharp, and corrosive, by a stagnation of the animal juices through sloth and indolence; whose membranes are irritated by pungent salts, whose mind is agitated by painful oscillations of the nervous (*b*) system, and whose nerves are mutually affected by the irregular passions of his mind. This ferment in the animal œconomy darkens and confounds the intellect. It produceth vain terrors and vain conceits, and stimulates the soul with mad desires, which, not being natural, nothing in nature can satisfy. No wonder, therefore, there are so many fine persons of both sexes, shining themselves, and shone on by fortune, who are inwardly miserable and sick of life.

(*a*) 66. (*b*) 86.

105. The hardness of stubbed vulgar constitutions, renders them insensible of a thousand things, that fret and gall those delicate people, who, as if their skin was peeled off, feel to the quick every thing that touches them. The remedy for this exquisite and painful sensibility is commonly sought from fermented, perhaps from distilled, liquors, which render many lives wretched, that would otherwise have been only ridiculous. The tender nerves, and low spirits of such poor creatures, would be much relieved by the use of tar-water, which might prolong and cheer their lives. I do therefore recommend to them the use of a cordial, not only safe and innocent, but giving health and spirit as surely as other cordials destroy them.

106. I do verily think, there is not any other medicine whatsoever, so effectual to restore a crazy constitution, and cheer a dreary mind, or so likely to subvert that gloomy empire of the spleen (*a*), which tyrannizeth over the better sort (as they are called) of these free nations; and maketh them, in spight of their liberty and property, more wretched slaves than even the subjects of absolute power, who breath clear air in a sunny climate. While men of low degree often enjoy a tranquillity and content, that no advantage of birth or fortune can equal. Such, indeed, was the case, while the rich alone could afford to be debauched; but when even beggars became debauchees, the case was altered.

107. The public virtue and spirit of the British legislature never shewed itself more conspicuous in any act, that in that for suppressing the immoderate use of distilled spirits among the people, whose strength and numbers constitute the true wealth of a nation: though evasive arts

(*a*) 103.

will

will, it is feared, prevail so long as distilled spirits of any kind are allowed, the character of Englishmen in general being that of Brutus, Quicquid vult, valde vult. But why should such a canker be tolerated in the vitals of a state, under any pretence or in any shape whatsoever? Better by far, the whole present set of distillers were pensioners of the public, and their trade abolished by law; since all the benefit thereof put together would not balance the hundredth part of its mischief.

108. To prove the destructive effects of such spirits with regard both to the human species and individuals, we need not go so far as our colonies, or the savage natives of America. Plain proof may be had nearer home. For, albeit there is in every town or district throughout England, some tough dram-drinker, set up as the Devil's decoy to draw in proselytes; yet the ruined health and morals, and the beggary of such numbers evidently shew, that we need no other enemy to compleat our destruction, than this cheap luxury at the lower end of the state, and that a nation lighted up at both ends must soon be consumed.

109. It is much to be lamented that our Insulars, who act and think so much for themselves, should yet, from grossness of air and diet, grow stupid or doat sooner than other people, who, by virtue of elastic air, water-drinking, and light food, preserve their faculties to extreme old age; an advantage which may perhaps be approached, if not equalled, even in these regions, by tar-water, temperance, and early hours; the last is a sure addition to life, not only in regard of time, which, being taken from sleep, the image of death, is added to the waking hours, but also in regard of longevity and duration in the vulgar

 sense.

ſenſe. I may ſay too, in regard of ſpirit and vivacity, which, within the ſame compaſs of duration, may truly and properly be affirmed to add to man's life: it being manifeſt, that one man, by a briſker motion of his ſpirits and ſucceſſion of his ideas, ſhall live more in one hour, than another in two: and that the quantity of life is to be eſtimated, not merely from the duration, but alſo from the intenſeneſs of living. Which intenſe living, or, if I may ſo ſay, lively life, is not more promoted by early hours as a regimen, than by tar-water as a cordial; which acts, not only as a ſlow medicine, but hath alſo an immediate and chearful (*a*) effect on the ſpirits.

110. It muſt be owned, that light attracted, ſecreted, and detained in tar (*b*), and afterwards drawn off in its fineſt balſamic particles, by the gentle menſtruum of cold water, is not a violent and ſudden medicine, always to produce its effect at once, (ſuch, by irritating, often do more miſchief than good) but a ſafe and mild alterative, which penetrates the whole ſyſtem, opens, heals, and ſtrengthens the remote veſſels, alters and propels their contents, and enters the minuteſt capillaries, and cannot therefore, otherwiſe than by degrees and in time, work a radical cure of chronic diſtempers. It gives nevertheleſs ſpeedy relief in moſt caſes, as I have found by my ſelf and many others. I have been ſurprized to ſee perſons, fallen away and languiſhing under a bad digeſtion, after a few weeks recover a good ſtomach, and with it fleſh and ſtrength, ſo as to ſeem renewed, by the drinking of tar-water. The ſtrength and quantity of this water to be taken by each individual perſon is beſt determined from experience. And as for the time

(*a*) 66. (*b*) 8, 29, 40.

of

of taking, I never knew any evil enſue from its being continued ever ſo long; but, on the contrary, many and great advantages, which ſometimes would not perhaps begin to ſhew themſelves till it had been taken two or three months.

111. We learn from Pliny, that in the firſt ferment of new wine or muſtum, the ancients were wont to ſprinkle it with powdered roſin, which gave it a certain ſprightlineſs, quædam ſaporis acumina. This was eſteemed a great improver of its odour and taſte, and was, I doubt not, of its ſalubrity alſo. The brown old roſin, that is to ſay, harden'd tar, as being more eaſily pulverized and ſifted, was moſt in requeſt for this purpoſe. They uſed likewiſe to ſeaſon their wine-veſſels with pitch or roſin. And I make no doubt, that if our vintners would contrive to medicate their wines with the ſame ingredients, they might improve and preſerve them, with leſs trouble and expence to themſelves, and leſs danger to others. He that would know more particulars of this matter may conſult Pliny and Columella. I ſhall only add, that I doubt not a ſimilar improvement may be made of malt liquor.

112. The ῥητίνη of Theophraſtus and reſina of Pliny are ſometimes uſed in a general ſenſe, to ſignify all ſorts of oily viſcid exſudations from plants or trees. The crude watery juice, that riſeth early in the ſpring, is gradually ripened and inſpiſſated by the ſolar heat, becoming in orderly ſucceſſion with the ſeaſons an oil, a balſam, and at laſt a reſin. And it is obſerved by chemiſts, that turpentine diſſolved over a gentle fire, is, by the conſtant operation of heat, ſucceſſively transformed into oil, balſam, pitch, and hard friable reſin, which will incorporate with oil or rectified ſpirit, but not with water.

113. Sir

113. Sir John Floyer remarks, that we want a method for the uſe of turpentine, and again, he who ſhall hit, ſaith he, on the pleaſanteſt method of giving turpentine, will do great cures in the gout, ſtone, catarrhs, dropſies, and cold ſcurvies, rheumatiſms, ulcers, and obſtructions of the glands. Laſtly, he ſubjoins, that for the uſe of altering and amending the juices and fibres, it muſt be given frequently, and in ſuch ſmall quantities at a time, and in ſo commodious a manner, as will agree beſt with the ſtomach (*a*), ſtay longeſt in the body, and not purge itſelf off; for large doſes (ſaith he) go through too quick, and beſides offend the head. Now the infuſion of tar or turpentine in cold water ſeems to ſupply the very method that was wanted, as it leaves the more unctuous and groſs parts behind (*b*), which might offend the ſtomach, inteſtines, and head; and as it may be eaſily taken, and as often, and in ſuch quantity, and ſuch degree of ſtrength, as ſuits the caſe of the patient. Nor ſhould it ſeem, that the fine ſpirit and volatile oil, obtained by infuſion of tar (*c*) is inferior to that of turpentine, to which it ſuperadds the virtue of wood ſoot, which is known to be very great with reſpect to the head and nerves; and this appears evident from the manner of obtaining tar (*d*). And as the fine volatile parts of tar or turpentine are drawn off by infuſion in cold water and eaſily conveyed throughout the whole ſyſtem of the human body; ſo it ſhould ſeem the ſame method may be uſed with all ſorts of balſams or reſins whatſoever, as the readieſt, eaſieſt, and moſt inoffenſive, as well as in many caſes the moſt effectual way of obtaining and imparting their virtues.

(*a*) 9. (*b*) 47. (*c*) 7, 42, 58. (*d*) 13.

114. After

114. After having ſaid ſo much of the uſes of tar, I muſt farther add, that being rubb'd on them it is an excellent preſervative of the teeth and gums; that it ſweetens the breath, and that it clears and ſtrengthens the voice. And, as its effects are various and uſeful, ſo there is nothing to be feared from the operation of an alterative ſo mild and friendly to nature. It was a wiſe maxim of certain ancient philoſophers, that diſeaſes ought not to be irritated by medicines. But no medicine diſturbs the animal œconomy leſs than this (a), which, if I may truſt my own experience, never produces any diſorder in a patient when rightly taken.

115. I knew indeed a perſon who took a large glaſs of tar-water juſt before breakfaſt, which gave him an invincible nauſea and diſguſt, although he had before received the greateſt benefit from it. But if the tar-water be taken and made in the manner preſcribed at the beginning of this eſſay, it will, if I miſtake not, have enough of the ſalt to be uſeful, and little enough of the oil to be inoffenſive. I mean my own manner of making it, and not the American; that ſometimes makes it too ſtrong, and ſometimes too weak; which tar-water, however it might ſerve as there uſed, merely for a preparative againſt the ſmall-pox, yet I queſtion whether it may be fitly uſed in all thoſe various caſes wherein I have found tar-water ſo ſucceſsful. Perſons more delicate than ordinary may render it palatable, by mixing a drop of the chemical oil of nutmegs, or a ſpoonful of mountain wine in each glaſs. It may not be amiſs to obſerve, that I have known ſome, whoſe nice ſtomachs could not bear it in the morning, take it at night going to bed without any inconvenience; and that with ſome it agrees beſt warm, with others cold. It may be

(a) 133.

made

made ſtronger for brute beaſts, as horſes, in whoſe diſorders I have found it very uſeful, I believe more ſo than that bituminous ſubſtance call'd Barbadoes tar.

116. In very dangerous and acute caſes much may be taken and often; as far as the ſtomach can bear. But in chronical caſes, about half a pint, night and morning, may ſuffice; or in caſe ſo large a doſe ſhould prove diſagreeable, half the quantity may be taken at four times, to wit, in the morning, at night going to bed, and about two hours after dinner and breakfaſt. A medicine of ſo great virtue in ſo many different diſorders, and eſpecially in that grand enemy, the fever, muſt needs be a benefit to mankind in general. There are nevertheleſs three ſorts of people to whom I would peculiarly recommend it: Sea-faring perſons, ladies, and men of ſtudious and ſedentary lives.

117. To ſailors and all ſea-faring perſons, who are ſubject to ſcorbutic diſorders and putrid fevers, eſpecially in long ſouthern voyages, I am perſuaded this tar-water would be very beneficial. And this may deſerve particular notice in the preſent courſe of marine expeditions, when ſo many of our country-men have periſhed by ſuch diſtempers, contracted at ſea and in foreign climates. Which, it is probable, might have been prevented, by the copious uſe of tar-water.

118. This ſame water will alſo give charitable relief to the ladies (*a*), who often want it more than the pariſh poor; being many of them never able to make a good meal, and ſitting pale, puny, and forbidden like ghoſts, at their own table, victims of vapours and indigeſtion.

119. Studious perſons alſo, pent up in narrow holes, breathing bad air, and ſtooping over their

(*a*) 103.

books,

books, are much to be pitied. As they are debarred the free use of air and exercise, this I will venture to recommend as the best succedaneum to both. Though it were to be wished, that modern scholars would, like the ancients, meditate and converse more in walks and gardens and open air, which, upon the whole, would perhaps be no hindrance to their learning, and a great advantage to their health. My own sedentary course of life had long since thrown me into an ill habit, attended with many ailments, particularly a nervous colic, which rendered my life a burden, and the more so, because my pains were exasperated by exercise. But since the use of Tar-water, I find, though not a perfect recovery from my old and rooted illness, yet such a gradual return of health and ease, that I esteem my having taken this medicine the greatest of all temporal blessings, and am convinced that, under Providence, I owe my life to it.

120. In the distilling of turpentine and other balsams by a gentle heat, it hath been observed, that there riseth first an acid spirit (*n*), that will mix with water; which spirit, except the fire be very gentle, is lost. This grateful acid spirit that first comes over, is, as a learned chemist and physician informs us, highly refrigeratory, diuretic, sudorific, balsamic or preservative from putrefaction, excellent in nephritic cases, and for quenching thirst, all which virtues are contained in the cold infusion, which draws forth from tar only its fine flower or quintessence, if I may so say, or the native vegetable spirit, together with a little volatile oil.

121. The distinguishing principle of all vegetables, that whereon their peculiar smell, taste, and specific properties depend, seems to be some

(*n*) 7.

extremely fine and subtile spirit, whose immediate vehicle is an exceeding thin volatile oil, which is itself detained in a grosser and more viscid resin or balsam, lodged in proper cells in the bark and seeds, and most abounding in autumn or winter, after the crude juices have been thoroughly concocted, ripened, and impregnated with solar light. The spirit itself is by some supposed to be an oil highly subtilized, so as to mix with water. But such volatile oil is not the spirit, but only its vehicle. Since aromatic oils, being long exposed to air, will lose their specific smell and taste, which fly off with the spirit or vegetable salt, without any sensible diminution of the oil.

122. Those volatile salts, that are set free and raised by a gentle heat, may justly be supposed essential (a), and to have pre-existed in the vegetable; whereas the lixivial fixed salts obtained by the incineration of the subject, whose natural constituent parts have been altered or destroyed by the extreme force of fire, are by later chemists, upon very good grounds, supposed not to have pre-existed therein; all such salts appearing, from the experiments of signor Redi, not to preserve the virtues of the respective vegetable subjects; and to be alike purgative and in an equal degree, whatsoever may be the shape of their points, whether sharp or obtuse. But although fixed or lixivious salts may not contain the original properties of the subject; yet volatile salts raised by a slight heat from vegetables are allowed to preserve their native virtues: and such salts are readily imbibed by water.

123. The most volatile of the salts, and the most attenuated part of the oil, may be supposed

the

the first and readiest to impregnate a cold infusion (*b*). And this will assist us to account for the virtues of tar-water. That volatile acid in vegetables, which resists putrefaction, and is their great preservative, is detained in a subtile oil miscible with water, which oil is itself imprisoned in the resin or grosser part of the tar, from which it is easily set free and obtained pure by cold water.

124. The mild native acids are observed more kindly to work upon, and more thoroughly to dissolve, metallic bodies, than the strongest acid spirits produced by a vehement fire; and it may be suspected, they have the same advantage as a medicine. And as no acid, by the observation of some of the best chemists, can be obtained from the substance of animals thoroughly assimilated, it should follow, that the acids received into a healthy body must be quite subdued and changed by the vital powers: but it is easier to subdue and assimilate (*c*) the gentler than the stronger acids.

125. I am very sensible, that on such subjects arguments fall short of evidence: and that mine fall short even of what they might have been, if I enjoyed better health, or those opportunities of a learned commerce, from which I am cut off in this remote corner. I shall nevertheless go on as I have begun, and proceed by reason, by conjecture, and by authority, to cast the best light I can on the obscure paths that lie in my way.

126. Sir Isaac Newton, Boerhaave, and Homberg are all agreed, that the acid is a fine subtile substance, pervading the whole terraqueous globe; which produceth divers kinds of bodies, as it is united to different subjects. This, according to

(*b*) 1, 7. (*c*) 48.

Homberg, is the pure salt, salt the principle, in it self similar and uniform, but never found alone. And although this principle be called the salt of the earth, yet it should seem it may more properly be called the salt of the air, since earth turned up and lying fallow receives it from the air. And it should seem that this is the great principle of vegetation, derived into the earth from all sorts of manures, as well as from the air. This acid is allowed to be the cause of fermentation in all fermented liquors. Why therefore, may it not be supposed to ferment the earth, and to constitute that fine penetrating principle, which introduces and assimilates the food of plants, and is so fugitive as to escape all the filtrations and perquisitions of the most nice observers?

127. It is the doctrine of Sir Isaac Newton and Monsieur Homberg, that, as the watry acid is that which renders salt soluble in water, so it is that same which joined to the earthy part makes it a salt. Let it therefore be considered, that the organs (*d*) of plants are tubes, the filling, unfolding, and distending whereof by liquors, doth constitute what is called the vegetation or growth of the plant. But earth itself is not soluble in water, so as to form one vegetable fluid therewith. Therefore the particles of earth must be joined with a watry acid, that is, they must become salts in order to dissolve in water; that so, in the form of a vegetable juice, they may pass through the strainers and tubes of the root into the body of the plant, swelling and distending its parts and organs, that is, increasing its bulk. Therefore the vegetable matter of the earth is in effect earth changed into salt. And to render earth

(*d*) 30, 31, 35.

fertile

fertile, is to cause many of its particles to assume a saline form.

128. Hence it is observed, there are more salts in the root than in the bark, more salts in vegetables during the spring, than in the autumn or winter, the crude saline juices being in the summer months partly evaporated, and partly ripened by the action and mixture of light. Hence also it appears, why the dividing of earth, so as to enlarge its surface, whereby it may admit more acid from the air, is of such use in promoting vegetation: And why ashes, lime, and burnt clay are found so profitable manures, fire being in reality the acid, as is proved in the sequel (*a*). Marls also and shells are useful, forasmuch as those alkaline bodies attract the acid, and raise an effervescence with it, thereby promoting a fermentation in the glebe. The excrements of animals and putrid vegetables do in like manner contribute to vegetation, by increasing the salts of the earth. And where fallows are well broken, and lye long to receive the acid of the air into all their parts; this alone will be sufficient to change many terrene particles into salts, and consequently render them soluble in water, and therefore fit aliment for vegetables.

129. The acid, saith Homberg, is always joined to some sulphur, which determines it to this or that species, producing different salts, as it is the vegetable, bituminous, or metallic sulphur. Even the alkaline, whether volatile or lixivial salts, are supposed to be nothing but this same acid strictly detained by oil and earth, in spight of the extreme force of fire, which lodgeth in them, without being able to dislodge some remains of the acid.

(*a*) 202.

130. Salts,

130. Salts, according to Sir Isaac Newton, are dry earth and watery acid united by attraction, the acid rendering them soluble in water (*f*). He supposeth the watery acid to flow round the terrestrial part, as the ocean doth round the earth, being attracted thereby, and compares each particle of salt, to a chaos whereof the innermost part is hard and earthy, but the surface soft and watery. Whatever attracts and is attracted most strongly is an acid in his sense.

131. It seems impossible to determine the figures of particular salts. All acid solvents together with the dissolved bodies are apt to shoot into certain figures. And the figures, in which the fossil salts crystallize, have been supposed the proper natural shapes of them and their acids. But Homberg hath clearly shewed the contrary: forasmuch as the same acid dissolving different bodies, assumes different shapes. Spirit of nitre, for instance, having dissolved copper, shoots into hexagonal crystals; the same having dissolved iron, shoots into irregular squares; and again, having dissolved silver, forms thin crystals of a triangular figure.

132. Homberg nevertheless holds in general, that acids are shaped like daggers, and alcalies like sheaths: and that moving in the same liquor, the daggers run into the sheaths fitted to receive them, with such violence as to raise that effervescence observed in the mixture of acids and alkalies. But it seems very difficult to conceive, how, or why the mere configuration of daggers and sheaths, floating in the same liquor, should cause the former to rush with such vehemence, and direct their points so aptly into the latter, any more than a parcel of spigots and fossets floating together in the same water, should rush one into the other.

(*f*) 127.

133. It should seem rather, that the vehement attraction which Sir Isaac Newton attributes to all acids, whereby he supposeth them to rush towards, penetrate, shake, and divide the most solid bodies, and to ferment the liquid of vegetables, could better account for this phænomenon. It is in this attraction, that Sir Isaac placeth all their activity, and indeed it should seem, the figures of salts were not of such efficacy in producing their effects, as the strong attractive powers whereby they are agitated and do agitate other bodies. Especially if it be true (what was before remarked) that lixivious salts are alike purgative, whatever may be the shape of their angles, whether more or less acute or obtuse.

134. Sir Isaac Newton accounts for the watery acids making earthy corpuscles soluble in water, by supposing the acid to be a mean between earth and water, its particles greater than those of water, and less than those of earth, and strongly to attract both. But perhaps there is no necessary reason for supposing the parts of the acid grosser than the parts of water, in order to produce this effect; may not this as well be accounted for, by giving them only a strong attraction or cohesion with the bodies to which they are joined?

135. The acid spirit or salt, that mighty instrument in the hand of nature, residing in the air, and diffused throughout that whole element, is discernible also in many parts of the earth, particularly in fossils, such as sulphur, vitriol, and allum; it was already observed from Homberg, that this acid is never found pure, but hath always sulphur joined with it, and is classed by the difference of its sulphurs, whether mineral, vegetable, or animal.

136. Salts are vulgarly reckoned the most active of chemical principles. But Homberg derives all

their

their activity from the sulphurs joined with them. From which also, as hath been said, he derives all their kinds and differences (*g*). Salt, water, oil, and earth seem to be originally the same in all vegetables. All the difference, according to the chemists, ariseth from a spirit residing in the oil, called the Rector or Archæus. This is otherwise called by chemists, ens primum, or the native spirit, whereon depend, and wherein are contained, the peculiar flavour and odour, the specific qualities and virtues of the plant.

137. These native spirits or vegetable souls are all breathed or exhaled into the air, which seems the receptacle as well as source of all sublunary forms, the great mass or chaos which imparts and receives them. The air, or atmosphere, that surrounds our earth, contains a mixture of all the active volatile parts of the whole habitable world, that is, of all vegetables, minerals, and animals. Whatever perspires, corrupts, or exhales, impregnates the air; which, being acted upon by the solar fire, produceth within itself all sorts of chemical operations, dispensing again those salts and spirits in new generations, which it had received from putrefactions.

138. The perpetual oscillations of this elastic and restless element operate without ceasing on all things that have life, whether animal or vegetable, keeping their fibres, vessels, and fluids in a motion always changing; as heat, cold, moisture, dryness, and other causes alter the elasticity of the air. Which accounts, it must be owned, for many effects. But there are many more which must be derived from other principles or qualities in the air. Thus iron and copper are corroded and gather rust in the air, and bodies of all sorts are dissolved or corrupted,

(*g*) 129.

which sheweth an acid to abound and diffuse itself throughout the air.

139. By this same air fire is kindled, the lamp of life preserved, respiration, digestion, nutrition, the pulse of the heart and motion of all the muscles seem to be performed. Air therefore is a general agent, not only exerting its own, but calling forth the qualities or powers of all other bodies, by a division, comminution, and agitation of their particles, causing them to fly off and become volatile and active.

140. Nothing ferments, vegetates, or putrefies without air, which operates with all the virtues of the bodies included in it; that is, of all nature; there being no drug, salutary or poisonous, whose virtues are not breathed into the air. The air therefore is an active mass of numberless different principles, the general source of corruption and generation; on one hand dividing, abrading, and carrying off the particles of bodies, that is, corrupting or dissolving them; on the other, producing new ones into being; destroying and bestowing forms without intermission.

141. The seeds of things seem to lye latent in the air, ready to appear and produce their kind, whenever they light on a proper matrix. The extremely small seeds of fern, mosses, mushrooms, and some other plants are concealed and wafted about in the air, every part whereof seems replete with seeds of one kind or other. The whole atmosphere seems alive. There is every where acid to corrode, and seed to engender. Iron will rust, and mold will grow in all places. Virgin earth becomes fertile, crops of new plants ever and anon shew themselves; all which demonstrates the air to be a common seminary and receptable of all vivifying principles.

142. Air may also be said to be the seminary of minerals and metals, as it is of vegetables. Mr. Boyle informs us, that the exhausted ores of tin and iron being exposed to the air become again impregnated with metal, and that ore of alum having lost its salt recovers it after the same manner. And numberless instances there are of salts produced by the air, that vast collection or treasury of active principles, from which all sublunary bodies seem to derive their forms, and on which animals depend for their life and breath.

143. That there is some latent vivifying spirit dispersed throughout the air, common experience sheweth; inasmuch as it is necessary both to vegetables and animals (*b*) whether terrestrial or aquatic, neither beasts, insects, birds, nor fishes being able to subsist without air. Nor doth all air suffice, there being some quality or ingredient, of which when air is deprived, it becometh unfit to maintain either life or flame. And this even though the air should retain its elasticity; which, by the bye, is an argument that air doth not act only as an antagonist to the intercostal muscles. It hath both that and many other uses. It gives and preserves a proper tone to the vessels: this elastic fluid promotes all secretions: its oscillations keep every part in motion: it pervades and actuates the whole animal system, producing great variety of effects, and even opposite in different parts, cooling at the same time and heating, distending and contracting, coagulating and resolving, giving and taking, sustaining life and impairing it, pressing without and expanding within, abrading some parts, at the same time insinuating and supplying others, producing various vibrations in the fibres, and fer-

(*b*) 138, 139.

ments

ments in the fluids; all which must needs ensue from such a subtile, active, heterogeneous and elastic fluid.

144. But there is, as we have observed, some one quality or ingredient in the air, on which life more immediately and principally depends. What that is, though men are not agreed, yet it is agreed that it must be the same thing that supports the vital and the common flame; it being found that when air, by often breathing in it, is become unfit for the one, it will no longer serve for the other. The like is observeable in poisonous damps or steams, wherein flame cannot be kindled. As is evident in the Grotto del cane near Naples. And here it occurs, to recommend the plunging them into cold water, as an experiment to be tried on persons affected by breathing a poisonous vapour in old vaults, mines, deep holes or cavities under ground. Which, I am apt to think, might save the lives of several, by what I have seen practised on a dog convulsed, and in all appearance dead, but instantly reviving on being taken out of the abovementioned grotto and thrown into a lake adjacent.

145. Air, the general menstruum and seminary, seemeth to be only an aggregate of the volatile parts of all natural beings, which variously combined and agitated produce many various effects. Small particles in a near and close situation strongly act upon each other, attracting, repelling, vibrating. Hence divers fermentations, and all the variety of meteors, tempests, and concussions both of earth and firmament. Nor is the microcosm less affected thereby. Being pent up in the viscera, vessels, and membranes of the body, by its salts, sulphurs, and elastic power, it engenders colics, spasms, hysteric disorders, and other maladies.

16. The specific quality of air is taken to be

permanent elasticity. Mr. Boyle is expresly of this opinion. And yet, whether there be any such thing as permanently elastic air may be doubted, there being many things which seem to rob the air of this quality, or at least lessen and suspend its exertion. The salts and sulphurs, for instance, that float in the air abate much of its elasticity by their attraction.

147. Upon the whole it is manifest, that air is no distinct element, but a mass or mixture of things the most heterogeneous and even opposite to each other (*m*), which become air, by acquiring an elasticity and volatility from the attraction of some active, subtile substance; whether it be called fire, æther, light, or the vital spirit of the world; in like manner as the particles of antimony, of themselves not volatile, are carried off in sublimation and rendered volatile, by cohering with the particles of sal ammoniac. But action and reaction being equal, the spring of this æthereal spirit is diminished by being imparted. Its velocity and subtilty are also less from its being mixed with grosser particles. Hence sound moves slower than light, as mud than water.

148. Whether air be only freed and fixed, or generated and destroyed, it is certain that air begins and ceases to exert and shew itself. Much by experiments seems to be generated, not only from animals, fruits, and vegetables, but also from hard bodies. And it is observed by Sir Isaac Newton, that air produced from hard bodies is most elastic. The transmutation of elements, each into other, hath been anciently held. In Plutarch we find it was the opinion of Heraclitus, that the death of fire was a birth to air, and the death of air a birth to water. This opinion is also maintained by

(*m*) 137, 145.

Sir

Sir Isaac Newton. Though it may be questioned, whether what is thought a change be not only a disguise.

149. Fire seems the most elastic and expansive of all bodies. It communicates this quality to moist vapours and dry exhalations, when it heats and agitates their parts, cohering closely with them, overcoming their former mutual attraction, and causing them, instead thereof, reciprocally to repel each other and fly asunder, with a force proportionable to that wherewith they had cohered.

150. Therefore in air we may conceive two parts, the one more gross, which was raised and carried off from the bodies of this terraqueous mass: the other a fine subtile spirit by means whereof the former is rendered volatile and elastic. Together they compose a medium, whose elasticity is less than that of pure æther, fire, or spirit, in proportion to the quantity of salts, vapours, and heterogeneous particles contained therein. Hence it follows, that there is no such thing as a pure simple element of air. It follows also, that on the highest mountains air should be more rare than in proportion to the vulgar rule, of the spaces being reciprocally as the pressures: and so in fact it is said to have been found, by the gentlemen of the French Academy of Sciences.

151. Æther, fire, or spirit being attracted and clogged by heterogeneous particles becometh less active; and the particles cohering with those of æther, become more active than before. Air therefore is a mass of various particles, abraded and sublimated from wet and dry bodies of all sorts, cohering with particles of æther; the whole permeated by pure æther, or light, or fire: for these words are used promiscuously by ancient philosophers.

152. This

152. This æther or pure invisible fire, the most subtile and elastic of all bodies, seems to pervade and expand itself throughout the whole universe. If air be the immediate agent or instrument in natural things, it is the pure invisible fire that is the first natural mover or spring, from whence the air derives its power (*a*). This mighty agent is every where at hand, ready to break forth into action, if not restrained and governed with the greatest wisdom. Being always restless and in motion, it actuates and enlivens the whole visible mass, is equally fitted to produce and to destroy, distinguishes the various stages of nature, and keeps up the perpetual round of generations and corruptions, pregnant with forms which it constantly sends forth and resorbs. So quick in its motions, so subtile and penetrating in its nature, so extensive in its effects, it seemeth no other than the vegetative soul or vital spirit of the world.

153. The animal spirit in man is the instrumental or physical cause both of sense and motion. To suppose sense in the world, would be gross and unwarranted. But loco-motive faculties are evident in all its parts. The Pythagoræans, Platonists, and Stoics held the world to be an animal. Though some of them have chosen to consider it as a vegetable. However the phænomena and effects do plainly shew there is a spirit that moves, and a mind or providence that presides. This providence, Plutarch saith, was thought to be in regard to the world, what the soul is in regard to man.

154. The order and course of things, and the experiments we daily make, shew there is a mind that governs and actuates this mundane system,

(*a*) 139, 149, 151.

as the proper real agent and cause. And that the inferior instrumental cause is pure æther, fire, or the substance of light (c) which is applied and determined by an infinite mind in the microcosm or universe, with unlimited power, and according to stated rules; as it is in the microcosm, with limited power and skill by the human mind. We have no proof either from experiment or reason, of any other agent or efficient cause than mind or spirit. When therefore we speak of corporeal agents or corporeal causes, this is to be understood in a different, subordinate, and improper sense.

155. The principles whereof a thing is compounded, the instrument used in its production, and the end for which it was intended, are all in vulgar use termed Causes, though none of them be strictly speaking agent or efficient. There is not any proof that an extended corporeal or mechanical cause doth really and properly act, even motion itself being in truth a passion. Therefore though we speak of this fiery substance as acting, yet it is to be understood only as a mean or instrument, which indeed is the case of all mechanical causes whatsoever. They are nevertheless sometimes termed agents and causes, although they are by no means active in a strict and proper signification. When, therefore, force, power, virtue, or action are mentioned as subsisting in an extended and corporeal or mechanical being, this is not to be taken in a true, genuine, and real, but only in a gross and popular sense, which sticks in appearances, and doth not analyse things to their first principles. In compliance with established language, and the use of the world, we must employ the popular current phrase. But then in regard to truth we ought to distinguish

(c) 29, 37, 136, 149.

its

its meaning. It may suffice to have made this declaration once for all, in order to avoid mistakes.

156. The calidum innatum, the vital flame, or animal spirit in man is supposed the cause of all motions, in the several parts of his body, whether voluntary or natural. That is, it is the instrument, by means whereof the mind exerts and manifests herself in the motions of the body. In the same sense may not fire be said to have force, to operate, and agitate the whole system of the world, which is held together and informed by one presiding mind, and animated throughout by one and the same fiery substance, as an instrumental and mechanical agent, not as a primary real efficient?

157. This pure spirit or invisible fire is ever ready to exert and shew itself in its effects (*d*), cherishing, heating, fermenting, dissolving, shining and operating in various manners, where a subject offers to employ or determine its force. It is present in all parts of the earth and firmament, though perhaps latent and unobserved, till some accident produceth it into act, and renders it visible in its effects.

158. There is no effect in nature, great, marvellous, or terrible, but proceeds from fire, that diffused and active principle, which at the same time that it shakes the earth and heavens, will enter, divide, and dissolve the smallest, closest, and most compacted bodies. In remote cavities of the earth it remains quiet, till perhaps an accidental spark from the collision of one stone against another kindles an exhalation, that gives birth to an earthquake or tempest, which splits mountains, or overturns cities. This same fire stands unseen in

(*d*) 152.

the

the focus of a burning glafs, till fubjects for it to act upon come in it's way, when it is found to melt, calcine, or vitrify the hardeft bodies.

159. No eye could ever hitherto difcern, and no fenfe perceive, the animal fpirit in a human body, otherwife than from it's effects. The fame may be faid of pure fire, or the fpirit of the univerfe, which is perceived only by means of fome other bodies, on which it operates, or with which it is joined. What the chemifts fay, of pure acids being never found alone, might as well be faid of pure fire.

160. The mind of man acts by an inftrument neceffarily. The τὸ ἡγεμονικὸν, or mind prefiding in the world, acts by an inftrument freely. Without inftrumental and fecond caufes, there could be no regular courfe of nature. And without a regular courfe, nature could never be underftood. Mankind muft always be at a lofs, not knowing what to expect, or how to govern themfelves, or direct their actions for the obtaining of any end. Therefore in the government of the world phyfical agents, improperly fo called, or mechanical, or fecond caufes, or natural caufes, or inftruments, are neceffary to affift, not the governor, but the governed.

161. In the human body the mind orders and moves the limbs: but the animal fpirit is fuppofed the immediate phyfical caufe of their motion. So likewife in the mundane fyftem, a mind prefides, but the immediate, mechanical, or inftrumental caufe, that moves or animates all it's parts, is the pure elementary fire or fpirit of the world. The more fine and fubtile part or fpirit is fuppofed to receive the impreffions of the firft mover, and communicate them to the groffer fenfible parts of this world. Motion, though in me-

taphyfical rigor and truth, a paffion or mere effect yet, in phyfics, paffeth for an action. And by this action all effects are fuppofed to be produced. Hence the various communications, determinations, accelerations of motion conftitute the laws of nature.

162. The pure æther or invifible fire contains parts of different kinds, that are impreffed with different forces, or fubjected to different laws of motion, attraction, repulfion, and expanfion, and endued with divers diftinct habitudes towards other bodies. Thefe feem to conftitute the many various qualities (*e*), virtues, flavours, odours, and colours, which diftinguifh natural productions. The different modes of cohefion, attraction, repulfion and motion, appear to be the fource from whence the fpecific properties are derived, rather than different fhapes or figures. This, as hath been already obferved, feems confirmed by the experiment of fixed falts operating one way, notwithftanding the difference of their angles. The original particles productive of odours, flavours, and other properties, as well as of colours, are, one may fufpect, all contained and blended together in that univerfal and original feminary of pure elementary fire; from which they are diverfly feparated and attracted, by the various fubjects of the animal, vegetable, and mineral kingdoms; which thereby become claffed into kinds, and endued with thofe diftinct properties, which continue till their feveral forms, or fpecific proportions of fire, return into the common mafs.

163. As the foul acts immediately on pure fire, fo pure fire operates immediately on air. That is, the abrafions of all terreftrial things being rendered volatile and elaftic by fire (*f*), and at the fame time leffening the volatility and expanfive force of the

(*e*) 37, 40, 44. (*f*) 149, 150, 152.

fire, whoſe particles they attract and adhere to (*k*), there is produced a new fluid, more volatile than water or earth, and more fixed than fire. Therefore the virtues and operations imputed to air muſt be ultimately attributed to fire, as that which imparts activity to air itſelf.

164. The element of æthereal fire or light ſeems to comprehend, in a mixed ſtate, the ſeeds, the natural cauſes and forms (*g*) of all ſublunary things. The groſſer bodies ſeparate, attract, and repel the ſeveral conſtituent particles of that heterogeneous element; which, being parted from the common maſs, make diſtinct eſſences, producing and combining together ſuch qualities and properties, as are peculiar to the ſeveral ſubjects, and thence often extracted in eſſential oils or odoriferous waters, from whence they exhale into the open air, and return into their original element.

165. Blue, red, yellow, and other colours, have been diſcovered by Sir Iſaac Newton to depend on the parted rays or particles of light. And in like manner, a particular odour or flavour ſeemeth to depend on peculiar particles of light or fire (*h*); as appears from heat's being neceſſary to all vegetation whatſoever, and from the extreme minuteneſs and volatility of thoſe vegetable ſouls or forms, flying off from the ſubjects without any ſenſible diminution of their weight. Theſe particles, blended in one common ocean, ſhould ſeem to conceal the diſtinct forms, but, parted and attracted by proper ſubjects, diſcloſe or produce them. As the particles of light, which, when ſeparated, form diſtinct colours, being blended are loſt in one uniform appearance.

(*k*) 147. (*g*) 43. (*h*) 40.

166. Agreeably thereto, an æthereal ſubſtance or fire was ſuppoſed by Heraclitus to be the ſeed of the generation of all things, or that from which all things drew their original. The Stoics alſo taught, that all ſubſtance was originally fire and ſhould return to fire: that an active ſubtile fire was diffuſed or expanded throughout the whole univerſe; the ſeveral parts whereof were produced, ſuſtained, and held together by it's force. And it was the opinion of the Pythagoræans, as Laertius informs us, that heat or fire was the principle of life animating the whole ſyſtem, and penetrating all the elements (*a*). The Platoniſts too, as well as the Pythagoræans, held fire to be the immediate natural agent, or animal ſpirit; to cheriſh, to warm, to heat, to enlighten, to vegetate, to produce the digeſtions, circulations, ſecretions, and organical motions in all living bodies, vegetable or animal, being effects of that element, which, as it actuates the macrocoſm, ſo it animates the microcoſm. In the Timæus of Plato, there is ſuppoſed ſomething like a net of fire and rays of fire in a human body. Doth not this ſeem to mean the animal ſpirit, flowing, or rather darting thro' the nerves?

167. According to the Peripatetics, the form of heaven, or the fiery æthereal ſubſtance, contains the forms of all inferior beings (*b*). It may be ſaid to teem with forms, and impart them to ſubjects fitted to receive them. The vital force thereof in the Peripatetic ſenſe is vital to all, but diverſly received according to the diverſity of the ſubjects. So all colours are virtually contained in the light; but their actual diſtinctions of blue, red, yellow, and the reſt, depend on the difference of the objects which it illuſtrates. Ariſtotle in the book De

(*a*) 152, 153. (*b*) 43.

mundo,

mundo, ſuppoſeth a certain fifth eſſence, an æthereal nature unchangeable and impaſſive; and next in order a ſubtile, flaming ſubſtance, lighted up, or ſet on fire by that æthereal and divine nature. He ſuppoſeth, indeed, that God is in heaven, but that his power, or a force derived from him, doth actuate and pervade the univerſe.

168. If we may credit Plutarch, Empedocles thought æther or heat to be Jupiter. Æther by the ancient philoſophers was uſed to ſignify promiſcuouſly ſometimes fire and ſometimes air. For they diſtinguiſhed two ſorts of air. Plato in the Timæus ſpeaking of air, ſaith there are two kinds, the one more fine and ſubtile, called æther; the other more groſs and replete with vapours. This æther, or purer medium, ſeems to have been the air or principle, from which all things, according to Anaximenes, derived their birth, and into which they were back again reſolved at their death. Hippocrates, in his treatiſe De diæta, ſpeaketh of a fire pure and inviſible; and this fire, according to him, is that which, ſtirring and giving movement to all things, cauſes them to appear, or, as he ſtyles it, come into evidence, that is, to exiſt, every one in it's time, and according to its deſtiny.

169. This pure fire, æther, or ſubſtance of light, was accounted in itſelf inviſible and imperceptible to all our ſenſes, being perceived only by it's effects, ſuch as heat, flame, and rarefaction. To which we may add, that the moderns pretend further to have perceived it by weight, inaſmuch as the aromatic oils which moſt abound with fire, as being the moſt readily and vehemently enflamed, are above all others the heavieſt. And by an experiment of Mr. Homberg's, four ounces of regulus of antimony, being calcined by a burning glaſs

for

for an hour together, were found to have imbibed and fixed seven drams of the substance of light.

170. Such is the rarefying and expansive force of this element, as to produce in an instant of time the greatest and most stupendous effects: a sufficient proof, not only of the power of fire, but also of the wisdom with which it is managed, and withheld from bursting forth every moment to the utter ravage and destruction of all things. And it is very remarkable, that this same element, so fierce and destructive, should yet be so variously tempered and applied, as to be withal the salutary warmth, the genial, cherishing, and vital flame of all living creatures. It is not therefore to be wondered that Aristotle thought the heat of a living body to be somewhat divine and celestial, derived from that pure æther to which he supposed the incorporeal deity (χωριςὸν εἶδος) to be immediately united, or on which he supposed it immediately to act.

171. The Platonists held their intellect resided in soul, and soul in an æthereal vehicle. And that as the soul was a middle nature reconciling intellect with æther; so æther was another middle nature, which reconciled and connected the soul with grosser bodies (*d*). Galen likewise taught, that admitting the soul to be incorporeal, it hath for it's immediate tegument or vehicle a body of æther or fire, by the intervention whereof it moveth other bodies and is mutually affected by them. This interior clothing was supposed to remain upon the soul, not only after death, but after the most perfect purgation, which in length of time, according to the followers of Plato and Pythagoras, cleansed the soul,

——purumque reliquit
Æthereum sensum atque auraï simplicis ignem.

(*d*) 152, 154.

This

This tunicle of the ſoul, whether it be called pure æther, or luciform vehicle, or animal ſpirit, ſeemeth to be that which moves and acts upon the groſs organs, as it is determined by the ſoul, from which it immediately receives impreſſion, and in which the moving force truly and properly reſides. Some moderns have thought fit to deride all that is ſaid of æthereal vehicles, as mere jargon or, words without a meaning. But they ſhould have conſidered, that all ſpeech concerning the ſoul is altogether, or for the moſt part, metaphorical; and that, agreeably thereunto, Plato ſpeaketh of the mind or ſoul, as a driver that guides and govern a chariot, which is, not unfitly, ſtyled αὐγοειδὲς, a luciform æthereal vehicle, or ὄχημα, terms expreſſive of the purity, lightneſs, ſubtilty and mobility of that fine celeſtial nature, in which the ſoul immediately reſides and operates.

172. It was a tenet of the Stoics, that the world was an animal, and that providence anſwered to the reaſonable ſoul in man. But then the providence or mind was ſuppoſed by them to be immediately reſident or preſent in fire, to dwell therein, and to act thereby. Briefly, they conceived God to be an intellectual and fiery ſpirit, πνεῦμα νοερὸν καὶ πυρῶδες. Therefore though they looked on fire (*f*) as the τὸ ἡγεμονικὸν, or governing principle of the world; yet it was not ſimply fire, but animated with a mind.

173. Such are the bright and lively ſignatures of a divine mind, operating and diſplaying itſelf in fire and light throughout the world, that, as Ariſtotle obſerves in his book De mundo, all things ſeem full of divinities, whoſe apparitions on all ſides ſtrike and dazzle our eyes. And it muſt be

(*f*) 166.

owned

owned, the chief philosophers and wise men of antiquity, how much soever they attributed to second causes and the force of fire, yet they supposed a mind or intellect always resident therein, active or provident, restraining it's force and directing it's operations.

174. Thus Hipocrates, in his treatise De diæta, speaks of a strong but invisible fire (*g*), that rules all things without noise. Herein, saith he, resides soul, understanding, prudence, growth, motion, dimunition, change, sleep, and waking. This is what governs all things and is never in repose. And the same author, in his tract De carnibus, after a serious preface, setting forth that he is about to declare his own opinion, expresseth it in these terms: "That which we call heat, θερμὸν, appears to me "something immortal, which understands all "things, which sees and knows both what is pre-"sent, and what is to come."

175. This same heat is also what Hippocrates calls nature, the author of life and death, good and evil. It is farther to be noted of this heat, that he maketh it the object of no sense. It is that occult, universal nature, and inward invisible force, which actuates and animates the whole world, and was worshipped by the ancients under the name of Saturn; which Vossius judges, not improbably, to be derived from the Hebrew word Satar, to lye hidden or concealed. And what hath been delivered by Hippocrates agrees with the notions of other philosophers: Heraclitus (*h*), for instance, who held fire to be the principle and cause of the generation of all things, did not mean thereby an inanimate element, but, as he termed it, πῦρ ἀείζωον, an ever-living fire.

(*g*) 168. (*h*) 166.

176. Theo-

176. Theophrastus, in his book De igne, distinguisheth between heat and fire. The first he considers as a principle or cause, not that which appeareth to sense as a passion or accident existing in a subject, and which is in truth the effect of that unseen principle. And it is remarkable, that he refers the treating of this invisible fire or heat, to the investigation of the first causes. Fire, the principle, is neither generated nor destroyed, is every where and always present (*a*); while its effects in different times and places shew themselves more or less, and are very various, soft, and cherishing, or violent and destructive, terrible or agreeable, conveying good and evil, growth and decay, life and death, throughout the mundane system.

177. It is allowed by all, that the Greeks derived much of their philosophy from the Eastern nations. And Heraclitus is thought by some to have drawn his principles from Orpheus, as Orpheus did from the Ægyptians; or, as others write, he had been auditor of Hippasus a Pythagorean, who held the same notion of fire, and might have derived it from Egypt by his master Pythagoras, who had travelled into Ægypt, and been instructed by the sages of that nation. One of whose tenets it was, that fire was the principle of all action; which is agreeable to the doctrine of the Stoics, that the whole of things is administered by a fiery intellectual spirit. In the Asclepian Dialogue, we find this notion, that all parts of the world vegetate by a fine subtil æther, which acts as an engine or instrument, subject to the will of the supreme God.

178. As the Platonists held intellect to be lodged in soul, and soul in æther (*b*); so it passeth

(*a*) 43. (*b*) 157.

for a doctrine of Trismegistus in the Pimander, that mind is cloathed by soul, and soul by spirit. Therefore as the animal spirit of man, being subtil and luminous, is the immediate tegument of the human soul, or that wherein and whereby she acts; even so the spirit of the world, that active fiery æthereal substance of light, that permeates and animates the whole system, is supposed to cloath the soul, which cloaths the mind of the universe.

179. The Magi likewise said of God, that he had light for his body and truth for his soul. And in the Chaldaic oracles, all things are supposed to be governed by a πῦρ νοερὸν or intellectual fire. And in the same oracles, the creative mind is said to be cloathed with fire, Ἑσσάμενος πυρὶ πῦρ, which oriental reduplication of the word fire, seems to imply the extreme purity and force thereof. Thus also in the Psalms, Thou art clothed with light as with a garment. Where the word rendered light might have been rendered fire, the Hebrew letters being the same with those in the word which signifies fire, all the difference being in the pointing, which is justly counted a late invention. That other scripture sentence is remarkable: Who maketh his ministers a flaming fire; which might, perhaps, be rendered, more agreeably to the context, as well as consistently with the Hebrew, after this manner: Who maketh flaming fire his ministers; and the whole might run thus: Who maketh the winds his messengers, and flaming fire his ministers.

180. A notion of something divine in fire, animating the whole world, and ordering its several parts, was a tenet of very general extent *(a)*,

(a) 156, 157, 163, 166, 167, 168, 170, 172, 173, 174, 175, 177, &c.

being

being embraced in the most distant times and places, even among the Chinese themselves; who make tien, æther, or heaven, the sovereign principle, or cause of all things, and teach, that the celestial virtue, by them called li, when joined to corporeal substance, doth fashion, distinguish, and specificate all natural beings. This li of the Chinese seems to answer the forms of the Peripatetics. And both bear analogy to the foregoing philosophy of fire.

181. The heaven is supposed pregnant with virtues and forms, which constitute and discriminate the various species of things. And we have more than once observed, that, as the light, fire, or celestial æther, being parted by refracting or reflecting bodies, produceth variety of colours; even so, that same apparently uniform substance, being parted and secreted by the attracting and repelling powers of the divers secretory ducts of plants and animals, that is, by natural chemistry, produceth or imparteth the various specific properties of natural bodies. Whence the tastes and odours and medicinal virtues so various in vegetables.

182. The tien is considered and adored by the learned Chinese, as living and intelligent æther, the πῦρ νοερὸν of the Chaldæans and the Stoics. And the worship of things celestial, the sun and stars, among the eastern nations less remote, was on account of their fiery nature, their heat and light, and the influence thereof. Upon these accounts, the sun was looked on by the Greek theologers as the spirit of the world, and the power of the world. The cleansing quality, the light and heat of fire are natural symbols of purity, knowledge, and power, or, if I may so say, the things them-

ſelves, ſo far as they are perceptible to our ſenſes, or in the ſame ſenſe as motion is ſaid to be action. Accordingly, we find a religious regard was paid to fire, both by Greeks and Romans, and indeed by moſt, if not all, the nations of the world.

183. The worſhip of Veſta at Rome was, in truth, the worſhip of fire.

> Nec tu aliud Veſtam quam vivam intellige flammam,

ſaith Ovid in his Faſti. And as in old Rome the eternal fire was religiouſly kept by virgins, ſo in Greece, particularly at Delphi and Athens, it was kept by widows. It was well known that Vulcan, or Fire, was worſhipped with great diſtinction by the Ægyptians. The Zabii or Sabeans are alſo known to have been worſhippers of fire. It appears too from the Chaldæan oracles, that fire was regarded as divine by the ſages of that nation. And it is ſuppoſed that Ur of the Chaldæans was ſo called from the Hebrew word ſignifying fire, becauſe fire was publickly worſhipped in that city. That a religious worſhip was paid to fire by the ancient Perſians and their Magi, is atteſted by all antiquity. And the ſect of Perſees, or old Gentils, of whom there are conſiderable remains at this day both in the Mogol's country and in Perſia, doth teſtify the ſame.

184. It doth not ſeem that their proſtrations before the perpetual fires, preſerved with great care in their Pyreia, or fire temples, were merely a civil reſpect, as Dr. Hyde would have it thought. Although he brings good proof that they do not invoke the fire on their altars, or pray to it, or call it God: and that they acknowledge a ſupreme inviſible deity. Civil reſpects are paid to things

as related to civil power: but ſuch relation doth not appear in the preſent caſe. It ſhould ſeem therefore, that they worſhip God as preſent in the fire, which they worſhip or reverence, not ultimately or for itſelf, but relatively to the ſupreme being. Which it is not unlikely was elſewhere the caſe at firſt; though the practice of men, eſpecially of the vulgar, might in length of time degenerate from the original inſtitution, and reſt in the object of ſenſe.

185. Doctor Hyde, in his hiſtory of the religion of the ancient Perſians, would have it thought, that they borrowed the uſe and reverence of perpetual fires, from the Jewiſh practice preſcribed in the Levitical law, of keeping a perpetual fire burning on the altar. Whether that was the caſe or not, thus much one may venture to ſay, it ſeems probable that whatever was the original of this cuſtom among the Perſians, the like cuſtoms among the Greeks and Romans were derived from the ſame ſource.

186. It muſt be owned there are many paſſages in holy ſcripture (*a*), that would make one think, the ſupreme being was in a peculiar manner preſent and manifeſt in the element of fire. Not to inſiſt that God is more than once ſaid to be a conſuming fire, which might be underſtood in a metaphorical ſenſe, the divine apparitions were by fire, in the buſh, at mount Sinai, on the tabernacle, in the cloven tongues. God is repreſented in the inſpired writings, as deſcending in fire, as attended by fire, or with fire going before him. Celeſtial things, as angels, chariots, and ſuch like phænomena are inveſted with fire, light, and ſplendor. Ezekiel in his viſions beheld

(*a*) 179.

fire and brightness, lamps, burning coals of fire, and flashes of lightening. In a vision of Daniel the throne of God appeared like a fiery flame, and his wheels like burning fire. Also a fiery flame issued and came forth from before him.

187. At the transfiguration, the apostles saw our Saviour's face shining as the sun, and his raiment white as light, also a lucid cloud or body of light, out of which the voice came; which visible light and splendor was, not many centuries ago, maintained by the Greek church, to have been divine, and uncreated, and the very glory of God: as may be seen in the history wrote by the emperor John Cantacuzene. And of late years bishop Patrick gives it as his opinion, that in the beginning of the world, the Shecinah or divine presence, which was then frequent and ordinary, appeared by light or fire. In commenting on that passage, where Cain is said to have gone out from the presence of the Lord, the bishop observes, that if Cain after this turned a downright idolater, as many think, it is very likely he introduced the worship of the sun, as the best resemblance he could find of the glory of the Lord, which was wont to appear in a flaming light. It would be endless to enumerate all the passages of holy scripture, which confirm and illustrate this notion, or represent the Deity as appearing and operating by fire. The misconstruction of which might possibly have misled the Gnostics, Basilidians, and other ancient heretics into an opinion, that Jesus Christ was the visible corporeal sun.

188. We have seen, that in the most remote ages and countries, the vulgar as well as the learned, the institutions of lawgivers as well as the reasonings of philosophers, have ever considered the

the element of fire in a peculiar light, and treated it with more than common regard, as if it were something of a very singular and extraordinary nature. Nor are there wanting authors of principal account among the moderns, who entertain like notions concerning fire, especially among those who are most conversant in that element, and should seem best acquainted with it.

189. Mr. Homberg the famous modern chemist, who brought that art to so great perfection, holds the substance of light or fire to be the true chemic principal sulphur (*a*), and to extend itself throughout the whole universe. It is his opinion that this is the only active principle: That mixed with various things it formeth several sorts of natural productions; with salts making oil, with earth bitumen, with mercury metal: That this principle of sulphur, fire, or the substance of light, is in itself imperceptible, and only becomes sensible as it is joined with some other principle, which serves as a vehicle for it: That, although it be the most active of all things, yet it is at the same time the most firm bond and cement to combine and hold the principles together, and give form to the mixed bodies: And, that in the analysis of bodies it is always lost, escaping the skill of the artist, and passing through the closest vessels.

190. Boerhaave, Niewenty't, and divers other moderns are in the same way of thinking. They with the ancients distinguish a pure, elementary, invisible fire from the culinary, or that which appears in ignited bodies (*b*). This last they will not allow to be pure fire. The pure fire is to be discerned by its effects alone; such as heat, dilatation of all solid bodies, and rarefaction of fluids,

(*a*) 129. (*b*) 163, 166.

the

the segregating heterogeneous bodies, and congregating those that are homogeneous. That therefore which smoakes and flames is not pure fire, but that which is collected in the focus of a mirrour or burning glass. This fire seems the source of all the operations in nature: without it nothing either vegetates, or putrefies, lives, or moves or ferments, is dissolved, or compounded or altered, throughout this whole natural world in which we subsist. Were it not for this, the whole would be one great stupid inanimate mass. But this active element is supposed to be every where, and always present, imparting different degrees of life, heat, and motion, to the various animals, vegetables, and other natural productions, as well as to the elements themselves, wherein they are produced and nourished.

191. As water acts upon salt, or aqua fortis upon iron, so fire dissolves all other bodies. Fire, air, and water are all three menstruums but the two last seem to derive all their force and activity from the first (*a*). And indeed there seems to be, originally or ultimately, but one menstruum in nature, to which all other menstruums may be reduced. Acid salts are a menstruum, but their force and distinct powers are from sulphur. Considered as pure, or in themselves, they are all of the same nature. But, as obtained by distillation, they are constantly joined with some sulphur, which characterizeth and cannot be separated from them. This is the doctrine of monsieur Homberg. But what is it that characterizeth or differenceth the sulphurs themselves? If sulphur be the substance of light, as that author will have it, whence is it that animal, vege-

(*a*) 149.

table,

table, and metallic sulphurs impart different qualities to the same acid salt? Can this be explained upon Homberg's principles? And are we not obliged to suppose, that light separated by the attracting and repelling powers in the strainers, ducts, and pores of those bodies, forms several distinct kinds of sulphur, all which, before such separation, were lost and blended together, in one common mass of light or fire seemingly homogeneous.

192. In the analysis of inflammable bodies, the fire or sulphur is lost, and the diminution of weight sheweth the loss (*a*). Oil is resolved into water, earth, and salt, none of which is inflammable. But the fire or vinculum which connected those things, and gave the form of oil, escapes from the artist. It disappears, but is not destroyed. Light or fire imprisoned made part of the compound, gave union to the other parts, and form to the whole. But having escaped, it mingles with the general ocean of æther, till being again parted and attracted, it enters and specificates some new subject of the animal, vegetable, or mineral kingdom. Fire therefore in the sense of philosophers is also fire, though not always flame.

193. Solar fire or light, in calcining certain bodies, is observed to add to their weight. There is therefore no doubt but light can be fixed, and enter the composition of a body. And though it should lye latent for a long time, yet, being set free from its prison, it shall still shew itself to be fire. Lead, tin, or regulus of antimony, being exposed to the fire of a burning glass, though they lose much in smoak and steam, are nevertheless found to be considerably increased in weight, which proves the introduction of light or fire in-

(*a*) 169.

to their pores. It is also observed, that urine produceth no phosphorus, unless it be long exposed to the solar light. From all which it may be concluded, that bodies attract and fix the light; whence it should seem, as some have observed, that fire without burning is an ingredient in many things, as water without wetting.

194. Of this there cannot be a better proof, than the experiment of Monsieur Homberg, who made gold of mercury, by introducing light into its pores, but at such trouble and expence, that I suppose no body will try the experiment for profit. By this junction of light and mercury, both bodies became fixed, and produced a third different from either, to wit, real gold. For the truth of which fact, I refer to the memoirs of the French academy of Sciences. From the foregoing experiment it appears, that gold is only a mass of mercury penetrated and cemented by the substance of light, the particles of those bodies attracting and fixing each other. This seems to have been not altogether unknown to former philosophers; Marsilius Ficinus the Platonist, in his commentary on the first book of the second Ennead of Plotinus, and others likewise before him, regarding mercury as the mother, and sulphur as the father of metals; and Plato himself in his Timæus describing gold to be a dense fluid with a shining yellow light, which well suits a composition of light and mercury.

195. Fire or light mixeth with all bodies (*a*), even with water; witness the flashing lights in the sea, whose waves seem frequently all on fire. Its operations are various according to its kind, quantity, and degree of vehemence. One degree

(*a*) 157.

keeps

keeps water fluid, another turns it into elastic air (*a*). And air itself seems to be nothing else but vapours and exhalations, rendered elastic by fire. Nothing flames but oil: and sulphur with water, salt, and earth compose oil; which sulphur is fire: therefore fire enclosed attracts fire, and causeth the bodies whose composition it enters to burn and blaze.

196. Fire collected in the focus of a glass operates in vacuo, and therefore is thought not to need air to support it. Calx of lead hath gone off with an explosion in vacuo, which Niewenty't and others take for a proof that fire can burn without air. But Mr. Hales attributes this effect to air enclosed in the red lead, and perhaps too in the receiver, which cannot be perfectly exhausted. When common lead is put into the fire in order to make red-lead, a greater weight of this comes out than was put in of common lead. Therefore the red-lead should seem impregnated with fire. Mr. Hales thinks it is with air. The vast expansion of compound aqua fortis, Mr. Niewenty't will have to proceed from fire alone. Mr. Hales contends that air must necessarily co-operate. Though by Niewenty't's experiment it should seem, the phosphorus burns equally, with and without air.

197. Perhaps they who hold the opposite sides in this question, may be reconciled by observing that air is in reality nothing more than particles of wet and dry bodies volatilised, and rendered elastic by fire (*b*). Whatever therefore is done by air must be ascribed to fire, which fire is a subtile invisible thing, whose operation is not to be discerned but by means of some grosser body, which

(*a*) 149. (*b*) 147, 150, 151.

serves not for a pabulum to nourish the fire, but for a vehicle to arrest and bring it into view. Which seems the sole use of oil, air, or any other thing, that vulgarly passeth for a pabulum or food of that element.

198. To explain this matter more clearly, it is to be observed, that fire, in order to become sensible, must have some subject to act upon. This being penetrated and agitated by fire affects us with light, heat, or some other sensible alteration. And this subject so wrought upon may be called culinary fire. In the focus of a burning glass exposed to the sun, there is real actual fire, though not discerned by the sense, till it hath somewhat to work on, and can shew itself in its effects, heating, flaming, melting, and the like. Every ignited body is, in the foregoing sense, culinary fire. But it will not therefore follow, that it is convertible into pure elementary fire. This, for ought that appears, may be ingenerable and incorruptible by the course of nature. It may be fixed and imprisoned in a compound (*a*), and yet retain its nature, though lost to sense, and though it return into the invisible elementary mass, upon the analysis of the compounded body: as is manifest in the solution of stone lime by water.

199. It should seem, therefore, that what is said of air's being the pabulum of fire, or being converted into fire, ought to be understood only in this sense; to wit, that air being less gross than other bodies, is of a middle nature, and therefore more fit to receive the impressions of a fine æthereal fire (*b*), and impart them to other things. According to the antients, soul serveth for a vehicle to

(*a*) 169, 192, 193. (*b*) 163.

in-

intellect (*a*), and light or fire for a vehicle to the soul; and, in like manner, air may be supposed a vehicle to fire, fixing it in some degree, and communicating its effects to other bodies.

200. The pure invisible fire or æther doth permeate all bodies, even the hardest and most solid, as the diamond. This alone, therefore, cannot, as some learned men have supposed, be the cause of muscular motion, by a mere impulse of the nerves communicated from the brain to the membranes of the muscles, and thereby to the enclosed æther, whose expansive motion, being by that means increased, is thought to swell the muscles, and cause a contraction of the fleshy fibres. This, it should seem, the pure æther cannot do immediately, and of itself, because, supposing its expansive motion to be increased, it must still pass through the membranes, and consequently not swell them, inasmuch as æther is supposed freely to pervade the most solid bodies. It should seem therefore, that this effect must be owing, not to pure æther, but to æther in some part fixed and arrested by the particles of air.

201. Although this æther be extremely elastic, yet as it is sometimes found by experience to be attracted, imprisoned, and detained in gross bodies (*b*), so we may suppose it to be attracted, and its expansive force diminished, though it should not be quite fixed, by the loose particles of air, which combining and cohering therewith may bring it down, and qualify it for intercourse with grosser things. Pure fire may be said to animate air, and air other things. Pure fire is invisible; therefore flame is not pure fire. Air is necessary both to life and flame. And it is found by experi-

(*a*) 178. (*b*) 169.

ment,

ment, that air loseth in the lungs the power of feeding flame. Hence it is concluded, that the same thing in air contributes both to life and flame. Vital flame survives culinary flame in vacuo: therefore it requires less of that thing to sustain it.

202. What this may be, whether some certain proportion, or some peculiar parts of æther, is not easy to say. But thus much seems plain, that whatever is ascribed to acid may be also ascribed to fire or æther. The particles of æther fly asunder with the greatest force: therefore, agreeably to Sir Isaac Newton's doctrine, when united they must attract each other with the greatest force. Therefore they constitute the acid. For whatsoever strongly attracts and is attracted, may be called an acid, as Sir Isaac Newton informs us in his tract De acido. Hence it should seem, that the sulphur of Homberg, and the acid of Sir Isaac are at bottom one and the same thing, to wit, pure fire or æther.

203. The vital flame or æthereal spirit, being attracted and imprisoned in grosser bodies, seemeth to be set free and carried off by the superior attraction of a subtil and pure flame. Hence, perhaps, it is that lightening kills animals, and turns spirituous liquors vapid in an instant.

204. Hippocrates, in his book concerning the Heart, observeth, that the soul of man is not nourished by meats and drinks from the lower belly, but by a pure and luminous substance, darting its rays and distributing a non-natural nourishment, as he terms it, in like manner as that from the intestines is distributed to all parts of the body. This luminous non-natural nourishment, though it be secreted from the blood, is expresly said not to come from the lower belly. It is plain, therefore,

he

he thought it came into the blood either by respiration, or by attraction through the pores. And it must be acknowledged, that somewhat igneous or æthereal brought by the air into the blood seems to nourish, though not the soul itself, yet the interior tunicle of the soul, the auraï simplicis ignem.

205. That there is really such a thing as vital flame, actually kindled, nourished, and extinguished like common flame, and by the same means, is an opinion of some moderns, particularly of Doctor Willis in his tract De sanguinis accensione: that it requires constant eventilation, through the trachea and pores of the body, for the discharge of a fuliginous and excrementitious vapour: and that this vital flame, being extremely subtil, might not be seen any more than shining flies or ignes fatui by day-light. And yet it hath sometimes become visible on divers persons, of which there are undoubted instances. This is Dr. Willis's notion: and perhaps there may be some truth in this, if it be so understood, as that light or fire might indeed constitute the animal spirit or immediate vehicle of the soul.

206. There have not been wanting those, who, not content to suppose light the most pure and refined of all corporeal beings, have gone farther, and bestowed upon it some attributes of a yet higher nature. Julianus the Platonic philosopher, as cited by Ficinus, saith, it was a doctrine in the theology of the Phœnicians, that there is diffused throughout the universe, a pellucid and shining nature pure and impassive, the act of a pure intelligence. And Ficinus himself undertakes to prove, that light is incorporeal, by several arguments: Because it enlightens and fills a great space in an instant, and without opposition: Because several

lights

lights meet without resisting each other: Because light cannot be defiled by filth of any kind: Because the solar light is not fixed in any subject: Lastly, because it contracts and expands itself so easily without collision, condensation, rarefaction, or delay throughout the wasted space. These reasons are given by Ficinus, in his comment on the first book of the second Ennead of Plotinus.

207. But it is now well known, that light moves, that its motion is not instantaneous: that it is capable of condensation, rarefaction, and collision: that it can be mixed with other bodies, enter their composition, and increase their weight (a). All which seem sufficiently to overthrow those arguments of Ficinus, and shew light to be corporeal. There appears indeed some difficulty at first sight, about the non-resistance of rays or particles of light occurring one to another, in all possible directions or from all points. Particularly, if we suppose the hollow surface of a large sphere, studded with eyes looking inwards one at another, it may perhaps seem hard to conceive, how distinct rays from every eye should arrive at every other eye without justling, repelling, and confounding each other.

208. But these difficulties may be got over by considering in the first place, that visible points are not mathematical points, and consequently, that we are not to suppose every point of space a radiating point. Secondly, by granting that many rays do resist and intercept each other, notwithstanding which the act of vision may be performed. Since as every point of the object is not seen, so it is not necessary that rays from every such point arrive at the eye. We often see

(a) 169, 192, 193.

an

an object, though more dimly, when many rays are intercepted by a gross medium.

209. Besides, we may suppose the particles of light to be indefinitely small, that is, as small as we please, and their aggregate to bear as small a proportion to the void as we please, there being nothing in this that contradicts the phænomena. And there needs nothing more in order to conceive the possibility of rays passing from and to all visible points, although they be not incorporeal. Suppose a hundred ports placed round a circular sea, and ships sailing from each port to every other; the larger the sea, and the smaller the vessels are supposed, the less danger will there be of their striking against each other. But as there is by hypothesis no limited proportion between the sea and the ships, the void and solid particles of light, so there is no difficulty that can oblige us to conclude the sun's light incorporeal from it's free passage; especially when there are so many clear proofs of the contrary. As for the difficulty, therefore, attending the supposition of a sphere studded with eyes looking at each other, this is removed only by supposing the particles of light exceeding small relatively to the empty spaces.

210. Plotinus supposeth, that from the sun's light which is corporeal, there springs forth another equivocal light which is incorporeal, and as it were the brightness of the former. Marsilius Ficinus also, observing it to be a doctrine in the Timæus of Plato, that there is an occult fire or spirit diffused throughout the universe, intimates that this same occult invisible fire or light is, as it were, the sight of the mundane soul. And Plotinus, in his fourth Ennead, sheweth it to be his opinion, that the world seeth it self and all it's

parts. The Platonic philosophers do wonderfully refine upon light, and soar very high: from coal to flame; from flame to light; from this visible light to the occult light of the celestial or mundane soul, which they supposed to pervade and agitate the substance of the univese by it's vigorous and expansive motion.

211. If we may believe Diogenes Laertius, the Pythagoræan philosophers thought there was a certain pure heat or fire, which had somewhat divine in it, by the participation whereof men became allied to the gods. And according to the Platonists, heaven is not defined so much by it's local situation, as by it's purity. The purest and most excellent fire, that is heaven, saith Ficinus. And again, the hidden fire that every where exerts it self, he calls celestial. He represents fire as most powerful and active, dividing all things, abhorring all composition or mixture with other bodies. And, as soon as it goes free, relapsing instantly into the common mass of celestial fire, which is every where present and latent.

212. This is the general source of life, spirit, and strength, and therefore of health to all animals, who constantly receive it's illapses cloathed in air, through the lungs and pores of the body. The same spirit, imprisoned in food and medicines, is conveyed into the stomach, the bowels, the lacteals, circulated and secreted by the several ducts, and distributed throughout the system (*a*). Plato, in his Timæus, enumerating the ignited juices, names wine in the first place, and tar in the second. But wine is pressed from the grape, and fermented by human industry. Therefore of all ignited juices purely natural, tar or resin must in his account be esteemed the first.

(*a*) 37, 42, 44.

213. The

213. The vivifying luminous æther exists in all places, even the darkest caverns, as is evident from hence, that many animals see in those dark places, and that fire may be kindled in them by the collision or attrition of bodies. It is also known, that certain persons have fits of seeing in the dark. Tiberius was said to have had this faculty or distemper. I my self knew an ingenious man, who had experienced it several times in himself. And doctor Willis, in his tract De sanguinis accensione, mentions another of his own knowledge. This luminous æther or spirit is therefore said by Virgil, to nourish or cherish the innermost earth, as well as the heavens and celestial bodies.

Principio cœlum ac terras, camposque liquentes,
Lucentemque globum Lunæ, Titaniaque astra
Spiritus intus alit.

214. The principles of motion and vegetation in living bodies seem to be delibations from the invisible fire or spirit of the universe (*a*). Which, though present to all things, is not nevertheless one way received by all; but variously imbibed, attracted, and secreted by the fine capillaries, and exquisite strainers in the bodies of plants and animals, whereby it becomes mixed and detained in their juices.

215. It hath been thought by somes observers of nature, that the fine glandular vessels admit from the common mass of the blood, only such juices as are homogeneous to those, with which they were originally imbued. How they came to be so imbued doth not appear. But thus much is plain; that fine tubes attract fluids, that the glands are fine tubes, and that they attract very

(*a*) 43, 157, 164, 171.

different juices from the common mass. The same holds also with regard to the capillary vessels (*a*) of vegetables; it being evident, that through the fine strainers in the leaves and all over the body of the plant, there be juices or fluids of a particular kind drawn in, and separated from the common mass of air and light. And that the most elaborate spirit, whereon the character or distinguishing virtue and properties of the plant depend, is of a luminous (*b*) and volatile nature, being lost or escaping into air or æther, from essential oils and odoriferous waters, without any sensible diminution of the subject.

216. As different kinds of secreted light or fire produce different essences, virtues, or specific properties; so also different degrees of heat produce different effects. Thus one degree of heat keeps the blood from coagulating, and another degree coagulates the blood. Thus a more violent fire hath been observed to set free and carry off that very light, which a more moderate fire had introduced and fixed in the calcined regulus of antimony. In like manner, one kind or quantity of this ætherial fiery spirit may be congenial and friendly to the spirits of a man, while another may be noxious.

217. And experience sheweth this to be true. For the fermented spirit of wine or other liquors produceth irregular motions, and subsequent depressions in the animal spirits. Whereas the luminous spirit lodged and detained in the native balsam of pines and firs, is of a nature so mild and benign, and proportioned to the human constitution, as to warm without heating, to cheer but not inebriate,

(*a*) 30, 31, 33, 35. (*b*) 37, 43.

briate, and to produce a calm and ſteddy joy like the effect of good news, without that ſinking of ſpirits, which is a ſubſequent effect of all fermented cordials. I may add, without all other inconvenience, except that it may, like any other medicine, be taken in too great a quantity for a nice ſtomach. In which caſe it may be right to leſſen the doſe, or to take it only once in the four and twenty hours, empty, going to bed) when it is found to be leaſt offenſive) or even to ſuſpend the taking of it for a time, till nature ſhall ſeem to crave it, and rejoice in it's benign and comfortable ſpirit.

218. Tar-water ſerving as a vehicle to this ſpirit is both diuretic and diaphoretic, but ſeems to work it's principal effect by aſſiſting the vis vitæ, as an alterative and cordial, enabling nature by an acceſſion of congenial ſpirit, to aſſimilate that which could not be aſſimilated by her proper force, and ſo to ſubdue the fomes morbi. And this ſhould ſeem in moſt caſes the beſt and ſafeſt courſe. Great evacuations weaken nature as well as the diſeaſe. And it is to be feared that they who uſe ſalivations and copious bleedings may, though they ſhould recover the diſtemper, in their whole life be never able to recover of the remedies.

219. It is true indeed, that in chronical caſes there is need of time to compleat a cure, and yet I have known this tar-water in diſorders of the lungs and ſtomach to prove a very ſpeedy remedy, and to allay the anxiety and heat of a fever in an inſtant; giving eaſe and ſpirits to the patient. This I have often experienced, not without ſurprize, at ſeeing theſe ſalutary effects follow ſo immediately in a fever on taking a glaſs of tar-water. Such is the force of theſe active vivifying principles contained in this balſam.

220. Force

220. Force or power, strickly speaking, is in the agent alone who imparts an equivocal force to the invisible elementary fire, or animal spirit (*a*) of the world, and this to the ignited body or visible flame, which produceth the sense of light and heat. In this chain the first and last links are allowed to be incorporeal: the two intermediate are corporeal, being capable of motion, rarefaction, gravity, and other qualities of bodies. It is fit to distinguish these things, in order to avoid ambiguity concerning the nature of fire.

221. Sir Isaac Newton, in his Optics, asks; Is not fire a body heated so hot as to emit light copiously? for what else, adds he, is a red hot iron than fire? Now it should seem, that to define fire by heat, would be to explain a thing by it self. A body heated so hot as to emit light is an ignited body, that is, hath fire in it, is penetrated and agitated by fire, but is not itself fire. And although it should in the third foregoing acceptation, or vulgar sense, pass for fire, yet it is not the pure elementary (*b*) fire in the second or philosophic sense, such as was understood by the sages of antiquity, and such as is collected in the focus of a burning glass; much less is it the vis, force, or power of burning, destroying, calcining, melting, vitrifying, and raising the perceptions of light and heat. This is truly and really in the incorporeal agent, and not in the vital spirit of the universe. Motion, and even power in an equivocal sense, may be found in this pure æthereal spirit, which ignites bodies, but is not itself the ignited body, being an instrument or medium (*c*) by which the real agent doth operate on grosser bodies.

(*a*) 153, 156, 157. (*b*) 190. (*d*) 160.

222. It

222. It hath been shewn in Sir Isaac Newton's Optics, that light is not reflected by impinging on bodies, but by some other cause. And to him it seems probable, that as many rays as impinge on the solid parts of the bodies, are not reflected but stifled and retained in the bodies. And it is certain, the great porosity of all known bodies affords room for much of this light or fire to be lodged therein. Gold itself, the most solid of all metals, seems to have far more pores than solid parts, from water being pressed through it in the Florentine experiment, from magnetic effluvia passing, and from mercury entering its pores so freely. And it is admitted that water, though impossible to be compressed, hath at least forty times more pores than solid parts. And as acid particles, joined with those of earth in certain proportions, are so closely united with them, as to be quite hid and lost to all appearance, as in mercurius dulcis and common sulphur, so also may we conceive the particles of light or fire to be absorbed and latent in grosser bodies.

223. It is the opinion of Sir Isaac Newton, that somewhat unknown remains in vacuo, when the air is exhausted. This unknown medium he calls æther. He supposeth it to be more subtil in its nature, and more swift in its motion, than light, freely to pervade all bodies, and by its immense elasticity to be expanded throughout all the heavens. Its density is supposed greater in free and open spaces, than within the pores of compact bodies. And, in passing from the celestial bodies to great distances, it is supposed to grow denser and denser continually; and thereby cause those great bodies to gravitate towards one another, and their respective parts towards their centers, every

body

body endeavouring to paſs from the denſer parts of the medium towards the rarer.

224. The extreme minuteneſs of the parts of this medium, and the velocity of their motion, together with its gravity, denſity, and elaſtic force, are thought to qualify it for being the cauſe of all the natural motions in the univerſe. To this cauſe are aſcribed the gravity and coheſion of bodies. The refraction of light is alſo thought to proceed from the different denſity and elaſtic force of this æthereal medium in different places. The vibrations of this medium alternately concurring with, or obſtructing the motions of the rays of light, are ſuppoſed to produce the fits of eaſy reflexion and tranſmiſſion. Light by the vibrations of this medium is thought to communicate heat to bodies. Animal motion and ſenſation are alſo accounted for by the vibrating motions of this ætherial medium, propagated thro' the ſolid capillaments of the nerves. In a word, all the phænomena and properties of bodies, that were before attributed to attraction, upon later thoughts ſeem aſcribed to this æther, together with the various attractions themſelves.

225. But in the philoſophy of Sir Iſaac Newton, the fits (as they are called) of eaſy tranſmiſſion and reflexion, ſeem as well accounted for by vibrations excited in bodies by the rays of light, and the refraction of light by the attraction of bodies. To explain the vibrations of light by thoſe of a more ſubtil medium, ſeems an uncouth explication. And gravity ſeems not an effect of the denſity and elaſticity of æther, but rather to be produced by ſome other cauſe; which Sir Iſaac himſelf inſinuates to have been the opinion even of thoſe ancients who took vacuum, atoms, and the gravity of atoms for the principles of their philoſophy, tacitly attri-

buting

buting (as he well observes) gravity to some other cause distinct from matter, from atoms, and consequently from that homogeneous æther or elastic fluid. The elasticity of which fluid is supposed to depend upon, to be defined and measured by its density; and this by the quantity of matter in one particle, multiplied by the number of particles contained in a given space; and the quantity of matter in any one particle or body of a given size to be determined by its gravity. Should not therefore gravity seem the original property and first supposed? On the other hand, if force be considered as prescinded from gravity and matter, and as existing only in points or centers, what can this amount to but an abstract spiritual incorporeal force?

226. It doth not seem necessary from the phænomena, to suppose any medium more active and subtil than light or fire. Light being allowed to move at the rate of about ten millions of miles in a minute, what occasion is there to conceive another medium of still smaller and more moveable parts. Light or fire seems the same with æther. So the ancients understood, and so the Greek word implies. It pervades all things (*a*), is every where present. And this same subtil medium, according to its various quantities, motions, and determinations, sheweth itself in different effects or appearances, and is æther, light, or fire.

227. The particles of æther fly asunder with the greatest force, therefore when united they must (according to the Newtonian doctrine) attract each other with the greatest force; therefore they are acids (*b*), or constitute the acid; but this united with earthy parts maketh alkali, as Sir Isaac teacheth in his tract De acido; alkali, as ap-

(*a*) 157. (*b*) 130.

 pears

pears in cantharides and lixivial salts, is a caustic; caustics are fire; therefore acid is fire; therefore æther is fire; and if fire, light. We are not therefore obliged to admit a new medium distinct from light, and of a finer and more exquisite substance, for the explication of phænomena, which appear to be as well explained without it. How can the density or elasticity of æther account for the rapid flight of a ray of light from the sun, still swifter as it goes farther from the sun? or how can it account for the various motions and attractions of different bodies? Why oil and water, mercury and iron repell, or why other bodies attract each other? or why a particle of light should repell on one side and attract on the other, as in the case of the Islandic crystal? To explain cohesion by hamate atoms is accounted ignotum per ignotius. And is it not as much so to account for the gravity of bodies by the elasticity of æther?

228. It is one thing to arrive at general laws of nature from a contemplation of the phænomena; and another to frame an hypothesis, and from thence deduce the phænomena. Those who supposed epicycles, and by them explained the motions and appearances of the planets, may not therefore be thought to have discovered principles true in fact and nature. And albeit we may from the premises infer a conclusion, it will not follow, that we can argue reciprocally, and from the conclusion infer the premises. For instance, supposing an elastic fluid, whose constituent minute particles are equidistant from each other and of equal densities and diameters, and recede one from another with a centrifugal force which is inversly as the distance of the centers, and admitting that from such supposition it must follow,

that

that the density and elastic force of such fluid are in the inverse proportion of the space it occupies when compressed by any force; yet we cannot reciprocally infer, that a fluid endued with this property must therefore consist of such supposed equal particles; for it would then follow, that the constituent particles of air were of equal densities and diameters; whereas it is certain, that air is an heterogeneous mass, containing in its composition an infinite variety of exhalations, from the different bodies which make up this terraqueous globe.

229. The phænomena of light, animal spirit, muscular motion, fermentation, vegetation, and other natural operations, seem to require nothing more than the intellectual and artificial fire of Heraclitus, Hippocrates, the Stoics (*a*), and other ancients. Intellect, superadded to ætherial spirit, fire, or light, moves, and moves regularly, proceeding, in a method as the Stoics, or increasing and diminishing by measure, as Heraclitus expressed it. The Stoics held that fire comprehended and included the spermatic reasons or forms (λόγους σπερματικοὺς) of all natural things. As the forms of things have their ideal existence in the intellect, so it should seem that seminal principles have their natural existence in the light (*b*), a medium consisting of heterogeneous parts, differing from each other in divers qualities that appear to sense, and not improbably having many original properties, attractions, repulsions, and motions, the laws and natures whereof are indiscernible to us, otherwise than in their remote effects. And this animated heterogeneous fire should seem a more adequate cause, whereby to explain the phæ-

(*a*) 166, 168. (*b*) 164.

nomena of nature, than one uniform æthereal medium.

230. Ariſtotle indeed excepts againſt the elements being animated. Yet nothing hinders why that power of the ſoul, ſtyled by him κινητική, or locomotive, may not reſide therein, under the direction of an intellect, in ſuch ſenſe, and as properly as it is ſaid to reſide in animal bodies. It muſt nevertheleſs be owned, that albeit that philoſopher acknowledgeth a divine force or energy in fire, yet to ſay that fire is alive, or that having a ſoul it ſhould not be alive, ſeem to him equally abſurd. See his ſecond book De partibus animalium.

231. The laws of attraction and repulſion are to be regarded as laws of motion, and theſe only as rules or methods obſerved in the productions of natural effects, the efficient and final cauſes whereof are not of mechanical conſideration. Certainly, if the explaining a phænomenon be to aſſign its proper efficient and final cauſe (*a*), it ſhould ſeem the mechanical philoſophers never explained any thing; their province being only to diſcover the laws of nature, that is, the general rules and methods of motion, and to account for particular phænomena by reducing them under, or ſhewing their conformity to ſuch general rules.

232. Some corpuſcularian philoſophers of the laſt age have indeed attempted to explain the formation of this world and its phænomena, by a few ſimple laws of mechaniſm. But if we conſider the various productions of nature, in the mineral, vegetable, and animal parts of the creation, I believe we ſhall ſee cauſe to affirm, that not any

(*a*) 154, 155, 160.

one

one of them has hitherto been, or can be accounted for on principles merely mechanical; and that nothing could be more vain and imaginary, than to suppose with Descartes, that merely from a circular motion's being impressed by the supreme agent on the particles of extended substance, the whole world with all its several parts, appurtenances, and phænomena, might be produced by a necessary consequence from the laws of motion.

233. Others suppose that God did more at the beginning, having then made the seeds of all vegetables and animals, containing their solid organical parts in miniature, the gradual filling and evolution of which, by the influx of proper juices, doth constitute the generation and growth of a living body. So that the artificial structure of plants and animals daily generated, requires no present exercise of art to produce it, having been already framed at the origin of the world, which with all its parts hath ever since subsisted, going like a clock or machine, by itself, according to the laws of nature, without the immediate hand of the artist. But how can this hypothesis explain the blended features of different species in mules and other mongrels? or the parts added or changed, and sometimes whole limbs lost by marking in the womb? or how can it account for the resurrection of a tree from its stump, or the vegetative power in its cutting? in which cases we must necessarily conceive something more than the mere evolution of a seed.

234. Mechanical laws of nature or motion direct us how to act, and teach us what to expect. Where intellect presides, there will be method and order, and therefore rules, which if not stated

and

and constant would cease to be rules. There is therefore a constancy in things, which is styled the course of nature (*a*). All the phænomena in nature are produced by motion. There appears an uniform working in things great and small, by attracting and repelling forces. But the particular laws of attraction and repulsion are various. Nor are we concerned at all about the forces, neither can we know or measure them otherwise than by their effects, that is to say, the motions, which motions only, and not the forces, are indeed in the bodies (*b*). Bodies are moved to or from each other, and this is performed according to different laws. The natural or mechanic philosopher endeavours to discover those laws by experiment and reasoning. But what is said of forces residing in bodies whether attracting or repelling, is to be regarded only as a mathematical hypothesis, and not as any thing really existing in nature.

235. We are not therefore seriously to suppose with certain mechanic philosophers, that the minute particles of bodies have real forces or powers by which they act on each other, to produce the various phænomena in nature. The minute corpuscles are impelled and directed, that is to say, moved to and from each other according to various rules or laws of motion. The laws of gravity, magnetism, and electricity are divers. And it is not known, what other different rules or laws of motion might be established by the author of nature. Some bodies approach together, others fly asunder, and perhaps some others do neither. When salt of tartar flows per deliquium, it is visible that the particles of water floating in the air

(*a*) 160. (*b*) 155.

are

are moved towards the particles of ſalt, and joined with them. And when we behold vulgar ſalt not to flow per deliquium, may we not conclude that the ſame law of nature and motion doth not obtain between its particles and thoſe of the floating vapours? A drop of water aſſumes a round figure, becauſe its parts are moved towards each other. But the particles of oil and vinegar have no ſuch diſpoſition to unite. And when flies walk in water without wetting their feet, it is attributed to a repelling force or faculty in the fly's feet. But this is obſcure, though the phænomenon be plain.

236. It is not improbable, and ſeems not unſupported by experiments, that, as in algebra, where poſitive quantities ceaſe there negative begin, even ſo in mechanics, where attracting forces ceaſe there repelling forces begin; or (to expreſs it more properly) where bodies ceaſe to be moved towards, they begin to be moved from each other. This Sir Iſaac Newton infers from the production of air and vapours, whoſe particles fly aſunder with ſuch vehement force. We behold iron move towards the loadſtone, ſtraws towards amber, heavy bodies towards the earth. The laws of theſe motions are various. And when it is ſaid, that all the motions and changes in the great world ariſe from attraction; the elaſticity of the air, the motion of water, the deſcent of heavy, and the aſcent of light bodies, being all aſcribed to the ſame principle; when from inſenſible attractions of moſt minute particles at the ſmalleſt diſtance are derived coheſion, diſſolution, coagulation, animal ſecretion, fermentation, and all chemical operations; and when it is ſaid, that without ſuch principles there never would have been any motion in the world, and without the

the continuance thereof all motion would cease. In all this we know or understand no more, than that bodies are moved according to a certain order, and that they do not move themselves.

237. So likewise, how to explain all those various motions and effects by the density and elasticity of æther, seems incomprehensible (*a*). For instance, why should the acid particles draw those of water and repell each other? why should some salts attract vapours in the air, and others not? why should the particles of common salt repell each other, so as not to subside in water? why should the most repellent particles be the most attractive upon contact? Or why should the repellent begin where the attractive faculty leaves off. These, and numberless other effects seem inexplicable on mechanical principles, or otherwise than by recourse to a mind or spiritual agent (*b*). Nor will it suffice from present phænomena and effects, through a chain of natural causes and subordinate blind agents, to trace a divine intellect as the remote original cause, that first created the world, and then set it a going. We cannot make even one single step in accounting for the phænomena, without admitting the immediate presence and immediate action of an incorporeal agent, who connects, moves, and disposes all things, according to such rules, and for such purposes as seem good to him.

238. It is an old opinion adopted by the moderns, that the elements and other natural bodies are changed each into other (*c*). Now, as the particles of different bodies are agitated by different forces, attracting and repelling, or, to speak more accurately, are moved by different laws, how can these forces

(*m*) 153, 162. (*b*) 154, 220. (*c*) 148.

or

or laws be changed, and this change accounted for by an elastic æther? Such a medium, distinct from light or fire, seemeth not to be made out by any proof, nor to be of any use in explaining the phænomena. But if there be any medium employed as a subordinate cause, or instrument in attraction, it would rather seem to be light (*k*); since by an experiment of Mr. Boyle, amber, that shewed no sign of attraction in the shade, being placed where the sun-beams shone upon it, immediately attracted light bodies. Besides, it hath been discovered by Sir Isaac Newton, and an admirable discovery it was, that light is an heterogeneous medium (*l*) consisting of particles endued with original distinct properties. And upon these, if I may venture to give my conjectures, it seemeth probable the specific properties of bodies, and the force of specific medicines may depend. Different sides of the same ray shall, one approach and the other recede from the Islandic crystal; can this be accounted for by the elasticity of a fine medium, or by the general laws of motion, or by any mechanical principles whatever? And if not, what should hinder but there may be specific medicines, whose operation depends not upon mechanical principles, how much soever that notion hath been exploded of late years?

239. Why may we not suppose certain idiosyncrasies, sympathies, oppositions, in the solids or fluids or animal spirit of a human body, with regard to the fine insensible parts of minerals or vegetables, impregnated by rays of light of different properties, not depending on the different size, figure, number, solidity, or weight of those particles,

(*k*) 152, 156. (*l*) 40, 181.

nor on the general laws of motion, nor on the density or elasticity of a medium; but merely and altogether on the good pleasure of the Creator, in the original formation of things? From whence divers unaccountable and unforeseen motions may arise in the animal œconomy; from whence also various peculiar and specific virtues may be conceived to arise, residing in certain medicines, and not to be explained by mechanical principles. For although the general known laws of motion are to be deemed mechanical, yet peculiar motions of the insensible parts, and peculiar properties depending thereon, are occult and specific.

240. The words attraction and repulsion may, in compliance with custom, be used where, accurately speaking, motion alone is meant. And in that sense it may be said, that peculiar attractions or repulsions in the parts, are attended with specific properties in the wholes. The particles of light are vehemently moved to or from, retained or rejected by objects. Which is the same thing as to say with Sir Isaac Newton, that the particles of acids are endued with great attractive force *(m)*, wherein their activity consists; whence fermentation and dissolution; and that the most repellent are, upon contact, the most attracting particles.

241. Gravity and fermentation are received for two most extensive principles. From fermentation are derived the motion and warmth of the heart and blood in animals, subterraneous heat, fires, and earthquakes, meteors and changes in the atmosphere. And, that attracting and repelling forces operate in the nutrition and dissolution of animal and vegetable bodies, is the doctrine both of Hip-

(m) 202.

pocrates

pocrates and Sir Isaac Newton. The former of these celebrated authors, in his treatise concerning diet or regimen, observes, that in the nourishment of man, one part repells and another attracts. And again, in the same treatise, two carpenters, saith he, saw a piece of timber; one draws, the other pushes; these two actions tend to one and the same end, though in a contrary direction, one up, the other down: This imitates the nature of man: πνεῦμα τὸ μὲν ἕλκει, τὸ δὲ ὠθέει.

242. It is the general maxim of Hippocrates, that the manner wherein nature acts consisteth in attracting what is meet and good, and in repelling what is disagreeable or hurtful. He makes the whole of the animal œconomy to be administered by the faculties or powers of nature. Nature alone, saith he, sufficeth for all things to animals. She knows of herself what is necessary for them. Whence it is plain, he means a conscious intelligent nature, that presides and moves the ætherial spirit. And tho' he declares all things are accomplished on man by necessity, yet it is not a blind fate or chain of mere corporeal causes, but a divine necessity, as he himself expresly calls it. And what is this but an over-ruling intelligent power that disposeth of all things?

243. Attraction cannot produce, and in that sense account for the phænomena, being itself one of the phænomena produced and to be accounted for *(n)*. Attraction is performed by different laws, and cannot therefore in all cases be the effect of the elasticity of one uniform medium. The phænomena of electrical bodies, the laws and variations of magnetism, and, not to mention other kinds, even

(n) 160, 235.

gravity, is not explained by elasticity, a phænomenon not less obscure than itself. But then, although it shews not the agent, yet it sheweth a rule and an alogy in nature to say, That the solid parts of animals are endued with attractive powers, whereby from contiguous fluids they draw like to like; and that glands have peculiar powers attractive of peculiar juices (*o*). Nature seems better known and explained by attractions and repulsions, than by those other mechanical principles of size, figure, and the like: that is, by Sir Isaac Newton, than Descartes. And natural philosophers excel, as they are more or less acquainted with the laws and methods observed by the Author of nature.

244. The size and shape of particles, and general laws of motion can never explain the secretions without the help of attraction, obscure perhaps as to its cause, but clear as a law. Numberless instances of this might be given: Lemery the younger thought himself obliged to suppose, the particles of light or fire (contrary to all reason) to be of a very gross kind, even greater than the pores of the burnt limestone, in order to account for their being detained or imprisoned therein; but this phænomenon is easily reduced to attraction. There would be no end of enumerating the like cases. The activity and force of ætherial spirit or fire by the laws of attraction is imparted to grosser particles (*p*), and thereby wonderfully supports the œconomy of living bodies. By such peculiar compositions and attractions it seems to be effected, that denser fluids can pass where air itself cannot (as oil through leather) and therefore through

(*o*) 41. (*p*) 152, 163.

the

the nicest and finest strainers of an animal or vegetable.

245. The ancients had some general conception of attracting and repelling powers (*q*) as natural principles. Galilæi had particularly considered the attraction of gravity, and made some discovery of the laws thereof. But Sir Isaac Newton by his singular penetration, profound knowledge in geometry and mechanics, and great exactness in experiments, hath cast a new light on natural science. The laws of attraction and repulsion were in many instances discovered, and first discovered, by him. He shewed their general extent, and therewith, as with a key, opened several deep secrets of nature, in the knowledge whereof he seems to have made a greater progress, than all the sects of corpuscularians together had done before him. Nevertheless, the principle of attraction itself is not to be explained by physical or corporeal causes.

246. The Cartesians attempted to explain it by the nisus of a subtil element, receding from the center of its motion, and impelling grosser bodies towards it. Sir Isaac Newton in his later thoughts seems (as was before observed) to have adopted somewhat not altogether foreign from this notion, ascribing that to his elastic medium (*r*) which Descartes did to his second element. But the great men of antiquity resolved gravity into the immediate action of an intelligent incorporeal being. To which also Sir Isaac Newton himself attests and subscribes, although he may perhaps sometimes be thought to forget himself, in his manner of speaking of physical agents, which in a strict sense are none at all, and in supposing real forces to exist in bodies, in

(*q*) 241, 242. (*r*) 237, 238.

which,

which, to ſpeak truly, attraction and repulſion ſhould be conſidered only as tendencies or motions, that is, as mere effects, and their laws as laws of motion.

247. Though it be ſuppoſed the chief buſineſs of a natural philoſopher to trace out cauſes from the effects, yet this is to be underſtood not of agents (s) but of principles, that is, of component parts, in one ſenſe, or of laws or rules, in another. In ſtrict truth, all agents are incorporeal, and as ſuch are not properly of phyſical conſideration. The Aſtronomer, therefore, the Mechanic, or the Chemiſt, not as ſuch, but by accident only, treat of real cauſes, agents or efficients. Neither doth it ſeem, as is ſuppoſed by the greateſt of mechanical philoſophers, that the true way of proceeding in their ſcience is, from known motions in nature to inveſtigate the moving forces. Foraſmuch as force is neither corporeal, nor belongs to any corporeal thing (t); nor yet to be diſcovered by experiments or mathematical reaſonings, which reach no farther than diſcernible effects, and motions in things paſſive and moved.

248. Vis or force is to the ſoul, what extenſion is to the body, ſaith ſaint Auguſtin, in his tract concerning the quantity of the Soul; and without force there is nothing done or made, and conſequently there can be no agent. Authority is not to decide in this caſe. Let any one conſult his own notions and reaſon, as well as experience, concerning the origin of motion, and the reſpective natures, properties, and differences of ſoul and body, and he will, if I miſtake not, evidently perceive, that there is nothing active in the latter. Nor are they natural

(s) 155. (t) 220.

agents or corporeal forces, which make the particles of bodies to cohere. Nor is it the business of experimental philosophers to find them out.

249. The mechanical philosopher, as hath been already observed, inquires properly concerning the rules and modes of operation alone, and not concerning the cause, forasmuch as nothing mechanical is or really can be a cause (*u*). And although a mechanical or mathematical philosopher may speak of absolute space, absolute motion, and of force as existing in bodies, causing such motion and proportional thereto; yet what these forces are, which are supposed to be lodged in bodies, to be impressed on bodies, to be multiplied, divided, and communicated from one body to another, and which seem to animate bodies like abstract spirits or souls, hath been found very difficult, not to say impossible, for thinking men to conceive and explain; as may be seen by consulting Borellus De vi percussionis, and Torricelli in his Lezioni academiche, among other authors.

250. Nor, if we consider the proclivity of mankind to realize their notions, will it seem strange that mechanic philosophers and geometricians should, like other men, be misled by prejudice, and take mathematical hypotheses for real beings existing in bodies, so far as even to make it the very aim and end of their science to compute or measure those phantoms; whereas it is very certain that nothing in truth can be measured * or computed, beside the very effects or motions themselves. Sir Isaac Newton asks, Have not the minute particles of bodies certain forces or powers by which they act on

(*u*) 236, 247.

* This subject is handled at large in my Latin tract De motu, published above twenty years ago.

one

one another, as well as on the particles of light, for producing most of the phænomema in nature? But in reality, those minute particles are only agitated according to certain laws of nature, by some other agent, wherein the force exists and not in them, which have only the motion; which motion in the body moved, the Peripatetics rightly judge to be a mere passion, but in the mover to be ἐνέργεια or act.

251. It passeth with many, I know not how, that mechanical principles give a clear solution of the phænomena. The Democritic hypothesis, saith doctor Cudworth, doth much more handsomely and intelligibly solve the phænomena, than that of Aristotle and Plato. But things rightly considered, perhaps it will be found not to solve any phænomenon at all. For all phænomena are, to speak truly, appearances in the soul or mind; and it hath never been explained, nor can it be explained, how external bodies, figures, and motions should produce an appearance in the mind. Those principles, therefore, do not solve, if by solving is meant assigning, the real, either efficient or final, cause of appearances, but only reduce them to general rules.

252. There is a certain analogy, constancy, and uniformity in the phænomena or appearances of nature, which are a foundation for general rules: and these are a grammar for the understanding of nature, or that series of effects in the visible world, whereby we are enabled to foresee what will come to pass, in the natural course of things. Plotinus observes, in his third Ennead, that the art of presaging is in some sort the reading of natural letters denoting order, and that so far forth as analogy obtains in the universe, there may be vaticination. And in reality, he that foretells the motions of the

pla-

planets, or the effects of medicines, or the result of chemical or mechanical experiments, may be said to do it by natural vaticination.

253. We know a thing when we understand it: and we understand it, when we can interpret or tell what it signifies. Strictly the sense knows nothing. We perceive indeed sounds by hearing, and characters by sight: but we are not therefore said to understand them. After the same manner, the phænomena of nature are alike visible to all: but all have not alike learned the connexion of natural things, or understand what they signify, or know how to vaticinate by them. There is no question, saith Socrates, in Theæteto, concerning that which is agreeable to each person; but concerning what will in time to come be agreeable, of which all men are not equally judges. He who foreknoweth what will be in every kind, is the wisest. According to Socrates, you and the cook may judge of a dish on the table equally well; but while the dish is making, the cook can better foretel what will ensue from this or that manner of composing it. Nor is this manner of reasoning confined only to morals or politics; but extends also to natural science.

254. As the natural connexion of signs with the things signified is regular and constant, it forms a sort of rational discourse (*a*), and is therefore the immediate effect of an intelligent cause. This is agreeable to the philosophy of Plato and other ancients. Plotinus indeed saith, that which acts naturally is not intellection, but a certain power of moving matter, which doth not know, but only do. And it must be owned, that, as faculties are multiplied by philosophers according to their operations, the will may be distinguished from the intellect.

(*a*) 152.

But it will not therefore follow, that the will, which operates in the courſe of nature, is not conducted and applied by intellect, although it be granted that neither will underſtands, nor intellect wills. Therefore, the phænomena of nature, which ſtrike on the ſenſes and are underſtood by the mind, form not only a magnificent ſpectacle, but alſo a moſt coherent, entertaining, and inſtructive diſcourſe; and to effect this, they are conducted, adjuſted, and ranged by the greateſt wiſdom. This language or diſcourſe is ſtudied with different attention, and interpreted with different degrees of ſkill. But ſo far as men have ſtudied and remarked its rules, and can interpret right, ſo far they may be ſaid to be knowing in nature. A beaſt is like a man who hears a ſtrange tongue, but underſtands nothing.

255. Nature, ſaith the learned Doctor Cudworth, is not maſter of art or wiſdom: Nature is ratio merſa et confuſa, reaſon immerſed and plunged into matter, and as it were fuddled in it and confounded with it. But the formation of plants and animals, the motions of natural bodies, their various properties, appearances, and viciſſitudes, in a word, the whole ſeries of things in this viſible world, which we call the courſe of nature, is ſo wiſely managed and carried on, that the moſt improved human reaſon cannot thoroughly comprehend even the leaſt particle thereof; ſo far is it from ſeeming to be produced by fuddled or confounded reaſon.

256. Natural productions, it is true, are not all equally perfect. But neither doth it ſuit with the order of things, the ſtructure of the univerſe, or the ends of providence, that they ſhould be ſo. General rules, we have ſeen (*a*), are neceſſary to

(*a*) 249, 252.

make

make the world intelligible: and from the constant observation of such rules, natural evils will sometimes unavoidably ensue: things will be produced in a slow length of time, and arrive at different degrees of perfection.

257. It must be owned, we are not conscious of the systole and diastole of the heart, or the motion of the diaphragm. It may not nevertheless be thence inferred, that unknowing nature can act regularly, as well as ourselves. The true inference is, that the self-thinking individual, or human person, is not the real author of those natural motions. And in fact no man blames himself if they are wrong, or values himself if they are right. The same may be said of the fingers of a musician, which some object to be moved by habit which understands not; it being evident, that what is done by rule must proceed from something that understands the rule; therefore, if not from the musician himself, from some other active intelligence, the same perhaps which governs bees and spiders, and moves the limbs of those who walk in their sleep.

258. Instruments, occasions, and signs (*b*) occur in, or rather make up, the whole visible course of nature. These, being no agents themselves, are under the direction of one agent concerting all for one end, the supreme good. All those motions, whether in animal bodies or in other parts of the system of nature, which are not effects of particular wills, seem to spring from the same general cause with the vegetation of plants, an aetherial spirit actuated by a mind.

259. The first poets and theologers of Greece and the East considered the generation of things, as ascribed rather to a divine cause; but the Physici

(*b*) 160.

to natural causes, subordinate to, and directed still by a divine; except some corporealists and mechanics, who vainly pretended to make a world without a God. The hidden force that unites, adjusts, and causeth all things to hang together, and move in harmony, which Orpheus and Empedocles styled love; this principle of union, is no blind principle, but acts with intellect. This divine love and intellect are not themselves obvious to our view, or otherwise discerned than in their effects. Intellect enlightens, Love connects, and the sovereign Good attracts all things.

260. All things are made for the supreme good, all things tend to that end: and we may be said to account for a thing, when we shew that it is so best. In the Phædon, Socrates declares it to be his opinion, that he, who supposed all things to have been disposed and ordered by a mind (*c*), should not pretend to assign any other cause of them. He blames physiologers for attempting to account for phænomena, particularly for gravity and cohesion, by vortexes and æther, overlooking the τὸ ἀγαθὸν and τὸ δέον, the strongest bond and cement which holds together all the parts of the universe, and not discerning the cause it self from those things which only attend it.

261. As in the microcosm, the constant regular tenor of the motions of the viscera and contained juices doth not hinder particular voluntary motions to be impressed by the mind on the animal spirit; even so in the mundane system, the steddy observance of certain laws of nature, in the grosser masses and more conspicuous motions, doth not hinder but a voluntarily agent may sometimes communicate particular impressions to the fine ætherial medium,

(*c*) 154, 160.

which

which in the world answers the animal spirit in man. Which two (if they are two) although invisible and inconceivably small, yet seem the real latent springs, whereby all the parts of this visible world are moved; albeit they are not to be regarded as a true cause, but only an instrument of motion; and the instrument not as a help to the creator, but only as a sign to the creature.

262. Plotinus supposeth that the soul of the universe is not the original cause or author of the species, but receives them from intellect, the true principle of order and distinction, the source and giver of forms. Others consider the vegetative soul only as some lower faculty of a higher soul, which animates the fiery ætherial spirit (*d*). As for the blots and defects which appear in the course of this world, which some have thought to proceed from a fatality or necessity in nature, and others from an evil principle, that same philosopher observes, that, it may be, the governing reason produceth and ordained all those things; and, not intending that all parts should be equally good, maketh some worse than others by design, as all parts in an animal are not eyes: and in a city, comedy, or picture, all ranks, characters, and colours are not equal or like; even so excesses, defects, and contrary qualities, conspire to the beauty and harmony of the world.

263. It cannot be denied, that with respect to the universe of things, we in this mortal state are like men educated in Plato's cave, looking on shadows with our backs turned to the light. But though our light be dim, and our situation bad, yet if the best use be made of both, perhaps something may be seen. Proclus, in his commentary on the theology of Plato, observes there are two

(*d*) 178.

sorts

ſorts of philoſophers. The one placed body firſt in the order of beings, and made the faculty of thinking depend thereupon, ſuppoſing that the principles of all things are corporeal: that body moſt really or principally exiſts, and all other things in a ſecondary ſenſe, and by virtue of that. Others, making all corporeal things to be dependent upon ſoul or mind, think this to exiſt in the firſt place and primary ſenſe, and the being of bodies to be altogether derived from, and preſuppoſe that of the mind.

264. Senſe and experience acquaint us with the courſe and analogy of appearances or natural effects. Thought, reaſon, intellect, introduce us into the knowledge of their cauſes. Senſible appearances, though of a flowing, unſtable, and uncertain nature, yet having firſt occupied the mind, they do, by an early prevention, render the after taſk of thought more difficult: and as they amuſe the eyes and ears, and are more ſuited to vulgar uſes and the mechanic arts of life, they eaſily obtain a preference, in the opinion of moſt men, to thoſe ſuperior principles, which are the later growth of the human mind arrived to maturity and perfection, but, not affecting the corporeal ſenſe, are thought to be ſo far deficient in point of ſolidity and reality; ſenſible and real to common apprehenſions being the ſame thing: although it be certain, that the principles of ſcience are neither objects of ſenſe nor imagination; and that intellect and reaſon are alone the ſure guides to truth.

265. The ſucceſsful curioſity of the preſent age, in arts and experiments and new ſyſtems, is apt to elate men, and make them overlook the ancients. But notwithſtanding that the encouragement and purſe of princes, and the united endeavours of great ſocieties in theſe later ages, have extended experi-

mental and mechanical knowledge very far, yet it muſt be owned, that the ancients too were not ignorant of many things (*e*), as well in phyſics as metaphyſics, which perhaps are more generally, though not firſt known in theſe modern times.

266. The Pythagoreans and Platoniſts had a notion of the true ſyſtem of the world. They allowed of mechanical principles, but actuated by ſoul or mind: they diſtinguiſhed the primary qualities in bodies from the ſecondary, making the former to be phyſical cauſes, and they underſtood phyſical cauſes in a right ſenſe: they ſaw that a mind infinite in power, unextended, inviſible, immortal, governed, connected, and contained all things: they ſaw there was no ſuch thing as real abſolute ſpace: that mind, ſoul, or ſpirit, truly and really exiſts: that bodies exiſt only in a ſecondary and dependent ſenſe: that the ſoul is the place of forms: that the ſenſible qualities are to be regarded as acts only in the cauſe, and as paſſions in us: they accurately conſidered the differences of intellect, rational ſoul, and ſenſitive ſoul, with their diſtinct acts of intellection, reaſoning, and ſenſation; points wherein the Carteſians and their followers, who conſider ſenſation as a mode of thinking, ſeem to have failed. They knew there was a ſubtil æther pervading the whole maſs of corporeal beings, and which was itſelf actually moved and directed by a mind: and that phyſical cauſes were only inſtruments, or rather marks and ſigns.

267. Thoſe ancient philoſophers underſtood the generation of animals to conſiſt in the unfolding and diſtending of the minute imperceptible parts or pre-exiſting animalcules; which paſſeth for a modern diſcovery: this they took for the work of nature, but

(*e*) 166, 167, 168, 241, 242, &c.

nature animate and intelligent (*f*): they underſtood that all things were alive and in motion: they ſuppoſed a concord and diſcord, union and diſunion in particles, ſome attracting, others repelling each other: and that thoſe attractions and repulſions, ſo various, regular, and uſeful, could not be accounted for, but by an intelligence preſiding and directing all particular motions, for the conſervation and benefit of the whole.

268. The Ægyptians, who imperſonated nature, had made her a diſtinct principle, and even deified her under the name of Iſis. But Oſiris was underſtood to be mind or reaſon, chief and ſovereign of all. Oſiris, if we may believe Plutarch, was the firſt, pure, unmixed, and holy principle, not diſcernible by the lower faculties; a glympſe whereof, like lightening darting forth, irradiates the underſtanding: with regard to which Plutarch adds, that Plato and Ariſtotle termed one part of philoſophy ἐποπτικὸν; to wit, when having ſoared above common mixed objects, and got beyond the precincts of ſenſe and opinion, they arrive to contemplate the firſt and moſt ſimple being, free from all matter and compoſition. This is that ȣσία ὄντως ȣσα of Plato, which employeth mind alone; which alone governs the world, and the ſoul is that which immediately informs and animates nature.

269. Although the Ægyptians did ſymbolically repreſent the ſupreme divinity ſitting on a lotus, and that geſture has been interpreted to ſignify the moſt holy and venerable being to be utterly at reſt repoſing within himſelf; yet, for any thing that appears, this geſture might denote dignity as well as repoſe. And it cannot be denied, that Jamblichus, ſo knowing in the Ægyptian notions,

(*f*) 172.

taught

taught there was an intellect that proceeded to generation, drawing forth the latent powers into light in the formation of things. Nor was this to be underſtood of an external world, ſubſiſting in real abſolute ſpace: For it was a doctrine of thoſe antient ſages, that ſoul was the place of forms, as may be ſeen in the twelfth book of the arcane part of divine wiſdom, according to the Ægyptians. This notion was embraced by divers philoſophers of Greece, who may be ſuppoſed to have derived it from the ſame ſource from whence many of their other opinions were drawn.

270. The doctrine of real abſolute external ſpace, induced ſome modern philoſophers to conclude it was a part or attribute of God, or that God himſelf was ſpace; inaſmuch as incommunicable attributes of the Deity appeared to agree thereto, ſuch as infinity, immutability, indiviſibility, incorporeity, being uncreated, impaſſive, without beginning or ending; not conſidering that all theſe negative properties may belong to nothing. For nothing hath no limits, cannot be moved or changed, or divided, is neither created nor deſtroyed. A different way of thinking appears in the Hermaic as well as other writings of the ancients. With regard to abſolute ſpace, it is obſerved in the Aſclepian dialogue, that the word Space or Place hath by itſelf no meaning; and again, that it is impoſſible to underſtand what ſpace alone or pure ſpace is. And Plotinus acknowledgeth no place but ſoul or mind, expreſly affirming that the ſoul is not in the world, but the world in the ſoul. And farther, the place of the ſoul, ſaith he, is not body, but ſoul is in mind, and body in ſoul. See the third chapter of the fifth book of the fifth Ennead.

271. Concerning absolute space, that phantome of the mechanic and geometrical philosophers (*b*), it may suffice to observe, that it is neither perceived by any sense, nor proved by any reason, and was accordingly treated by the greatest of the ancients as a thing merely visionary. From the notion of absolute space springs that of absolute motion*; and in these are ultimately founded the notions of external existence, independence, necessity, and fate. Which fate, the idol of many moderns, was by old philosophers differently understood, and in such a sense, as not to destroy the αὐτεξούσιον of God or man. Parmenides, who thought all things to be made by necessity or fate, understood justice and providence to be the same with fate; which, how fixed and cogent soever with respect to man, may yet be voluntary with respect to God. Empedocles declared fate to be a cause using principles and elements. Heraclitus taught, that fate was the general reason that runs through the whole nature of the universe; which nature he supposed to be an æthereal body, the seed of the generation of all things. Plato held fate to be the eternal reason or law of nature. Chrysippus supposed that fate was a spiritual power which disposed the world in order; that it was the reason and law of those things which are administred by providence.

(*b*) 250.

* Our judgment in these matters is not to be over-born by a presumed evidence of mathematical notions and reasonings, since it is plain, the mathematicians of this age embrace obscure notions, and uncertain opinions, and are puzzled about them, contradicting each other and disputing like other men: witness their doctrine of fluxions, about which, within these ten years, I have seen published about twenty tracts and dissertations, whose authors being utterly at variance, and inconsistent with each other, instruct by-standers what to think of their pretensions to evidence.

272. All the foregoing notions of fate, as represented by Plutarch, plainly ſhew that thoſe antient philoſophers did not mean by fate a blind, head-long, unintelligent principle, but an orderly ſettled courſe of things conducted by a wiſe and provident mind. And as for the Ægyptian doctrine, it is indeed aſſerted in the Pimander, that all things are produced by fate. But Jamblichus, who drew his notions from Ægypt, affirms, that the whole of things is not bound up in fate; but that there is a principle of the ſoul higher than nature, whereby we may be raiſed to an union with the gods, and exempt ourſelves from fate. And in the Aſclepian dialogue it is expreſly ſaid, that fate follows the decrees of God. And indeed, as all the motions in nature are evidently the product of reaſon *(c)*, it ſhould ſeem there is no room for neceſſity, in any other ſenſe than that of a ſteddy regular courſe.

273. Blind fate and blind chance are at bottom much the ſame thing, and one no more intelligible than the other. Such is the mutual relation, connection, motion, and ſympathy of the parts of this world, that they ſeem as it were animated and held together by one ſoul: and ſuch is their harmony, order, and regular courſe, as ſheweth the ſoul to be governed and directed by a mind. It was an opinion of remote antiquity that the world was an animal *(d)*. If we may truſt the Hermaic writings, the Ægyptians thought all things did partake of life. This opinion was alſo ſo general and current among the Greeks, that Plutarch aſſerts, all others held the world to be an animal, and governed by providence, except Leucippus, Democritus, and Epicurus. And although an animal, contain-

(c) 154. *(d)* 153, 172.

ing all bodies within itſelf, could not be touched or ſenſibly affected from without; yet it is plain they attributed to it an inward ſenſe and feeling, as well as appetites and averſions; and that from all the various tones, actions, and paſſions of the univerſe, they ſuppoſed one ſymphony, one animal act and life to reſult.

274. Jamblichus declares the world to be one animal, in which the parts, however diſtant each from other, are nevertheleſs related and connected by one common nature. And he teacheth, what is alſo a received notion of the Pythagoreans and Platonics, that there is no chaſm in nature, but a chain or ſcale of beings riſing by gentle uninterrupted gradations from the loweſt to the higheſt, each nature being informed and perfected by the participation of a higher. As air becomes igneous, ſo the pureſt fire becomes animal, and the animal ſoul becomes intellectual, which is to be underſtood not of the change of one nature into another, but of the connection of different natures, each lower nature being, according to thoſe philoſophers, as it were a receptable or ſubject for the next above it to reſide and act in.

275. It is alſo the doctrine of the Platonic philoſophers, that intellect is the very life of living things, the firſt principle and exemplar of all, from whence, by different degrees, are derived the inferior claſſes of life; firſt the rational, then the ſenſitive, after that the vegetal, but ſo as in the rational animal there is ſtill ſomewhat intellectual, again in the ſenſitive there is ſomewhat rational, and in the vegetal ſomewhat ſenſitive, and laſtly in mixt bodies, as metals and mineral, ſomewhat of vegetation: By which means the whole is thought to be more perfectly connected. Which

doctrine implies, that all the faculties, instincts, and motions of inferior beings, in their several respective subordinations, are derived from, and depend upon mind and intellect.

276. Both Stoics and Platonics held the world to be alive, though sometimes it be mentioned as a sentient animal, sometimes as a plant or vegetable. But in this, notwithstanding what hath been surmised by some learned men, there seems to be no atheism. For so long as the world is supposed to be quickened by elementary fire or spirit, which is itself animated by soul, and directed by understanding, it follows that all parts thereof originally depend upon, and may be reduced unto, the same indivisible stem or principle, to wit, a supreme mind; which is the concurrent doctrine of Pythagoræans, Platonics, and Stoics.

277. There is according to those philosophers a life infused throughout all things: the πῦρ νοερὸν, πῦρ τεχνικὸν, an intellectual and artificial fire (*e*), an inward principle, animal spirit, or natural life producing and forming within as art doth without, regulating, moderating, and reconciling the various motions, qualities, and parts of this mundane system. By virtue of this life the great masses are held together in their orderly courses, as well as the minutest particles governed in their natural motions, according to the several laws of attraction, gravity, electricity, magnetism, and the rest. It is this gives instincts, teaches the spider her web, and the bee her honey. This it is that directs the roots of plants to draw forth juices from the earth, and the leaves and cortical vessels to separate and attract such particles of air, and elementary fire, as suit their respective natures.

278. Nature seems to be not otherwise distin-

(*e*) 166, 168, 174, 175, &c.

guiſhed from the anima mundi, than as life is from ſoul, and, upon the principles of the oldeſt philoſophers, may not improperly or incongruouſly be ſtyled the life of the world. Some Platonics, indeed, regard life as the act of nature, in like manner as intellection is of the mind or intellect. As the firſt intellect acts by underſtanding, ſo nature according to them acts or generates by living. But life is the act of the ſoul, and ſeems to be very nature itſelf, which is not the principle, but the reſult of another, and higher principle, being a life reſulting from ſoul, as cogitation from intellect.

279. If nature be the life of the world, animated by one ſoul, compacted into one frame, and directed or governed in all parts by one mind: This ſyſtem cannot be accuſed of atheiſm; tho' perhaps it may of miſtake or impropriety. And yet, as one preſiding mind gives unity to the infinite aggregate of things, by a mutual communion of actions and paſſions, and an adjuſtment of parts, cauſing all to concur in one view to one and the ſame end, the ultimate and ſupreme good of the whole, it ſhould ſeem reaſonable to ſay, with Ocellus Lucanus the Pythagorean, that as life holds together the bodies of animals, the cauſe whereof is the ſoul; and as a city is held together by concord, the cauſe whereof is law; even ſo the world is held together by harmony, the cauſe whereof is God. And in this ſenſe, the world or univerſe may be conſidered either as one animal (*f*) or one city.

280. Ariſtotle diſapproves the opinion of thoſe who hold a ſoul to be diffuſed throughout the world; and for this reaſon, becauſe the elements are not alive. Tho' perhaps it may not be eaſy to prove, that blood and animal ſpirit are more alive in man, than water and fire in the world. That phi-

(*f*) 172, 277.

losopher, in his books of the soul, remarks upon an opinion set forth in the Orphics, of the soul's entering from the universe into living creatures, being born by winds, that this cannot be true of plants or of certain animals which do not breath. But air vessels are by later experiments allowed to be found in all plants and animals. And air may in some sort not improperly be said, to be the carrier or vehicle of the soul, inasmuch as it is the vehicle of fire, which is the spirit immediately moved and animated by the soul (*g*).

281. The living fire, the living omniform seminary of the world, and other expressions of the like nature occurring in the ancient and Platonic philosophy, how can they be understood exclusive of light or elemental fire, the particles of which are known to be heterogeneous, and, for ought we know, may some of them be organized, and, notwithstanding their wonderful minuteness, contain original seeds, which, being formed and sown in a proper matrix, do gradually unfold and manifest themselves, still growing to a just proportion of the species.

282. May not this æthereal seminary, consistently with the notions of that philosophy, which ascribed much of generation to celestial influence, be supposed to impregnate plants and animals with the first principles, the stamina, or those animalcules which Plato, in his Timæus, saith are invisible for their smallness, but, being sown in a proper matrix, are therein gradually distended and explicated by nourishment, and at length the animals brought forth to light. Which notion hath been revived and received of late years by many, who perhaps are not aware of its antiquity, or that it was to be found in Plato. Timæus Locrensis in

(*g*) 163, 171.

his book of the soul of the world, supposeth even souls to be derived from the celestial luminaries, excepting only the rational or intellectual part. But what influence or influx is there from the celestial bodies, which hath not light for its vehicle (*a*)?

283. What other nature there should be intermediate between the soul of the world (*b*) and this gross corporeal system, which might be the vehicle of life, or, to use the language of philosophers, might receive or be impressed with the forms of things, is difficult to comprehend. It is a vulgar remark, that the works of art do not bear a nice microscopical inspection, but the more helps are used, and the more nicely you pry into natural productions, the more do you discover of the fine mechanism of nature, which is endless or inexhaustible; new and other parts, more subtile and delicate than the precedent, still continuing to offer themselves to view. And these microscopical observations have confirmed the ancient theory concerning generation, delivered in the Timæus of Plato. But that theory or hypothesis, how agreeable soever to modern discoveries, is not alone sufficient to explain the phænomena, without the immediate action of a mind. And Ficinus, notwithstanding what himself and other Platonics, say of a plastic nature, is obliged to own, that with the mundane force or soul it is to be understood there is joined an intelligence, upon which the seminal nature constantly depends, and by which it is governed.

284. Alcinous, in his tract of the doctrine of Plato, saith that God hath given the world both mind and soul: others include both in the word soul, and suppose the soul of the world to be God.

(*a*) 43. (*b*) 171.

Philo-

Philo appears to be of this opinion in several parts of his writings. And Virgil, who was no stranger to the Pythagorean and Platonic tenets, writes to the same purpose.

> Deum namque ire per omnes
> Terrasque tractusque maris cœlumque profundum.
> Hinc pecudes armenta, viros, genus omne ferarum,
> Quemque sibi tenues nascentem arcessere vitas.

Thus much the schools of Plato and Pythagoras seem agreed in, to wit, that the soul of the world (*b*) whether having a distinct mind of its own, or directed by a superior mind (*c*) doth embrace all its parts, connect them by an invisible and indissoluble chain, and preserve them ever well adjusted, and in good order.

285. Naturalists, whose proper province it is to consider phænomena, experiments, mechanical organs and motions, principally regard the visible frame of things or corporeal world, supposing soul to be contained in body. And this hypothesis may be tolerated in physics, as it is not necessary in the arts of dialling or navigation to mention the true system or earth's motion. But those who, not content with sensible appearances, would penetrate into the real and true causes (the object of theology, metaphysics, or the philosophia prima) will rectify this error, and speak of the world as contained by the soul, and not the soul by the world.

286. Aristotle hath observed there were indeed some who thought so grosly, as to suppose the universe to be one only corporeal and extended nature: but in the first book of his Metaphy-

(*b*) 153, 172. (*c*) 154, 279.

sics he justly remarks they were guilty of a great mistake; forasmuch as they took into their account the elements of corporeal beings alone; whereas there are incorporeal beings also in the universe; and while they attempted to assign the causes of generation and corruption, and account for the nature of all things, they did at the same time destroy the very cause of motion.

287. It is a doctrine among other speculations contained in the Hermaic writings, that all things are one. And it is not improbable that Orpheus, Parmenides, and others among the Greeks, might have derived their notion of τὸ ἓν, THE ONE, from Ægypt. Tho' that subtil metaphysician Parmenides, in his doctrine of ἓν ἑστὼς, seems to have added something of his own. If we suppose, that one and the same mind is the universal principle of order and harmony throughout the world, containing and connecting all its parts, and giving unity to the system, there seems to be nothing atheistical or impious in this supposition.

288. Number is no object of sense: it is an act of the mind. The same thing in a different conception is one or many. Comprehending God and the creatures in one general notion, we may say that all things together make one universe, or τὸ πᾶν. But if we should say, that all things make one God; this would, indeed, be an erroneous notion of God, but would not amount to atheism, so long as mind or intellect was admitted to be the τὸ ἡγεμονικὸν, the governing part. It is nevertheless more respectful, and consequently the truer notion of God, to suppose him neither made up of parts, nor to be himself a part of any whole whatsoever.

289. All those, who conceived the universe to be an animal, must in consequence of that notion,

suppose

ſuppoſe all things to be one. But to conceive God to be the ſentient ſoul of an animal, is altogether unworthy and abſurd. There is no ſenſe, nor ſenſory, nor any thing like a ſenſe or ſenſory in God. Senſe implies an impreſſion from ſome other being, and denotes a dependence in the ſoul which hath it. Senſe is a paſſion; and paſſions imply imperfection. God knoweth all things, as pure mind or intellect, but nothing by ſenſe, nor in nor through a ſenſory. Therefore to ſuppoſe a ſenſory of any kind, whether ſpace or any other, in God, would be very wrong, and lead us into falſe conceptions of his nature. The preſuming there was ſuch a thing as real abſolute uncreated ſpace, ſeems to have occaſioned that modern miſtake. But this preſumption was without grounds.

290. Body is oppoſite to ſpirit or mind. We have a notion of ſpirit from thought and action. We have a notion of body from reſiſtance. So far forth as there is real power, there is ſpirit. So far forth as there is reſiſtance, there is inability or want of power; that is, there is a negation of ſpirit. We are embodied, that is, we are clogged by weight, and hindered by reſiſtance. But in reſpect of a perfect ſpirit, there is nothing hard or impenetrable: there is no reſiſtance to the Deity: nor hath he any body: nor is the ſupreme being united to the world, as the ſoul of an animal is to its body, which neceſſarily implieth defect, both as an inſtrument, and as a conſtant weight and impediment.

291. Thus much it conſiſts with piety to ſay, that a divine agent doth by his virtue permeate and govern the elementary fire or light (*d*), which ſerves as an animal ſpirit to enliven and actuate the

(*d*) 157, 172.

whole mass, and all the members of this visible world. Nor is this doctrine less philosophical than pious. We see all nature alive or in motion. We see water turned into air, and air rarified and made elastic (*e*) by the attraction of another medium, more pure indeed, more subtil, and more volatile than air. But still, as this is a moveable, extended, and, consequently, a corporeal being (*f*), it cannot be itself the principle of motion, but leads us naturally and necessarily to an incorporeal spirit or agent. We are conscious that a spirit can begin, alter, or determine motion, but nothing of this appears in body. Nay the contrary is evident both to experiment and reflection.

292. Natural phænomena are only natural appearances. They are, therefore, such as we see and perceive them. Their real and objective natures are, therefore, the same; passive without any thing active, fluent and changing without any thing permanent in them. However, as these make the first impressions, and the mind takes her first flight and spring, as it were, by resting her foot on these objects, they are not only first considered by all men, but most considered by most men. They and the phantomes that result from those appearances, the children of imagination grafted upon sense, such for example as pure space (*i*), are thought by many the very first in existence and stability, and to embrace and comprehend all other beings.

293. Now although such phantomes as corporeal forces, absolute motions, and real spaces, do pass in physics for causes and principles (*g*), yet are they in truth but hypotheses, nor can they be the objects of real science. They pass nevertheless in physics conversant about things of sense, and con-

(*e*) 149, 152, 200. (*f*) 207. (*i*) 270. (*g*) 220, 249, 250.

fined

fined to experiments and mechanics. But when we enter the province of the philosophia prima, we discover another order of beings, mind and its acts, permanent being, not dependent on corporeal things, nor resulting, nor connected, nor contained; but containing, connecting, enlivening the whole frame; and imparting those motions, forms, qualities, and that order and symmetry to all those transient phænomena, which we term the course of nature.

294. It is with our faculties as with our affections: what first seizes, holds fast (*a*). It is a vulgar theme, that man is a compound of contrarieties, which breed a restless struggle in his nature, between flesh and spirit, the beast and the angel, earth and heaven, ever weighed down and ever bearing up. During which conflict the character fluctuates: when either side prevails, it is then fixed for vice or virtue. And life from different principles takes a different issue. It is the same in regard to our faculties. Sense at first besets and overbears the mind. The sensible appearances are all in all, our reasonings are employed about them; our desires terminate in them; we look no farther for realities or causes; till intellect begins to dawn, and cast a ray on this shadowy scene. We then perceive the true principle of unity, identity, and existence. Those things that before seemed to constitute the whole of being, upon taking an intellectual view of things, prove to be but fleeting phantomes.

295. From the outward form of gross masses which occupy the vulgar, a curious inquirer proceeds to examine the inward structure and minute parts, and from observing the motions in nature, to discover the laws of those motions. By the way he frames his hypothesis and suits his language to

(*a*) 264.

this

this natural philosophy. And these fit the occasion and answer the end of a maker of experiments or mechanic, who means only to apply the powers of nature, and reduce the phænomena to rules. But if, proceeding still in his analysis and inquiry, he ascends from the sensible into the intellectual world, and beholds things in a new light and a new order, he will then change his system, and perceive, that what he took for substances and causes are but fleeting shadows; that the mind contains all, and acts all, and is to all created beings the source of unity and identity, harmony and order, existence and stability.

296. It is neither acid, nor salt, nor sulphur, nor air, nor æther, nor visible corporeal fire (*b*), much less the phantome fate, or necessity, that is the real agent, but by a certain analysis, a regular connection and climax, we ascend through all those mediums to a glympse of the first mover, invisible, incorporeal, unextended, intellectual source of life and being. There is, it must be owned, a mixture of obscurity and prejudice in human speech and reasonings. This is unavoidable, since the veils of prejudice and error are slowly and singly taken off one by one. But if there are many links in the chain which connects the two extremes of what is grosly sensible and purely intelligible, and it seem a tedious work, by the slow helps of memory, imagination, and reason, oppressed and overwhelmed, as we are, by the senses, through erroneous principles and long ambages of words and notions, to struggle upwards into the light of truth; yet as this gradually dawns, further discoveries still correct the style, and clear up the notions.

297. The mind, her acts and faculties, furnish a new and distinct class of objects (*c*) from the

(*b*) 155. (*c*) 163, 266.

contemplation whereof arise certain other notions, principles, and verities, so remote from, and even so repugnant to, the first prejudices which surprize the sense of mankind, that they may well be excluded from vulgar speech and books, as abstract from sensible matters, and more fit for the speculation of Truth, the labour and aim of a few, than for the practice of the world, or the subjects of experimental or mechanical inquiry. Nevertheless, though, perhaps, it may not be relished by some modern readers, yet the treating in physical books concerning metaphysical and divine matters can be justified by great authorities among the ancients; not to mention, that he, who professedly delivers the elements of a science, is more obliged to method and system, and tied down to more rigorous laws, than a mere essay writer. It may, therefore, be pardoned if this rude essay doth, by insensible transitions, draw the reader into remote inquiries and speculations, that were not thought of, either by him or by the author, at first setting out.

298. There are traces of profound thought as well as primæval tradition in the Platonic, Pythagoræan, Ægyptian, and Chaldaic philosophy (*p*). Men in those early days were not overlaid with languages and literature. Their minds seem to have been more exercised, and less burdened, than in later ages; and, as so much nearer the beginning of the world, to have had the advantage of patriarchal lights handed down through a few hands. It cannot be affirmed indeed (how probable soever it may seem) that Moses was that same Mochus, with whose successors, priests and prophets, Pythagoras is said to have conversed at Sidon. Yet the study of philosophy appears to be of very great antiquity and remote original; inasmuch as Timæus

(*p*) 179, 266.

Locrensis,

Locrensis, that ancient Pythagorean, author of the book concerning the soul of the world, speaks of a most ancient philosophy, even in his time, ἁ πρεσβύστα φιλοσοφία, stirring up and recovering the soul from a state of ignorance to the contemplation of divine things. And though the books attributed to Mercurius Trismegistus were none of them wrote by him, and are allowed to contain some manifest forgeries; yet it is also allowed, that they contain tenets of the ancient Ægyptian philosophy, though dressed perhaps in a more modern garb. To account for which, Jamblichus observes, that the books under his name contain indeed mercurial opinions, though often expressed in the style of the Greek philosophers; as having been translated from the Ægyptian tongue into Greek.

299. The difference of Isis from Osiris (*d*) resembles that of the moon from the sun, of the female from the male, of natura naturata (as the schoolmen speak) from natura naturans. But Isis, though mostly taken for nature, yet (as the Pagan divinities were very fluctuating things) it sometimes signified τὸ πᾶν. And we find in Mountfaucon an Isis of the ordinary form with this inscription Θεᾶ παντός. And in the mensa Isiaca, which seems to exhibit a general system of the religion and superstition of the Ægyptians, Isis on her throne possesseth the center of the table. Which may seem to signify, that the universe or τὸ πᾶν was the center of the ancient secret religion of the Ægyptians; their Isis or τὸ πᾶν comprehending both Osiris the author of nature, and his work.

300. Plato and Aristotle considered God as abstracted or distinct from the natural world. But the Ægyptians considered God and nature as ma-

(*d*) 268.

king

king one whole, or all things together as making one univerſe. In doing which they did not exclude the intelligent mind, but conſidered it as containing all things. Therefore, whatever was wrong in their way of thinking, it doth not, nevertheleſs, imply or lead to Atheiſm.

301. The human mind is ſo much clogged, and born downward, by the ſtrong and early impreſſions of ſenſe (*a*), that it is wonderful, how the ancients ſhould have made even ſuch a progreſs, and ſeen ſo far into intellectual matters, without ſome glimmering of a divine tradition. Whoever conſiders a parcel of rude ſavages left to themſelves, how they are ſunk and ſwallowed up in ſenſe and prejudice, and how unqualified by their natural force to emerge from this ſtate, will be apt to think that the firſt ſpark of philoſophy was derived from heaven; and that it was (as a Heathen writer expreſſeth it) θεοπαράδοτος φιλοσοφία.

302. The lapſed ſtate of human kind is a thing to which the ancient philoſophers were not ſtrangers. The λύσις, the φυγή, the παλιγγενεσία ſhew that the Egyptians and Pythagoreans, the Platoniſts and Stoics, had all ſome notion of this doctrine, the outlines of which ſeem to have been ſketched out in thoſe tenets. Theology and philoſophy gently unbind the ligaments, that chain the ſoul down to the earth, and aſſiſt her flight towards the ſovereign Good. There is an inſtinct or tendency of the mind upwards, which ſheweth a natural endeavour to recover and raiſe ourſelves, from our preſent ſenſual and low condition, into a ſtate of light, order, and purity.

303. The perceptions of ſenſe are groſs: but even in the ſenſes there is a difference. Though harmony and proportion are not objects of ſenſe,

(*a*) 264.

yet the eye and the ear are organs, which offer to the mind such materials, by means whereof she may apprehend both the one and the other. By experiments of sense we become acquainted with the lower faculties of the soul; and from them, whether by a gradual (*a*) evolution or ascent, we arrive at the highest. Sense supplies images to memory. These become subjects for fancy to work upon. Reason considers and judges of the imaginations. And these acts of reason become new objects to the understanding. In this scale, each lower faculty is a step that leads to one above it. And the uppermost naturally leads to the Deity, which is rather the object of intellectual knowledge than even of the discursive faculty, not to mention the sensitive. There runs a chain throughout the whole system of beings. In this chain one link drags another. The meanest things are connected with the highest. The calamity therefore is neither strange nor much to be complained of, if a low sensual reader shall, from mere love of the animal life, find himself drawn on, surprised and betrayed into some curiosity concerning the intellectual.

304. There is, accordingto Plato, properly no knowledge, but only opinion concerning things sensible and perishing (*b*), not because they are naturally abstruse and involved in darkness, but because their nature and existance is uncertain, ever fleeting and changing; or rather, because they do not in strict truth exist at all, being always generating, or in fieri, that is, in a perpetual flux, without any thing stable or permanent in them to constitute an object of real science. The Pythagoreans and Platonics distinguish between τὸ γιγνόμενον and τὸ ὄν, that which is ever generated and that which exists. Sensible things and corporeal forms

(*a*) 275. (*b*) 263, 264.

are

are perpetually producing and perishing, appearing and disappearing, never resting in one state, but always in motion and change; and therefore in effect, not one being but a succession of beings: while τὸ ὂν is understood to be somewhat of an abstract or spiritual nature, and the proper object of intellectual knowledge. Therefore as there can be no knowledge of things flowing and instable, the opinion of Protagoras and Theætetus, that sense was science, is absurd. And indeed nothing is more evident, than that the apparent sizes and shapes, for instance, of things are in a constant flux, ever differing as they are viewed at different distances, or with glasses more or less accurate. As for those absolute magnitudes and figures, which certain Cartesians and other moderns suppose to be in things, that must seem a vain supposition, to whoever considers, it is supported by no argument of reason, and no experiment of sense.

305. As understanding perceiveth not, that is, doth not hear, or see, or feel, so sense knoweth not: And although the mind may use both sense and fancy, as means whereby to arrive at knowledge, yet sense or soul, so far forth as sensitive, knoweth nothing. For, as it is rightly observed in the Theætetus of Plato, science consists not in the passive perceptions, but in the reasoning upon them, τῷ περὶ ἐκείνων συλλογισμῷ.

306. In the ancient philosophy of Plato and Pythagoras, we find distinguished three sorts of objects: In the first place a form or species that is neither generated nor destroyed, unchangeable, invisible, and altogether imperceptible to sense, being only understood by the intellect. A second sort there is ever fluent and changing (g), generating and perishing, appearing and vanishing. This

(f) 263. (g) 292, 293.

is comprehended by sense and opinion. The third kind is matter which, as Plato teacheth, being neither an object of understanding nor of sense, is hardly to be made out by a certain spurious way of reasoning λογισμῷ τινι νόθῳ μόγις πιϛόν. See his Timæus. The same doctrine is contained in the Pythagoric treatise De anima mundi, which distinguishing ideas, sensible things, and matter, maketh the first to be apprehended by intellect, the second by sense, and the last, to wit, matter, λογισμῷ νόθῳ· whereof Themistius the Peripatetic assigns the reason. For, saith he, that act is to be esteemed spurious, whose object hath nothing positive, being only a mere privation, as silence or darkness. And such he accounteth matter.

307. Aristotle maketh a threefold distinction of objects according to the three speculative sciences. Physics he supposeth to be conversant about such things as have a principle of motion in themselves; mathematics about things permanent but not abstracted; and theology about being abstracted and immoveable; which distinction may be seen in the ninth book of his Metaphysics. Where by abstracted, χωριϛὸν, he understands separable from corporeal beings and sensible qualities.

308. That philosopher held that the mind of man was a tabula rasa, and that there were no innate ideas. Plato, on the contrary, held original ideas in the mind, that is, notions which never were or can be in the sense, such as being, beauty, goodness, likeness, parity. Some perhaps may think the truth to be this: That there are properly no ideas or passive objects in the mind, but what were derived from sense: but that there are also besides these her own acts or operations; such are notions.

309. It is a maxim of the Platonic philosophy, that

that the ſoul of man was originally furniſhed with native inbred notions, and ſtands in need of ſenſible occaſions, not abſolutely for producing them, but only for awakening, rouſing, or exciting into act what was already pre-exiſtent, dormant, and latent in the ſoul; as things are ſaid to be laid up in the memory, though not actually perceived, until they happen to be called forth and brought into view by other objects. This notion ſeemeth ſomewhat different from that of innate ideas, as underſtood by thoſe moderns who have attempted to explode them. To underſtand and to be, are according to Parmenides the ſame thing. And Plato, in his ſeventh letter, makes no difference between νοῦς and ἐπιστήμη, mind and knowledge. Whence it follows, that mind, knowledge, and notions, either in habit or in act, always go together.

310. And albeit Ariſtotle conſidered the ſoul in its original ſtate as a blank paper, yet he held it to be the proper place of forms, τὴν ψυχὴν εἶναι τόπον εἰδῶν (a). Which doctrine firſt maintained by others he admits, under this reſtriction, that it is not to be underſtood of the whole ſoul, but only of the νοητικὴ; as is to be ſeen in his third book De anima. Whence, according to Themiſtius in his commentary on that treatiſe, it may be inferred, that all beings are in the ſoul. For, ſaith he, the forms are the beings. By the form every thing is what it is. And he adds, it is the ſoul that imparteth forms to matter; τὴν ὕλην μορφῶσα ποικίλαις μορφαῖς. Therefore they are firſt in the ſoul. He further adds, that the mind is all things, taking the forms of all things it becomes all things by intellect and ſenſe. Alexander Aphrodiſæus ſaith as much, affirming the mind to be all things, κατά τε τὸ νοεῖν καὶ τὸ αἰσθάνεσθαι. And

(n) 269.

this

this in fact is Ariſtotle's own doctrine in his third book De anima, where he alſo aſſerts, with Plato, that actual knowledge and the thing known are all one: *το αυτο δε εϛιν η κατ ἐνέργειαν ἐπιϛήμη τῷ πϱάγματι*. Whence it follows that the things are where the knowledge is, that is to ſay, in the mind. Or, as it is otherwiſe expreſſed, that the ſoul is all things. More might be ſaid to explain Ariſtotle's notion, but it would lead too far.

311. As to an abſolute actual exiſtence (*b*) of ſenſible or corporeal things, it doth not ſeem to have been admitted either by Plato or Ariſtotle. In the Theætetus we are told, that if any one ſaith a thing is or is made, he muſt withal ſay, for what, or of what, or in reſpect of what, it is or is made; for, that any thing ſhould exiſt in itſelf or abſolutely, is abſurd. Agreeably to which doctrine it is alſo farther affirmed by Plato, that it is impoſſible a thing ſhould be ſweet, and ſweet to no body. It muſt nevertheleſs be owned with regard to Ariſtotle, that, even in his Metaphyſics there are ſome expreſſions which ſeem to favour the abſolute exiſtence of corporeal things. For inſtance, in the eleventh book ſpeaking of corporeal ſenſible things, What wonder, ſaith he, if they never appear to us the ſame, no more than to ſick men, ſince we are always changing, and never remain the ſame ourſelves? And again, he ſaith, Senſible things, although they receive no change in themſelves, do nevertheleſs in ſick perſons produce different ſenſations and not the ſame. Theſe paſſages would ſeem to imply a diſtinct and abſolute exiſtence of the objects of ſenſe.

312. But it muſt be obſerved, that Ariſtotle diſtinguiſheth a twofold exiſtence, potential and actual. It will not, therefore, follow, that, ac-

(*b*) 264, 292, 294.

cording

cording to Aristotle, because a thing is, it must actually exist. This is evident from the eighth book of his Metaphysics, where he animadverts on the Megaric philosophers, as not admitting a possible existence distinct from the actual: from whence, saith he, it must follow, that there is nothing cold or hot or sweet or any sensible thing at all, where there is no perception. He adds, that in consequence of that Megaric doctrine, we can have no sense but while we actually exert it: we are blind when we do not see, and therefore both blind and deaf several times in a day.

313. The ἐντελέχειαι πρῶται of the Peripatetics, that is, the sciences, arts, and habits, were by them distinguished from the acts or ἐντελέχειαι δεύτεραι, and supposed to exist in the mind, though not exerted or put into act. This seems to illustrate the manner in which Socrates, Plato, and their followers conceived innate (c) notions to be in the soul of man. It was the Platonic doctrine, that human souls or minds descended from above, and were sowed in generation, that they were stunned, stupified, and intoxicated by this descent and immersion into animal nature. And that the soul, in this ὀνείρωξις, or slumber, forgets her original notions, which are smothered and oppressed by many false tenets and prejudices of sense. Insomuch that Proclus compares the soul, in her descent invested with growing prejudices, to Glaucus diving to the bottom of the sea, and there contracting divers coats of sea-weed, coral, and shells, which stick close to him and conceal his true shape.

314. Hence, according to this philosophy, the mind of man is so restless to shake off that slumber, to disengage and emancipate herself from those prejudices and false opinions, that so straitly

(c) 309.

beset

beset and cling to her, to rub off those covers, that disguise her original form, and to regain her primæval state and first notions: Hence, that perpetual struggle to recover the lost region of light, that ardent thirst and endeavour after truth and intellectual ideas, which she would neither seek to attain, nor rejoice in, nor know when attained, except she had some prænotion or anticipation of them, and they had lain innate and dormant like habits and sciences in the mind, or things laid up, which are called out and roused by recollection or reminiscence. So that learning seemeth in effect reminiscence.

315. The Peripatetics themselves distinguish between reminiscence and mere memory. Themistius observes that the best memories commonly go with the worst parts; but that reminiscence is most perfect in the most ingenious minds. And notwithstanding the tabula rasa *(d)* of Aristotle, yet some of his followers have undertaken to make him speak Plato's sense. Thus Plutarch the Peripatetic teacheth, as agreeable to his master's doctrine, that learning is reminiscence, and that the νοῦς καθ' ἕξιν is in children. Simplicius also, in his commentary on the third book of Aristotle περὶ ψυχῆς, speaketh of a certain interiour reason in the soul, acting of itself, and originally full of its own proper notions, πλήρης ἀφ' ἑαυτοῦ τῶν οἰκείων γνώσεων.

316. And as the Platonic philosophy supposed intellectual notions to be originally inexistent or innate in the soul *(e)*, so likewise it supposed sensible qualities to exist (though not originally) in the soul, and there only. Socrates saith to Theætetus, You must not think the white colour that you see is in any thing without your eyes, or in your eyes,

(d) 308. *(e)* 309, 314.

or

or in any place at all. And in the Timæus Plato teacheth, that the figure and motion of the particles of fire dividing the parts of our bodies, produce that painful sensation we call heat. And Plotinus, in the sixth book of his second Ennead, observes, that heat and other qualities are not qualities in the things themselves, but acts: that heat is not a quality, but act, in the fire: that fire is not really what we perceive in the qualities light, heat, and colour. From all which it is plain, that whatever real things they supposed to exist independent of the soul, those were neither sensible things, nor cloathed with sensible qualities.

317. Neither Plato nor Aristotle by matter, ὕλη, understood corporeal substance, whatever the moderns may understand by that word. To them certainly it signified no positive actual being. Aristotle describes it as made up of negatives, having neither quantity, nor quality, nor essence. And not only the Platonists and Pythagoreans, but also the Peripatetics themselves declare it to be known neither by sense, nor by any direct and just reasoning, but only by some spurious or adulterine method, as hath been observed before. Simon Portius, a famous Peripatetic of the sixteenth century, denies it to be any substance at all, for, saith he, nequit per se subsistere, quia sequeretur, id quod non est in actu esse in actu. If Jamblichus may be credited, the Ægyptians supposed matter so far from including ought of substance or essence, that, according to them, God produced it by a separation from all substance, essence, or being, ἀπὸ οὐσιότητος ἀποσχισθείσης ὑλότητος. That matter is actually nothing, but potentially all things, is the doctrine of Aristotle, Theophrastus, and all the antient Peripatetics.

318. According to those philosophers, matter is

only a pura potentia, a mere poſſibility. But Anaximander, ſucceſſor to Thales, is repreſented as having thought the ſupreme Deity to be infinite matter. Nevertheleſs though Plutarch calleth it matter, yet it was ſimply τὸ ἄπειρον, which means no more than infinite or indefinite. And although the moderns teach that ſpace is real and infinitely extended; yet if we conſider that it is no intellectual notion, nor yet perceived by any of our ſenſes, we ſhall perhaps be inclined to think with Plato in his Timæus, that this alſo is the reſult of λογισμὸς νόθος, or ſpurious reaſoning, and a kind of waking dream. Plato obſerves that we dream, as it were, when we think of place, and believe it neceſſary, that whatever exiſts ſhould exiſt in ſome place. Which place or ſpace (*f*) he alſo obſerves is μετ' ἀναισθησίας ἁπτὸν, that is to be felt as darkneſs is ſeen, or ſilence heard, being a mere privation.

319. If any one ſhould think to infer the reality or actual being of matter from the modern tenet, that gravity is always proportionable to the quantity of matter, let him but narrowly ſcan the modern demonſtration of that tenet, and he will find it to be a vain circle, concluding in truth no more than this, that gravity is proportionable to weight, that is to it ſelf. Since matter is conceived only as defect and mere poſſibility; and ſince God is abſolute perfection and act; it follows there is the greateſt diſtance and oppoſition imaginable between God and matter. Inſomuch that a material God would be altogether inconſiſtent.

320. The force that produces, the intellect that orders, the goodneſs that perfects all things, is the ſupreme being. Evil, defect, negation, is not the object of God's creative power. From

(*f*) 250, 270.

motion

motion the Peripatetics trace out a first immoveable mover. The Platonics make God author of all good, author of no evil, and unchangeable. According to Anaxagoras there was a confused mass of all things in one chaos, but mind supervening, ἐπελθὼν, distinguished and divided them. Anaxagoras, it seems, ascribed the motive faculty to mind, which mind some subsequent philosophers have accurately discriminated from soul and life, ascribing to it the sole faculty of intellection.

321. But still God was supposed the first agent, the source and original of all things, which he produceth, not occasionally or instrumentally, but with actual and real efficacy. Thus, the treatise De secretiore parte divinæ sapientiæ secundum Ægyptios, in the tenth book, saith of God, that he is not only the first agent, but also that he it is who truly acts or creates, qui vere efficit.

322. Varro, Tully, and St. Augustin understand the soul to be vis, the power, or force, that acts moves, enlivens. Now although, in our conception, vis, or spirit, might be distinguished from mind, it would not thence follow, that it acts blindly or without mind, or that it is not closely connected with intellect. If Plutarch is to be trusted in his account of the opinions of philosophers, Thales held the mind of the world to be God: Democritus held the soul of the world to be an igniform deity (*g*): Pythagoras taught that God was the monad and the good, or τ' ἀγαθὸν: Socrates also and Plato pronounced him to be the τὸ ἓν (*h*), the single, self-originate one, essentially good. Each of which appellations and forms of speech directly tends to, and determines in mind; εἰς τὸν νοῦν σπεύδει, saith Plutarch.

323. Whence that author concludes, that in the sense

(*g*) 166, 168, 277. (*h*) 287.

of those philosophers God is a mind, χωριστὸν εἶδος, not an abstract idea compounded of inconsistencies and prescinded from all real things, as some moderns understand abstraction; but a really existing spirit, distinct or separate from all sensible and corporeal beings. And although the Stoics are represented as holding a corporeal deity, or that the very system of the world is God, yet it is certain they did not, at bottom, dissent from the forementioned doctrine; inasmuch as they supposed the world to be an animal (*a*), consisting of soul or mind as well as body.

324. This notion was derived from the Pythagoreans, who held the world, as Timæus Locrus teacheth, to be one perfect animal, endued with soul and reason: but then they believed it to have been generated: whereas the Stoics looked on the world as the supreme God, including therein mind or intellect. For the elementary fire, or, if one may so speak, the animal spirit of the world, seemeth, according to them, to have been the vehicle of the soul (*b*), the vehicle of intellect or νοῦς; since they styled the Divinity πῦρ νοερὸν (*c*), or intellectual fire.

325. The Ægyptians, if we may credit the Hermaic writings, maintained God to be all things, not only actual but possible. He is styled by them, that which is made and that which is unmade. And therein it is said, Shall I praise thee for those things thou hast made manifest, or for the things thou hast hidden? therefore, in their sense, to manifest, was to create; the things created having been before hidden in God.

326. Now whether the νοῦς be abstracted from the sensible world, and considered by it self, as distinct from, and presiding over the created sy-

(*a*) 276, 279. (*b*) 277, 284. (*c*) 272.

stem,

stem, or whether the whole universe, including mind together with the mundane body, is conceived to be God (*d*), and the creatures to be partial manifestations of the divine essence, there is no atheism in either case, whatever misconceptions there may be; so long as mind or intellect is understood to preside over, govern, and conduct the whole frame of things. And this was the general prevailing opinion among the philosophers.

327. Nor if any one, with Aristotle in his Metaphysics, should deny that God knows any thing without himself; seeing that God comprehends all things, could this be justly pronounced an atheistical opinion. Nor even was the following notion of the same author to be accounted atheism, to wit, that there are some things beneath the knowledge of God, as too mean, base, and vile; however wrong this notion may be, and unworthy of the divine perfection.

328. Might we not conceive that God may be said to be all in divers senses; as he is the cause and origine of all beings; as the νȣς is the νοητὰ, a doctrine both of Platonics and Peripatetics (*e*); as the νȣς is the place of all forms, and as it is the same which comprehends, and orders (*f*), and sustains the whole mundane system. Aristotle declares, that the divine force or influence permeates the intire universe (*g*), and that what the pilot is in a ship, the driver in a chariot, the præcentor in a choir, the law in a city, the general in an army, the same God is in the world. This he amply sets forth in his book De mundo, a treatise which having been anciently ascribed to him, ought not to be set aside from the difference of style, which (as Patricius rightly observes) being in a letter to

(*d*) 300. (*e*) 309, 310. (*f*) 320. (*g*) 173.

a king,

a king, might well be ſuppoſed to differ from the other dry and crabbed parts of his writings.

329. And although there are ſome expreſſions to be met with in the philoſophers, even of the Platonic and Ariſtotelic ſects, which ſpeak of God as mixing with, or prevading all nature and all the elements; yet this muſt be explained by force and not by extenſion, which was never attributed to the mind (*b*) either by Ariſtotle or Plato. This they always affirmed to be incorporeal: and, as Plotinus remarks, incorporeal things are diſtant each from other not by place, but (to uſe his expreſſion) by alterity.

330. Theſe diſquiſitions will probably ſeem dry and uſeleſs, to ſuch readers as are accuſtomed to conſider only ſenſible objects. The employment of the mind on things purely intellectual is to moſt men irkſome: whereas the ſenſitive powers, by conſtant uſe, acquire ſtrength. Hence, the objects of ſenſe more forcibly affect us (*k*), and are too often counted the chief good. For theſe things men fight, cheat, and ſcramble. Therefore, in order to tame mankind, and introduce a ſenſe of virtue, the beſt humane means is to exerciſe their underſtanding, to give them a glympſe of another world, ſuperior to the ſenſible, and while they take pains to cheriſh and maintain the animal life, to teach them not to neglect the intellectual.

331. Prevailing ſtudies are of no ſmall conſequence to a ſtate, the religion, manners, and civil government of a country ever taking ſome bias from its philoſophy, which affects not only the minds of its profeſſors and ſtudents, but alſo the opinions of all the better ſort, and the practice of the whole people, remotely and conſequentially, indeed, though not inconſiderably. Have not the

(*b*) 290, 293, 297, 319. (*k*) 264, 294.

polemic

polemic and ſcholaſtic philoſophy been obſerved to produce controverſies in law and religion? And have not Fataliſm and Sadduciſm gained ground, during the general paſſion for the corpuſcularian and mechanical philoſophy, which hath prevailed for about a century? This indeed might uſefully enough have employed ſome ſhare of the leiſure and curioſity of inquiſitive perſons. But when it entered the ſeminaries of learning as a neceſſary accompliſhment, and moſt important part of education, by engroſſing men's thoughts, and fixing their minds ſo much on corporeal objects, and the laws of motion, it hath, however undeſignedly, indirectly, and by accident, yet not a little indiſpoſed them for ſpiritual, moral, and intellectual matters. Certainly had the philoſophy of Socrates and Pythagoras prevailed in this age, among thoſe who think themſelves too wiſe to receive the dictates of the goſpel, we ſhould not have ſeen intereſt take ſo general and faſt hold on the minds of men, nor public ſpirit reputed to be γενναῖαν εὐήθειαν, a generous folly, among thoſe who are reckoned to be the moſt knowing, as well as the moſt getting, part of mankind.

332. It might very well be thought ſerious trifling to tell my readers, that the greateſt men had ever an high eſteem for Plato; whoſe writings are the touchſtone of a haſty and ſhallow mind; whoſe philoſophy has been the admiration of ages; which ſupplied patriots, magiſtrates, and lawgivers to the moſt flouriſhing ſtates, as well as fathers to the church, and doctors to the ſchools. Albeit in theſe days, the depths of that old learning are rarely fathomed, and yet it were happy for theſe lands, if our young nobility and gentry, inſtead of modern maxims, would imbibe the notions of the great men of antiquity. But in theſe free-thinking times many an empty head is

ſhook

ſhook at Ariſtotle and Plato, as well as at the holy ſcriptures. And the writings of thoſe celebrated ancients are by moſt men treated on a foot with the dry and barbarous lucubrations of the ſchoolmen. It may be modeſtly preſumed, there are not many among us, even of thoſe who are called the better ſort, who have more ſenſe, virtue, and love of their country than Cicero, who in a letter to Atticus could not forbear exclaiming, O Socrates et Socratici viri! nunquam vobis gratiam referam. Would to God many of our countrymen had the ſame obligations to thoſe Socratic writers! Certainly where the people are well educated, the art of piloting a ſtate is beſt learned from the writings of Plato. But among bad men, void of diſcipline and education, Plato, Pythagoras and Ariſtotle themſelves, were they living, could do but little good. Plato hath drawn a very humorous and inſtructive picture of ſuch a ſtate; which I ſhall not tranſcribe for certain reaſons. But whoever has a mind, may ſee it in page 78. of the ſecond tome of Aldus's edition of Plato's works.

333. Proclus, in the firſt book of his commentary on the theology of Plato, obſerves, that, as in the myſteries, thoſe who are initiated, at firſt meet with manifold and multiform gods, but being entered and thoroughly initiated they receive the divine illumination and participate the very deity; in like manner, if the ſoul look abroad ſhe beholds the ſhadows and images of things; but returning into herſelf ſhe unravels and beholds her own eſſence: At firſt ſhe ſeemeth only to behold her ſelf: but having penetrated farther, ſhe diſcovers the mind. And again, ſtill farther advancing into the innermoſt ſanctuary of the ſoul, ſhe contemplates the θεῶν γένος. And this, he ſaith, is the moſt excellent of all human acts, in the ſilence and repoſe of the faculties of the ſoul to tend upwards to the very divinity; to approach and

be

be closely joined with that which is ineffable and superior, to all beings. When come so high as the first principle she ends her journey and rests. Such is the doctrine of Proclus.

334. But Socrates in the first Alcibiades teacheth on the other hand, that the contemplation of God is the proper means to know or understand our own soul. As the eye, saith he, looking stedfastly at the visive part or pupil of another eye, beholds itself, even so the soul beholds and understands herself, while she contemplates the Deity which is wisdom and virtue or like thereunto. In the Phædon Socrates speaks of God as being τἀγαθὸν and τὸ δέον (*a*), the good and the decent. Plotinus represents God as order; Aristotle as law.

335. It may seem perhaps to those, who have been taught to discourse about substratums, more reasonable and pious to attribute to the Deity a more substantial being, than the notional entities of wisdom, order, law, virtue, or goodness, which being only complex ideas, framed and put together by the understanding, are its own creatures, and have nothing substantial, real, or independent in them. But it must be considered, that in the Platonic system, order, virtue, law, goodness, and wisdom are not creatures of the soul of man, but innate and originally existent therein, not as an accident in a substance, but as light to enlighten, and as a guide to govern. In Plato's style, the term idea doth not merely signify an inert inactive object of the understanding, but is used as synonymous with αἴτιον and ἀρχὴ, cause and principle. According to that philosopher, goodness, beauty, virtue and such like, are not figments of the mind, nor mere mixed modes, nor yet abstract ideas in the modern sense, but the most real beings, intellectual and unchangeable; and therefore more real than the fleeting transient objects of sense (*b*), which wanting

(*a*) 260, 220. (*b*) 306.

ſtability cannot be ſubjects of ſcience (*d*), much leſs of intellectual knowledge.

336. By Parmenides, Timæus, and Plato a diſtinction was made, as hath been obſerved already, between genitum and ens. The former ſort is always generating or in fieri (*e*), but never exiſts, becauſe it never continues the ſame, being in a conſtant change, ever periſhing and producing. By entia they underſtand things remote from ſenſe, inviſible and intellectual, which never changing are ſtill the ſame, and may therefore be ſaid truly to exiſt: ȣσία, which is generally tranſlated ſubſtance, but more properly eſſence, was not thought to belong to things ſenſible and corporeal, which have no ſtability; but rather to intellectual ideas, tho' diſcerned with more difficulty, and making leſs impreſſion on a mind ſtupified and immerſed in animal life, than groſs objects that continually beſet and ſollicit our ſenſes.

337. The moſt refined human intellect exerted to its utmoſt reach, can only ſeize ſome imperfect glympſes (*f*) of the divine ideas, abſtracted from all things corporeal, ſenſible, and imaginable. Therefore Pythagoras and Plato treated them in a myſterious manner, concealing rather than expoſing them to vulgar eyes; ſo far were they from thinking, that thoſe abſtract things, altho' the moſt real, were the fitteſt to influence common minds, or become principles of knowledge, not to ſay duty and virtue, to the generality of mankind.

338. Ariſtotle and his followers have made a monſtrous repreſentation of the Platonic ideas; and ſome of Plato's own ſchool have ſaid very odd things concerning them. But if that philoſopher himſelf was not read only, but ſtudied alſo with care, and made his own interpreter, I believe the prejudice that now lies againſt him would ſoon wear off (*g*) or be even

(*d*) 264, 266, 297. (*e*) 304, 306. (*f*) 313, 330. (*g*) 309, 313.

con-

converted into a high eſteem for thoſe exalted notions and fine hints, that ſparkle and ſhine throughout his writings; which ſeem to contain not only the moſt valuable learning of Athens and Greece, but alſo a treaſure of the moſt remote traditions and early ſcience of the eaſt.

339. In the Timæus of Plato mention is made of ancient perſons, authors of traditions, and the offſpring of the gods. It is very remarkable, that in the account of the creation contained in the ſame piece, it is ſaid that God was pleaſed with his work, and that the night is placed before the day. The more we think, the more difficult ſhall we find it to conceive, how mere man, grown up in the vulgar habits of life, and weighed down by ſenſuality, ſhould ever be able to arrive at ſcience, without ſome tradition *(b)* or teaching, which might either ſow the ſeeds of knowledge, or call forth and excite thoſe latent ſeeds that were originally ſown in the ſoul.

340. Human ſouls in this low ſituation, bordering on mere animal life, bear the weight and ſee through the duſk of a groſs atmoſphere, gathered from wrong judgments daily paſſed, falſe opinions daily learned, and early habits of an older date than either judgment or opinion. Through ſuch a medium the ſharpeſt eye cannot ſee clearly *(i)*. And if by ſome extraordinary effort the mind ſhould ſurmount this duſky region, and ſnatch a glympſe of pure light, ſhe is ſoon drawn backward and depreſſed by the heavineſs of the animal nature, to which ſhe is chained. And if again ſhe chanceth, amidſt the agitation of wild fancies and ſtrong affections, to ſpring upwards, a ſecond relapſe ſpeedily ſucceeds into this region of darkneſs and dreams.

341. Nevertheleſs, as the mind gathers ſtrength by repeated acts, we ſhould not deſpond, but continue to exert the prime and flower of our faculties,

(b) 298, 301, 302. *(i)* 292, 293, 294.

 ſtill

ſtill recovering, and reaching on, and ſtruggling into the upper region, whereby our natural weakneſs and blindneſs may be in ſome degree remedied, and a taſte attained of truth and intellectual life. Beſide the conſtant prevailing opinion of the greateſt men of antiquity, that there is both an univerſal ſpirit author of life and motion, and an univerſal mind enlightening and ordering all things, it was a received tenet among them, that there is alſo τὸ ἓν or τἀγαθὸν (*a*), which they looked on as the fons deitatis, the firſt hypoſtaſis in the divinity.

342. The one, or τὸ ἓν, being immutable and indiviſible, always the ſame and entire, was therefore thought to exiſt truly and originally, and other things only ſo far as they are one and the ſame, by participation of the τὸ ἓν. This gives unity, ſtability, reality to things (*b*). Plato deſcribes God, as Moſes, from his being. According to both, God is he who truly is, ὁ ὄντως ὤν. Change and diviſion were eſteemed defects or bad. Evil ſcatters, divides, deſtroys: Good, on the contrary, produceth concord and union, aſſembles, combines, perfects, and preſerves entire. The ſeveral beings which compoſe the univerſe are parts of the ſame ſyſtem, they combine to carry on one end, and perfect one whole. And this aptneſs and concurrence thereunto furniſhes the partial particular idea of good in the diſtinct creatures. Hence it might have come to paſs, that τἀγαθὸν and τὸ ἓν were regarded as one and the ſame.

343. Light and ſight (ſaith Plato in the ſixth book of his Republic) are not the ſun; even ſo truth and knowledge are not the good itſelf, altho' they approach thereunto. And again, what the ſun is in a viſible place with reſpect to ſight and things ſeen, that ſame is τἀγαθὸν or good in an intelligible place, with reſpect to underſtanding and things underſtood.

(*a*) 329. (*b*) 264, 306.

Therefore

Therefore the good or one is not the light that enlightens, but the ſource of that light.

344. Every moment produceth ſome change in the parts of this viſible creation. Something is added or diminiſhed, or altered in eſſence, quantity, quality, or habitude. Wherefore all generated beings were ſaid by the ancients to be in a perpetual flux (c). And that which, on a confuſed and general view, ſeems one ſingle conſtant being, ſhall upon a nearer inſpection appear a continued ſeries of different beings. But God remains for ever one and the ſame. Therefore God alone exiſts. This was the doctrine of Heraclitus, Plato, and other ancients.

345. It is the opinion of Plato and his followers, that in the ſoul of man, prior and ſuperior to intellect, there is ſomewhat of an higher nature, by virtue of which we are one; and that by means of our one or unit, we are moſt cloſely joined to the Deity. And, as by our intellect we touch the divine intellect, even ſo by our τὸ ἓν or unit the very flower of our eſſence, as Proclus expreſſeth it, we touch the firſt one.

346. According to the Platonic philoſophy, ens and unum are the ſame. And conſequently our minds participate ſo far of exiſtence as they do of unity. But it ſhould ſeem that perſonality is the indiviſible center of the ſoul or mind, which is a monad ſo far forth as ſhe is a perſon. Therefore perſon is really that which exiſts, inaſmuch as it participates of the divine unity. In man the monad or indiviſible is the αὐτὸ τὸ αὐτὸ the ſelf ſame ſelf or very ſelf, a thing, in the opinion of Socrates, much and narrowly to be inquired into and diſcuſſed, to the end that, knowing ourſelves, we may know what belongs to us and our happineſs.

347. Upon mature reflexion the perſon or mind of all created beings ſeemeth alone indiviſible, and to partake moſt of unity. But ſenſible things are rather conſidered as one than truly ſo, they being in a perpe-

(c) 304, 336.

tual

tual flux or succession, ever differing and various. Nevertheless, all things together may be considered as one universe (*d*), one by the connection, relation, and order of its parts, which is the work of mind, whose unit is by Platonic supposed a participation of the first τὸ ἕν.

348. Socrates, in the Theætetus of Plato, speaketh of two parties of philosophers, the ῥέοντες and οἱ τοῦ ὅλου στασιῶται, the flowing philosophers, who held all things to be in a perpetual flux, always generating and never existing; and those others, who maintained the universe to be fixed and immoveable. The difference seems to have been this, that Heraclitus, Protagoras, Empedocles, and in general those of the former sect, considered things sensible and natural; whereas Parmenides and his party considered τὸ πᾶν, not as the sensible but as the intelligible world (*e*), abstracted from all sensible things.

349. In effect, if we mean by things the sensible objects, these, it is evident, are always flowing; but if we mean things purely intelligible, then we may say on the other hand, with equal truth, that they are immoveable and unchangeable. So that those, who thought the whole or τὸ πᾶν to be ἓν ἑστὼς a fixed or permanent one, seem to have understood the whole of real beings, which, in their sense, was only the intellectual world, not allowing reality of being to things not permanent.

350. The displeasure of some readers may perhaps be incurred, by surprising them into certain reflexions and inquiries for which they have no curiosity. But perhaps some others may be pleased, to find a dry subject varied by digressions, traced through remote inferences, and carried into ancient times, whose hoary maxims (*f*) scattered in this essay are not proposed as principles, but barely as hints to awaken and exercise the inquisitive reader, on points not beneath the at-

(*d*) 287, 288. (*e*) 293, 294, 295. (*f*) 298, 301.

tention of the ablest men. Those great men, Pythagoras, Plato, and Aristotle, the most consummate in politics, who founded states, or instructed princes, or wrote most accurately on publick government, were at the same time most acute at all abstracted and sublime speculations; the clearest light being ever necessary to guide the most important actions. And whatever the world thinks, he who hath not much meditated upon God, the human mind, and the Summum bonum, may possibly make a thriving earth-worm, but will most indubitably make a sorry patriot and a sorry statesman.

351. According to the nice metaphysics of those ancient philosophers, τὸ ἓν, being considered as what was first and simplest in the Deity, was prescinded even from entity to which it was thought prior and superior; and is therefore by the Platonics styled super-essential. And in the Parmenides it is said, τὸ ἓν doth not exist; which might seem to imply a negation of the divine being. The truth is, Zeno and Parmenides argued, that a thing existing in time was older and younger than itself; therefore the constant immutable τὸ ἓν did not exist in time; and if not in time, then in none of the differences of time past, present, or to come; therefore we cannot say that it was, is, or will be. But nevertheless it is admitted in the same Parmenides, that τὸ νῦν is every where present to τὸ ἓν: that is, instead of a temporary succession of moments, there is one eternal now, or punctum stans, as it is termed by the schoolmen.

352. The simplicity of τὸ ἓν (the Father in the Pythagoric and Platonic trinity) is conceived such as to exclude intellect or mind, to which it is supposed prior. And that hath created a suspicion of atheism in this opinion. For, saith the learned doctor Cudworth, shall we say that the first hypostasis or person is ἄνους and ἄλογος, senseless and irrational, and altogether devoid of mind and understanding? or would

(f) 298, 301.

not

not this be to introduce a kind of mysterious atheism? To which it may be answered, that whoever acknowledgeth the universe to be made and governed by an eternal mind, cannot be justly deemed an atheist (g). And this was the tenet of those ancient philosophers. In the Platonic doctrine, the generation of the νοῦς or λόγος was not contingent but necessary, not temporary but from everlasting. There never was a time supposed wherein τὸ ἓν subsisted without intellect, the priority having been understood only as a priority of order or conception, but not a priority of age. Therefore, the maintaining a distinction of priority between τὸ ἓν and νοῦς doth not infer, that the one ever existed without the other. It follows, therefore, that the father or τὸ ἓν may, in a certain sense, be said to be ἄνους without atheism, or without destroying the notion of a deity; any more than it would destroy the notion of a human soul, if we should conceive a distinction between self and intellect, or intellect and life. To which we may farther add, that it is a doctrine of Platonics, and agrees with their master's tenets, to say that τὸ ἓν, or the first hypostasis, contains all excellence and perfection, whereof it is the original source, and is eminenter, as the schools speak, intellect and life, as well as goodness; while the second hypostasis is essentially intellect, and by participation, goodness and life; and the third, life essentially, and by participation, goodness and intellect.

353. Therefore, the whole being considered, it will not seem just, to fix the imputation of atheism upon those philosophers, who held the doctrine of τὸ ἓν; whether it be taken in an abstracted or collective, a metaphysical or merely vulgar meaning (h); that is, whether we prescind unity from essence and intellect, since metaphysical distinctions of the divine attributes do not in reality divide them: or whether we consider the universal system of beings, as one, since the union, connexion, and order of its members,

(g) 154, 276, 279, 287. (h) 300.

bers, do manifestly infer a mind or intellect to be the cause thereof.

354. THE ONE or Τὸ ἓν may be conceived either by composition or division. For as, on the one hand, we may say the world or universe is one whole, or one animal; so we may, on the other hand, consider THE ONE, τὸ ἓν, by division or abstraction, as somewhat in the order of things prior to mind. In either sense there is no atheism, so long as mind is admitted to preside and direct the animal; and so long as the unum or τὸ ἓν is supposed not to exist without mind (*a*). So that neither Heraclitus, nor Parmenides, nor Pythagoras, nor Plato, neither the Ægyptians, nor Stoics, with their doctrine of a divine whole or animal, nor Xenophanes with his ἓν καὶ πᾶν, are justly to be accounted atheists. Therefore modern atheism, be it of Hobbes, Spinosa, Collins, or whom you will, is not to be countenanced by the learning and great names of antiquity.

355. Plato teacheth, that the doctrine concerning the one or unite is a means to lead and raise the mind (*b*) to the knowledge of him who truly is. And it is a tenet both of Aristotle and Plato, that identity is a certain unity. The Pythagoreans also, as well as the Platonic philosophers, held unum and ens to be the same. Consistently with which that only can be said to exist, which is one and the same. In things sensible and imaginable, as such, there seems to be no unity, nothing that can be called one, prior to all act of the mind; since they being in themselves aggregates, consisting of parts, or compounded of elements, are in effect many. Accordingly it is remarked by Themistius, the learned interpreter of Aristotle, that to collect many notions into one, and to consider them as one, is the work of intellect, and not of sense or fancy.

356. Aristotle himself, in his third book of the

(*a*) 287, 288. (*b*) 294, 295.

Soul, saith it is the mind that maketh each thing to be one, τὸ δὲ ἓν ποιοῦν τοῦτο ὁ νοῦς ἕκαστον. How this is done, Themistius is more particular, observing, that as being conferreth essence, the mind by virtue of her simplicity conferreth simplicity upon compounded beings. And, indeed, it seemeth that the mind, so far forth as person, is individual (*a*), therein resembling the divine one by participation, and imparting to other things what itself participates from above. This is agreeable to the doctrine of the ancients, however the contrary opinion of supposing number to be an original primary quality in things, independent of the mind, may obtain among the moderns.

357. The Peripatetics taught, that in all divisible things there was somewhat indivisible, and in all compounded things somewhat simple. This they derived from an act of the mind. And neither this simple indivisible unite, nor any sum of repeated unites, consequently no number, can be separated from the things themselves, and from the operation of the mind. Themistius goeth so far as to affirm, that it cannot be separated from the words or signs; and, as it cannot be uttered without them, so, saith he, neither can it be conceived without them. Thus much upon the whole may be concluded, that, distinct from the mind and her operations, there is in created beings neither unite nor number.

358. Of inferior beings the human mind, self, or person, is the most simple and undivided essence (*b*). And the supreme father is the most perfect one. Therefore the flight of the mind towards God is called by the Platonics φυγὴ μόνου πρὸς μόνον. The supreme being, saith Plotinus, as he excludes all diversity, is ever alike present. And we are then present to him, when, recollected and abstracted from the world and sensible objects, we are most free and disengaged (*c*) from all variety. He adds, that in the intuition of

(*a*) 345, 346, 347. (*b*) 347. (*c*) 268.

the

the supreme Deity the soul finds her wished for end and repose; which that philosopher calls awaking out of his body into himself.

359. In the tenth book of the arcane, or divine wisdom of the Ægyptians, we are taught that the supreme being is not the cause of any created thing; but that he produced or made the word; and that all created beings were made by the word, which is accordingly styled the cause of all causes: and that this was also the doctrine of the Chaldæans. Plato, likewise, in his letter to Hermias, Erastus, and Coriscus, speaks of God the ruler and cause of all things, as having a father: And in his Epinomis, he expresly teacheth that the word or λόγος made the world. Accordingly saint Augustine in his commentary on the beginning of saint John's Gospel, having declared that Christ is the wisdom of God by which all things were made, observes that this doctrine was also found in the writings of philosophers, who taught that God had an only begotten Son, by whom are all things.

360. Now, though Plato had joined with an imagination the most splendid and magnificent, an intellect not less deep and clear; yet it is not to be supposed, that either he or any other philosophers of Greece or the East, had by the light of nature attained an adequate notion of the Holy Trinity, nor even that their imperfect notion, so far as it went, was exactly just; nor perhaps that those sublime hints, which dart forth like flashes of light in the midst of a profound darkness, were originally struck from the hard rock of human reason; but rather derived, at least in part, by a divine tradition (a) from the author of all things. It seems a remarkable confirmation of this, what Plotinus observes in his fifth Ennead, that this doctrine of a Trinity, father, mind, and soul, was no late invention, but an ancient tenet.

(a) 298, 301.

361. Certain it is, that the notion of a Trinity is to be found in the writings of many old heathen philosophers, that is to say, a notion of three divine hypostases. Authority, light, and life did, to the eye of reason, plainly appear to support, pervade, and animate the mundane system or macrocosm. The same appeared in the microcosm, preserving soul and body, enlightening the mind, and moving the affections. And these were conceived to be necessary, universal principles, co-existing and co-operating in such sort, as never to exist asunder, but on the contrary to constitute one Sovereign of all things. And, indeed, how could power or authority avail or subsist without knowledge? or either without life and action?

362. In the administration of all things there is authority to establish, law to direct, and justice to execute. There is first the source of all perfection, or fons deitatis, secondly the supreme Reason, order, or λόγος, and lastly the Spirit, which quickens and inspires. We are sprung from the father, irradiated or enlightened by the son, and moved by the spirit. Certainly, that there is father, son, and spirit; that these bear analogy to the sun, light, and heat; and are otherwise expressed by the terms, principle, mind, and soul; by one, or τὸ ἓν, intellect, and life; by good, word, and love; and that generation was not attributed to the second hypostasis, the νοῦς or λόγος, in respect of time (*g*), but only in respect of origine and order, as an eternal necessary emanation; these are the express tenets of Platonists, Pythagoreans, Ægyptians, and Chaldæans.

363. Though it may be well presumed there is nothing to be found on that sublime subject in human writings, which doth not bear the sure signatures of humanity; yet it cannot be denied, that several fathers of the church have thought fit to illustrate the christian doctrine of the Holy Trinity by simi-

litudes

litudes and expreſſions borrowed from the moſt eminent heathens, whom they conceived to have been no ſtrangers to that myſtery; as hath been plainly proved by Beſſarion, Eugubinus, and Doctor Cudworth.

364. Therefore, how unphiloſophical ſoever that doctrine may ſeem to many of the preſent age, yet it is certain, the men of greateſt fame and learning among the ancient philoſophers held a Trinity in the Godhead. It muſt be owned, that upon this point ſome later Platoniſts of the Gentile world ſeem to have bewilder'd themſelves (as many Chriſtians have alſo done) while they purſued the hints derived from their predeceſſors, with too much curioſity.

365. But Plato himſelf conſidered that doctrine as a venerable myſtery, not to be lightly treated of or raſhly divulged. Wherefore in a letter to Dionyſius he writes (as he himſelf profeſſeth) ænigmatically and briefly in the following terms, which he giveth for a ſummary of his notion concerning the ſupreme being, and which being capable of divers ſenſes, I leave to be decyphered by the learned reader: περὶ τὸν πάντων βασιλέα πάντ' ἐστι, καὶ ἐκείνου ἕνεκα πάντα, καὶ ἐκεῖνο αἴτιον ἁπάντων τῶν καλῶν, δεύτερον δὲ περὶ τὰ δεύτερα, καὶ τρίτον περὶ τὰ τρίτα. Plato enjoins Dionyſius over and over, with great earneſtneſs, not to ſuffer what he communicates concerning the myſtery of the divine nature, to fall into illiterate or vulgar hands; giving it withal as a reaſon for this caution, that nothing would ſeem more ridiculous or abſurd to the common run of mankind. He adds, that in regard writings might miſcarry, the prudent way was to write nothing at all on thoſe matters, but to teach and learn them by word of mouth: for which reaſon, ſaith he, I have never wrote any thing thereon; nor is there, nor ſhall there ever be any thing of Plato's extant on that ſubject. He farther adds, as for what hath been now ſaid, it belongs all to Socrates.

366. And, indeed, what this philosopher in his Phædrus speaketh of the super-celestial region, and the divinity resident therein, is of a strain not to be relished or comprehended by vulgar minds; to wit, essence really existent, object of intellect alone, without colour, without figure, without any tangible quality. He might very justly conceive that such a description must seem ridiculous to sensual men.

367. As for the perfect intuition of divine things, that he supposeth to be the lot of pure souls, beholding by a pure light, initiated, happy, free, and unstained from those bodies, wherein we are now imprisoned like oysters. But in this mortal state, we must be satisfied to make the best of those glympses (*b*) within our reach. It is Plato's remark in his Theætetus, that while we sit still we are never the wiser, but going into the river and moving up and down, is the way to discover its depths and shallows. If we exercise and bestir ourselves, we may even here discover something.

368. The eye by long use comes to see even in the darkest cavern: and there is no subject so obscure, but we may discern some glympse of truth by long poring on it. Truth is the cry of all, but the game of a few. Certainly where it is the chief passion, it doth not give way to vulgar cares and views; nor is it contented with a little ardour in the early time of life, active perhaps to pursue, but not so fit to weigh and revise. He that would make a real progress in knowledge, must dedicate his age as well as youth, the later growth as well as first fruits, at the altar of truth.

Cujusvis est errare, nullius nisi insipientis in errore perseverare. Cic.

(*b*) 335, 337.

F I N I S.

CONTENTS.

TAR-WATER, how made, Sect. 1
How much to be taken at a time, 3. 116. 217
How long to be continued, 110
How made palatable, 115
A preservative and preparative against the small-pox, 2
Useful in it, 74
A cure for foulness of blood, ulceration of bowels, lungs, consumptive coughs, pleurisy, peripneumony, erysipelas, asthma, indigestion, cachectic and hysteric cases, gravel, dropsy, and all inflammations, 4—7
Answers all the purposes of Elixir proprietatis, Stoughton's drops, best turpentines, decoction of the woods, and mineral waters, 53. 61—65
And of the most costly balsams, 21. 22. 62. 63
May be given to children, 67
Of great use in the gout, 68. 80
In fevers, 75—77. 114
Cures a gangrene as well as erysipelas, 82, 83
The scurvy and all hypocondriac disorders, 86—109
Whence this English malady proceeds, 88, 89
High food how prejudicial, 66. 104
More particularly spirituous liquors, 103. 106—108
Tar-water a preservative for the teeth and gums, 114
Is particularly recommended to sea-faring persons, ladies, and men of studious and sedentary lives, 117—119
Its specific virtues consist in its volatile salts, 8. 123
Tar preserves trees from the biting of goats, and other injuries, Sect. 11
Its virtues heretofore known, but only in part, 9. 11. 111
Tar, whence produced, 10—17
Rosin, whence, 18—19
Turpentine, what, 20
Tar mixt with honey, a cure for a cough, 21
Rosin an effectual cure for a bloody flux, 79
Recommended to vintners to medicate their wines with, 111
Method to cure persons affected by breathing a pestilential vapour, 144
Scotch firs what, and how they might be improved, 25
Pine and fir, different species of each, 26—28
The wonderful structure of trees, 29—38
Juices produced with the least violence best, 46
Myrrh soluble by the human body would prolong life, 49
Tar-water, by what means, and in what manner, it operates, 50—57
Is a soap at once and a vinegar, 59
Soap, opium, and mercury, tho' they bid fair for universal medicines, in what respects dangerous, 69—71
Aromatic flavours of vegetables depend on light as much as colours, 40. 162. 214, 5
Analogy between the specific qualities of vegetable juices and colours, 165. 181
A fine subtile spirit, the distinguishing principle of all vegetables, 121
What the principle of vegetation, and how promoted, 126—8

Theory

CONTENTS.

Theory of acids, salts, and alcalies, Sect. 129—136. 227

Air the common seminary of all vivifying principles, 137—144

Air, of what it consists, 147—151. 195—7

Pure æther, or invisible fire, the spirit of the universe, which operates in every thing, 152—62

The world how understood to be an animal, 152—156. 166. 175. 262. 273—9

Opinion of the ancients concerning it, 166—75. 229

And of the Chinese conformable to them, 180—82

What meant by the forms of the Peripatetics, 167. 310

Fire worshipped among various nations, 183—5

Opinion of the best modern chemists concerning it, 189—90

Ultimately the only menstruum in nature, 191

Adds to the weight of bodies, and even gold made by the introduction of it into quicksilver, 169. 192—6

Pure elementary fire how inherent in bodies without being subject to the senses, 198---201

Opinion of Hippocrates and Dr. Willis of a vital flame, 204, 5

The theory of Ficinus and others concerning light, 206—13

Sir Isaac Newton's hypothesis of a subtle æther examined, 221. 228. 237. 246.

Pure æther the same with his acid, 130. 202. 227

No accounting for natural phænomena, either by attraction and repulsion, or by elastic æther, without the presence of an incorporeal agent, 231—38. 246. 249. 294—97

The doctrine of all things unfolding themselves from seeds ill founded, Sect. 233

More ancient than many are aware, 282

Nature better explained by attraction than by Descartes's principles of size and figure, 243, 4

Attraction in some degree discovered by Galilæi, 245

Phænomena are but appearances in the soul, not to be accounted for upon mechanical principles, 251, 2. 310

The ancients not ignorant of many things in physics and metaphysics, which we think the discovery of modern times, 265—69

Had some advantages beyond us, 298

Of absolute space, and fate, 270—3

Of the anima mundi of Plato, 276—84. 322

What meant by the Ægyptian Isis and Osiris, 268. 299

Plato's and Aristotle's threefold distinction of objects, 306, 7

Their opinion of ideas being innate, or not, 308, 9

Neither of them believed the absolute existence of corporeal things, 311, 12. 316—18

The study of the philosophy of Socrates and Pythagoras would have secured the minds of men from that selfishness which the mechanic philosophy has introduced, 331, 32

The study of Plato recommended, 332. 338

Who agrees with Scripture in many particulars, 339

His opinion of the Deity, and particularly of a Trinity, agreeable to revelation, 341—365

An Authentick

NARRATIVE

Of the SUCCESS of

TAR-WATER,

In curing a great NUMBER and

VARIETY of DISTEMPERS,

WITH

REMARKS,

AND

OCCASIONAL PAPERS

Relative to the Subject.

To which are subjoined,

Two LETTERS from the Author of *SIRIS*,

Shewing the Medicinal Properties of TAR-WATER, and the best Manner of making it.

By *THOMAS PRIOR*, Esq;

To do good, and to communicate, forget not. HEB. xiii. 16.

DUBLIN Printed,

LONDON Re-printed,

For W. INNYS, C. HITCH, and M. COOPER, in *Pater-noster-row*; and C. DAVIS, in *Holbourn*. MDCCXLVI.

[Price Two Shillings.]

To His Excellency

PHILIP,

Earl of CHESTERFIELD,

Lord Lieutenant General, and General Governor of *IRELAND*.

HIGH Stations furniſh great Opportunities of doing Good, where there is a Head to diſcern, and a Heart to apply. Your Excellency is eminent for both. Since your Arrival in this Kingdom, you have acquired a thorough Knowledge of its Intereſts, which you apply to the Service of his Majeſty, and the Public; in ſuch a Manner, that your Adminiſtration will be always remembered with Gratitude and Honour. Your Management, ſo generous of your own, and ſo frugal of the public Treaſure, joined with

with a conduct so open and sincere, without the least Tincture or Suspicion of private Views, leave us at a Loss to determine, which to admire most, the true Policy, or the Probity of our Governor.

That benevolent and disinterested Spirit, which distinguishes your Character, hath emboldened me to address this small Treatise to your Excellency: which, as it is calculated to promote the public Good, coincides so far with your own Views, as to seem entitled to some Share of your Protection and Patronage.

I am,

With the greatest Respect,

Your Excellency's most Obedient,

and most Humble Servant,

THOMAS PRIOR.

An AUTHENTICK ACCOUNT OF THE EFFECTS OF *TAR-WATER.*

1. HAVING publiſhed, in the *Dublin Journal* of the Third of *July*, 1744, Remarks on an Advertiſement, and upon certain Affidavits mentioned therein, concerning the Effects of Tar-water in *Stephens*'s Hoſpital, and having promiſed to communicate to the Public, an Account of ſeveral Perſons, who have been entirely cured, or greatly relieved by the Uſe of Tar-water only, together with their Names, Places of Abode, and Nature of their Ailments; I now addreſs myſelf to the Performance of my Promiſe, which hitherto has been delayed by many intervening Affairs, and by the Length of Time that was requiſite to obtain full Information in a Multitude of Caſes that daily occurred; but this Delay hath given me an Opportunity of procuring a more par-

ticular and exact Account of the Cases of many Patients, and the Progress of their Relief, which must give more Satisfaction, than a short imperfect Detail of the Effects of Tar-water on the first Tryals could possibly afford. And finding that new Tryals and Discoveries were made of the Virtues of Tar-water in many different Distempers, and that some Patients, who drank it for one Ailment only, yet found surprising and unexpected Relief in other Ailments they laboured under, I thought it proper to wait for the full Effect of those Tryals, and to find out if others, in the like Cases, had not also received the same Benefit; which would be a farther Confirmation of the Efficacy of Tar-water in such Distempers.

2. Many, on the general Invitation given in the Journal above-mentioned, several others, on particular Application, very freely communicated their Ailments and Reliefs for the good of Mankind. Some, who had received Benefit by Tar-water on the first drinking of it, chose to postpone sending their Accounts, till they had received the full Benefit they expected by a longer Use of it. Some, especially of the Female Sex, communicated their Cases, and the Benefit they received, yet were unwilling to have their Names mentioned in public. Some Cases required a long Use of Tar-water, before any Judgment could be formed of the Efficacy of it, and before a Cure could be effected. It was also suggested by some, who decried the Use of Tar-water, that whatever seeming Benefit some might have received on their first drinking of it, yet, that towards the Fall of the Leaf, or the Winter following, they would feel fatal Consequences from it, insinuating, at the same time, that it was dangerous to drink it in the Dog-days, or in cold Weather, by which Means several were prevailed upon to lay aside the drinking of it for some Months; but finding

ing no such Consequences, they have since resumed the drinking of it with great Advantage.

3. For these, and many other Reasons, the Publication of the Effects of Tar-water has been so long deferred; but now that we find many Thousands have drank Tar-water, and great Numbers have received Benefit thereby; since Time, Experience, and many Tryals (the surest Guides in Cases of this Nature) have established the Credit and Use of this Medicine, it would be a Prejudice to the Public, and an Injury to Mankind, to defer any longer the Publication of the many unexpected and surprising Cures effected by Tar-water. And as particular Instances and Facts, within the Knowledge and Observation of every one, make stronger Impressions than general Assertions and Reasonings can do; it is with great Satisfaction I can inform the Public, that I am furnished with a great Number of authentic Accounts of the Effects of Tar-water, (more perhaps than ever happened in the Case of any other Medicine in so short a time) and that chiefly from the Patients themselves, most of them Men of Character and Integrity, who, besides the Pleasure of recounting the Benefits they received, had no other View in communicating their Cases, but to promote the Good of others, and particularly of those, who might have the Misfortune of labouring under the same Disorders.

4. Having no other View in publishing this Narrative, but to promote the same good Intentions, I can assure the Public, that I have, with the greatest Candor and Impartiality, laid before them the Facts and Cases, as they were communicated to me; for which Purpose I beg Leave to publish the Letters of particular Gentlemen, who have been so good as to give a Detail of their own Disorders, or of those of their Neighbours and Acquaintance, and of the Benefit they received; the Originals of which may

 be

be viewed in my Hands, and I hope thoſe Gentlemen will excuſe the Liberty I have taken in publiſhing their Letters, which, as they were deſigned for the Good of Mankind, ſo I do not in the leaſt doubt, but that they were communicated with the ſame beneficent Intentions; and as they come from Gentlemen of Character and Worth, they will not fail to be much regarded, make the following Narrative more Authentick, and be the Means of promoting the good of Thouſands.

5. From ſome, I had the Accounts of their Caſes from their own Mouths; and any one, who will give himſelf the Trouble of enquiring, may be ſatisfied of the Truth thereof from the Perſons themſelves, whoſe Names are herein mentioned. Some Gentlemen in the Country hearing of the Succeſs of Tar-water among their Neighbours, made a ſtrict Enquiry, and were pleaſed to ſend me Accounts of ſeveral relieved thereby. I have alſo taken Notice of the Caſes of ſeveral Perſons, without mentioning their Names, in Compliance with their Deſires not to have their Names publiſhed; but if any ſhould be deſirous to know who the Perſons are, whoſe Names are omitted, I ſhall be ready, for their private Satisfaction, to let them know ſo much.

6. At firſt many Caſes occurred, of Perſons troubled with Colds, Coughs, Difficulty of Breathing, want of Reſt and Appetite, which were ſoon removed by the Uſe of Tar-water; but as it may be thought, that theſe Ailments might be removed by Exerciſe, Air, proper Diet, or other Medicines, without being beholden to Tar-water, I have omitted moſt of thoſe Caſes, though the Quickneſs and Eaſe with which they were relieved, and the Number of the Cures, muſt greatly recommended the Uſe of this Medicine. Thoſe Caſes were thought too ſlight to lay any Streſs upon: But the Inſtances produced in this Narrative, are, for the moſt part,

Caſes

Cases of the most grievous and dangerous Distempers, Acute and Chronical; such as the Gout, King's-Evil, inveterate Scurvies, and Ulcers, confirmed Asthmas, and Coughs, Fevers, Pleurisies, Rheumatisms, and Colics, *&c.* which rarely give Way to any Medicines; those in common Use having generally failed in the Instances herein mentioned; but they all, in a great measure, yielded to the Power and Efficacy of Tar-water, as will appear by the subsequent Narrative.

7. But, in order to lay the Whole in a fair Light before the Reader, I shall beg Leave, by Way of Introduction, to re-publish the *Affidavit*, and my *Remarks* thereon, which gave the first Occasion of writing on this Subject, together with some Observations, published in *England*, relating to that *Affidavit*, and shall then proceed to give an ample Account of the Effects of Tar-water, according to Promise.

8. The said *Remarks* were as follow:

Remarks *on a late* Advertisement, *and upon certain* Affidavits *mentioned therein*, *concerning the Effects of Tar-water in* Stephens's *Hospital.*

9. The *Advertisement* was published in the *Dublin Journal* of the Second of *June*, 1744, in the following Words, *viz.* "We are very well informed, that many voluntary *Affidavits* have been made before Alderman *Walker*, of the unsuccessful Use of Tar-water in Dr. *Stephens*'s Hospital, by Numbers of Patients in that House, setting forth, that, after a long Series of using Tar-water, in the most strict and regular manner, none found themselves in any wise better, but many of them much worse; and that these *Affidavits* are in the Hands of the Visitors of the Hospital, and may, at any Time, be viewed by the Curious in this Matter."

10. Being surprized to hear, that in *Stephens*'s Hospital alone, none found themselves any way

better, and many of them worse, by the Use of Tar-water, when, at the same Time, great Numbers both in Town and Country had received great Benefit thereby; and being fully persuaded, by the surprizing Benefits which many of my Acquaintance have received, and daily do receive by Tar-water, that it is a useful and most safe Medicine; my regard to Truth and the good of Mankind induced me to make an Enquiry into the Contents of those Affidavits, on which so much stress had been laid in the Advertisement.

11. I accordingly addressed myself to the visiting Physicians of the Hospital, who shewed me the original Affidavits, and gave me leave to take Copies of them, and at the same time declared, that the said Advertisement was published without his Knowledge.

12. That the Public may be better able to judge of the Force of those Affidavits, and the Truth of the Advertisement, I shall here publish one of them, which may serve for the rest, all of them being written in the same Form and Words, except an Addition to three of them, which I shall also take notice of. The Affidavit I shall mention, is in the following Words:

County of the City of *Dublin.* } *Sylvester Dowdal*, one of the Patients in *Stephens's* Hospital, came this Day before me, and made Oath, that he constantly drank the Tar-water by the Directions of Dr. *Lebunte*, for about nine Weeks, and deposed that he hath not found any Benefit thereby.

Sworn before me the 25th of *May*, 1744.
William Walker.

His
Syl O Dowdal
Mark.

13. The

13. The Doctor informed me, that the said *Dowdal* had an Imposthume in his Stomach, and mentioned the Disease which the others laboured under, and said the Patients began to drink the Water on the 26th of *March*, and that some, who were ordered to drink the Water, neglected so to do.

14. There were but six Affidavits in all, the Depositions of the remaining Five, which were taken at the same Time, are to the following Purpose:

15. " *James Martin*, in a high Degree of Leprosy, swears he drank Tar-water near six Weeks without any Benefit.

16. " *Bartholomew Hughs*, in an Asthma and Consumption of the Lungs, drank Tar-water seven Weeks without any Benefit as to his Shortness of Breath, which was his principal Disorder.

17. " *Mary Malone*, for the Itch, drank the Tar-water five Weeks, without any Benefit; but being put into another Course for three Weeks, finds herself much better.

18. " *Patrick Shaghnussy*, for an inveterate Itch, drank Tar-water six Weeks, found no Benefit, but found himself much worse; but being put into another Course finds himself much better.

19. " Ma.——in the foul Disease, drank Tar-water six Weeks, without any Benefit, but found herself much worse; but being put into another Course, finds herself much better."

20. This is the Substance of the Affidavits, whereof four were made by Persons that could not write their Names.

21. When Tar-water first began to obtain some Vogue, it was expected, that the Learned would have left it to its own Fate, as was done in the Case of Quicksilver, and *Ward*'s Pill; and indeed one would have thought, that an Opposition to a Me-

dicine of this Nature, must have been either needless or criminal: If the Medicine be bad, it will die away of itself; if good, it is plainly unwarrantable to oppose it. How far this Opposition, coming from a Quarter that may possibly be suspected of having some Interest in the Matter, can be reconciled with the Rules of Prudence, is submitted to the publick Consideration: The Doctor, who is known to be a Man of Worth and Skill in his Profession, acted very properly, and with good Intention, in prescribing this Water, to be taken, even in the worst Cases, in the Hospital; and I hear he has prescribed it to others, out of the Hospital, with Success; but the Use that others have made of what he had done, without his Knowledge, gives room for making the following *Remarks*.

22. It is said in the *Advertisement*, that many voluntary *Affidavits* have been made by Numbers of Patients in the Hospital, setting forth, that "after a "long Series of using Tar-water, in the most strict "and regular manner, none found themselves in any "wise better, but many of them much worse." Now upon comparing the *Advertisement* with the *Affidavits*, we can find no Words in the latter to support those Assertions; not a Word of a *long Series*, or *the most strict and regular Manner*, or that *none received Benefit*; and it was impossible that any one Patient could safely swear, that none in the House received the least Benefit, whatever he might have said of his own Case; And by the Words mentioned in the *Advertisement*, that many voluntary *Affidavits* have been made by *Numbers of Patients* in that House, one might have expected to have met with a numerous Train of such *Affidavits*; but behold, they are dwindled to Six only, by which it appears, that the *Advertisement* doth no way tally with the *Affidavits*, nor can be supported or warranted by them. Six of the most desperate Cases in the whole Hospital,

were culled out for the Affidavits, and these made the only Tests of the Virtues of Tar-water, upon so short a Trial as five or six Weeks; altho' the Distempers were inveterate and chronical, and plainly required a Length of Time to effect a Cure. Did ever any prudent Man try the Force of a Medicine at first, in desperate Cases only! What Medicine in the World could stand, if a few Instances of its Unsuccessfulness were sufficient to destroy its Credit? or what would become of the Practice, or Credit of Physicians, if Instances of their failing to cure, by the Medicines they prescribe, should be urged against their Medicines or Practice? were not several of the said Patients in the Hospital without Relief many Months before they drank Tar-water?

23. It does not appear by the Affidavits, that Justice was done to Tar-water in Quantity, in Time, in accompanying it with any outward Wash of Tar-water, as was proper in the Case of outward Sores, or in acknowledging that it concurred in the Cure of the Itch; in which last Case Tar-water, by driving the Venom from the Blood to the Surface, will increase the Sores for a time, and make ignorant Patients think themselves worse. And probably this very Thing facilitated and proved the main Part of the Cure; for as soon as they were anointed with Brimstone, they found themselves better; and it is not probable they would have been kept in the Hospital so long before they drank Tar-water, if a bare outward anointing could have cured them. The Conduct of the Advertisers doth not appear to be very fair; in order to discourage the Use of Tar-water, they say that none of the Patients in the Hospital received any Benefit by Tar-water, though they produce Affidavitsof but Six of them, and those in desperate Cases; but they take not the least Notice at the same time of any Persons who received any Benefit by it: In this Point they are intirely silent;

I ap-

I appeal to the Publick, if this be fair and equal Dealing, but we ſhall take Care to ſupply that Defect: They themſelves know, and the whole City can teſtify, the many Inſtances of Perſons of all Ranks, who have received the greateſt Benefit by Tar-water, and this in a great Variety of Caſes.

24. In Proof whereof, for the Good of Mankind, and for the ſake of Truth, we ſhall publiſh a Liſt of thoſe within our Knowledge, who have been either intirely cured, or greatly relieved by the Uſe of Tar-water alone, with the Places of their Abode, and in what Ailments they received Benefit; that every other Perſon, who may have the ſame Sort of Ailment, may know what Perſons to apply to, and be informed of the Particulars of their Cure, and thereby may have an Opportunity of obtaining the like Relief themſelves; and in order to make the Liſt as complete as poſſible, it is earneſtly deſired, that they who have received Benefit by Tar-water, would be ſo good and humane, as to ſend their Names, and Places of Abode, to *Thomas Prior*, Eſq; at his Houſe in *Bolton-Street*; and at the ſame Time it is alſo deſired, that they who have received any Harm by Tar-water, (if any ſuch there be) would be ſo good to ſend their Names, and Places of Abode, in like manner; and we have the greateſt Hopes of being gratified in this Particular, as we have no other View or Intention in this Affair, but, on the one hand, to do all the Good in our Power, and on the other, to guard againſt all the Evils that may poſſibly happen, and ſo do equal Juſtice to the Publick.

25. By what we have already experienced, and daily do experience, of the good Effects of Tar-water, we have great Reaſon to be perſuaded, and greater ſtill to rejoice, that the World is bleſt with a Medicine, ſo efficacious as ſeldom to fail of Succeſs, ſo general as to relieve in moſt Diſeaſes, ſo ſafe as never to be attended with Danger, and yet ſo cheap, as to

be

be in the Power of the poorest Person to purchase, and we hope in GOD, that every Day's Experience will, more and more, confirm us in this Persuasion.

26. The aforesaid Advertisement from *Stephens*'s Hospital, being publish'd in the *English* News-papers, moved a Gentleman, in the *North* of *England*, to send a Letter to the Publishers of the *Newcastle Journal*, which they printed in their Journal, with a Preface, and was after re-printed in the *Dublin Journal* on the 21st of *August*, in the Words following:

27. "There appears so benevolent a Design in the following Letter, that should we delay the Publication of it, we might be accused, not only of Ingratitude to the ingenious Author, but of Injustice to the Public."

To the Publishers of the Newcastle Journal.

Gentlemen,

28. I was moved with no little Indignation and Concern, at reading a sly inveterate Paragraph against Tar-water, in a late *Newcastle Courant*, published, it seems originally for an Article of News, in the Papers of *Dublin*: But what Quarter it should come from there, together with the Purposes intended it should answer, are plain enough to be guessed at: To obviate, therefore, as much as in me lies, the ill Effects of so malevolent a Design, I think myself indispensibly obliged, as well by the Ties of Justice and Gratitude, to the excellent Writer upon the extensive Virtues of Tar-water, and Discoverer of its powerful Effects, as by those of Charity and Benevolence to my Fellow-Creatures and Sufferers, to make known to the Public, through the Means of your Paper, the inestimable Benefits that have accrued to me and mine, from the Use of it.

29. I had long laboured under these following complicated Distempers, *viz.* Palsy, Colic, Rheumatism,

matiſm, Gravel and Piles; in all which Caſes I found ſurpriſing Relief from Tar-water, and that in conſiderably leſs time than a Month from beginning to drink it. And it has worked ſtill greater Effects upon my Wife, who was infeſted to the higheſt Degree, with that *Engliſh* Plague, the Scurvy, together with a large Train of Diſorders, naturally incident to ſuch a Height of it; from which, by the ſame Means, and in the ſame Compaſs of Time, ſhe is recovered in ſuch a Manner, as amazes all who were acquainted with her Condition; and that for the Time it has been effected in, both ſhe and myſelf are reſtored to Health, in a Degree infinitely beyond our moſt ſanguine Expectations; the Truth whereof I am ready to atteſt to any one who ſhall require it of me; moreover I have been a Witneſs of its extraordinary ſalutary Effects in ſome of my Acquaintance, to a Degree little ſhort of our own: So happy an Experience, therefore, both in myſelf and others, of its wonderful Operation and Force, leaves me not the leaſt room to doubt that Tar-water is the moſt ſovereign, and extenſive Remedy, and Cure for Diſeaſes in general; ſafeſt to be taken, as well as the eaſieſt in the Operation, that ever was found out in the whole *Materia Medica*; and as ſuch, may be recomended to the World, notwithſtanding the ſiniſter Paragraph above mentioned. And, if it is not an Abſurdity to ſuppoſe ſuch a Thing in Nature as a *Panacea*, nothing ſurely, ever bid ſo fair as this for that Character before. In my thus praiſing Tar-water, I think I cannot be ſuſpected to be actuated by any other Intereſt than the general Welfare and Happineſs of the human Species, willing them to ſhare and enjoy the precious Effects of it equally with myſelf. I purpoſely forbore, Gentlemen, troubling you with this ſooner, becauſe I would firſt be well warranted in my own Mind for whatever I had to ſay upon the

Subject, that I might not in the least invade the bounds of Truth, which in all Cases, and especially in so delicate an Affair as this, every one ought to be very cautious of.

30. I shall conclude with the good Bishop's own Words, (selected from his admirable Treatise of *Siris*, for the generous disinterested Present whereof, together with the invaluable Services likely to result therefrom, the World will for ever remain the Debtor;) *viz.* "Men may censure and object as they "please, but I appeal to Time and Experiment. "Effects misimputed, Cases wrong told, Circum-"stances overlooked, perhaps too, Prejudices and "Partialities against Truth, may for a Time prevail, "and keep her at the Bottom of her Well: From "whence, nevertheless, she emergeth sooner or la-"ter, and strikes the Eyes of all, who do not keep "them shut." I am, Gentlemen, yours, *&c.*

N.B. If the Genuiness of the above Letter should be doubted, or any one desire further Information concerning it, the Author, who lives in the County of *Durham*, has authorized us to satisfy any Person, upon Application to the Printer of this Paper.

31. This Instance shews that many different Ailments in the same Person, and a Complication of Distempers, may be all cured at the same Time by the same Medicine.

23. *William Ward* of *Cockerton* near *Darlington* in the County of *Durham*, Esq; having seen the aforesaid Advertisement and Remarks in the *Newcastle Journal*, was pleased to communicate his Case and Relief in several Letters, according to the Progress of his Cure. And his Case being very singular and worth taking Notice of, I take this Opportunity of publishing Extracts of his Letters in his own Words, which are as follow:

From

From his Letter, dated *June* 8, 1744.

33. " I began to drink Tar-water for an Asthma this Day Fortnight, and take it Night and Morning a Glass, whereof three make a Pint. I find it opens my Body gently, about two Stools a Day; but I have had my Fits, as often and violently as before. I am not so weak as to think I was to have found a perceptible Benefit in so short a Space, but shall still continue it; I have had my Asthma upwards of twelve Years, but not so violent as at present, and for seven Years last; in which Time I have not been in Bed, or at most, not above three or four Hours once in a Year, when I have flattered myself with being tolerably well; and then, as soon as I awaked, I found by the Head of the Bed, I was quite loaden, as I thought, with Phlegm, though a dry Asthma; so that I was obliged to get up and have Recourse to a Pipe of Tobacco, which I use all the Time I am ill, for I have no Ease when I do not smoak. I am seldom without a Fit above three or four Days, and continue as long in it, and as soon as Rain comes I am easy; I have it also against the least Change of Weather.

My Father has it, and my Grand-mother died of it; so that I have less Hopes of a Cure, as it seems to be hereditary. I have tried many of the most eminent Physicians in *England*, but never found Benefit. I have had Issues in my Shoulders, and at present one under each Breast, but cannot say I reap any Advantage. The Medicines I have taken are innumerable."

From his Letter, dated *July* 27, 1744.

" I now relate to you the Success I have met with from the Tar-water. The first Month I took it my Fits were as violent and frequent as usual. The second Month I had not one Fit, but one Night,

Night, which was very eaſy; and I believe I might have continued to have found a daily Benefit, if I had not been obliged to attend at the Aſſizes; where I have received a moſt violent Cold, which has brought on both my Aſthma and a Cough: So that at preſent I am very ill, but am taking all the Care I can now to recover myſelf; for I found ſo much Pleaſure in that Month's Eaſe, that no Temptation can induce me to ſwerve from Rules. I can't ſo much as lye back in an eaſy Chair; for I have a Table ſet by the Side of my Chair, with Pillows on it, ſo I lay my Arm on them, and my Head on my Arm; and if I am very ill, can't even reſt that Way, ſo that no Bed can be contrived for me to reſt on yet; and though I ſay above, that I had not a Fit for a Month, yet if I lay back in my Chair then, it made me uneaſy in two Minutes: I drank Tar-water frequently in the Day, but not a Quarter of a Pint at a time, for I find it agrees better with my Stomach than drinking a larger Quantity; and in the Day, I may take ſuch a Quantity five or ſix times, as agrees with me. I muſt beg to take Notice of one very great Effect it has had on me (which I hope is a good Symptom:)

35. Before I drank the Tar-water, my Feet were always as cold as Ice, ſo that I had not the leaſt Perſpiration in them; for if I had not waſhed them for a Year, they were as clean and dry as the back of my Hand: But now, in the laſt Month I was ſo eaſy, I found my Feet ſweat very copiouſly, and found, in wearing a Pair of new Stockings only a Week, that all the Soals were worn and mouldered away; and what was left was very red, as if I had burnt them.

36. I beg Pardon for dwelling ſo long upon this Particular, as it was ſo ſurpriſing; and my Apothecary telling me, when I related it to him, that he was ſure I ſhould be cured by drinking the Tar-

Tar-water, as it had this Effect; for it was what he and all my Physicians had drove at, to make me have a Perspiration in my Feet, which was never in their Power to get, not even by sitting with my Feet in warm Water."

Extract from his Letter of *September* 18, 1744.

37. "As to my present State of Health, I have the Pleasure to tell you, I was in Bed the 10th, 11th, 12th, and 15th Instant at Night; I went to Bed about eight a Clock, and lay until seven the next Morning, as well as ever I was in my Life; and found, when I awaked, I was lying on my Back; and am quite another Man."

Extract from his Letter of *January* 16, 1744.

38. "I find the least Cold does me Harm, and therefore keep close to my House, which is no Inconveniency to me, since I am all Air and Vivacity, which before was a meer State of Hebetude. I was obliged to go on the 4th of *November* last into *Northumberland*, when it was very cold with Snow; and as the Roads would not admit of Wheels, I was compelled to go on Horse-back; and when I had rode a Mile easily (for it is only since I took Tar-water I could ride above a Mile on Horseback) I found I was able to go faster, and put on so fast, that I observed by my Watch, that I rode at the Rate of six Miles an Hour. My Journey was thirty six Miles, which I completed between the Hours of Ten in the Morning, and Four in the Afternoon, without drawing Bridle; I rested one Day, and came home on the 6th of *November* in the same Time.

This I declare upon my Honour to be Fact, and which was as great a Surprize to myself as others."

39. So extraordinary a Case as this, and so well vouched by the Patient himself, gives us Reason to believe,

believe, that any Aſthma whatſoever may be cured by a Courſe of Tar-water, and at the ſame Time ſhews, that People ought to wait for the Effect of this Medicine, and not lay it aſide on a ſhort Trial; though it is very probable, as will appear by other Inſtances, that if Mr. *Ward* had drank a greater Quantity of Tar-water at firſt, and avoided catching cold, he would have been much ſooner relieved.

As I had a few more Caſes, and printed Accounts from *England*, which ſhew the Power and Efficacy of Tar-water in a high Degree, I ſhall beg Leave to introduce them in this Part of the Narrative, before I mention *Iriſh* Caſes. The Singularity of the Caſes, will, I doubt not, juſtify my exceeding the firſt Intentions, of publiſhing only ſuch Accounts, as occurred to me in this Kingdom.

Extract of a Letter from *John Hardcaſtle*, Eſq; of *Haughton*, near *Darlington*, in the County of *Durham*, a Civilian.

40. "My Diſorder began with violent Pains in my Breaſt, which, being removed by Fomentation, were ſucceeded by a great Cough. I was, in ſome Time, almoſt freed from it; but within two or three Days after it was ſtopped, I was ſuddenly ſeized with a Palpitation of the Heart, in a very high Degree, which laſted, with very little Intermiſſion, for two Days. That Diſorder being partly calmed by bleeding, my Cough returned again with as much Force as ever. I became much emaciated, loſt my Appetite, grew very weak, and had frequent Sweats; my Urine was loaded, during this Illneſs, with a large Quantity of red Matter, which, when evaporated to Dryneſs, did not ſeem, to the Touch, to be of the Nature of Sand or Gravel, but rather like Loam or fine Clay. The Phyſician declared my Caſe ſcorbutic, and treated it accordingly. As I had been

long following the Prefcriptions of the Phyfician I confulted, I cannot impute my Recovery, with any Certainty, wholly to Tar-water. But, I think, the fenfible, and moft immediate Alteration I perceived in myfelf after taking it, leaves me no room to doubt, that Alteration was caufed by the Tar. It refrefhed my Stomach with a kindly and agreeable Warmth, reftored my Appetite, and, in all Probability, caufed a good Digeftion: As thefe gradually increafed, my Cough declined, my Sweats abated, and my Strength returned.

41. Having received feveral Letters from *Liverpool*, giving an Account of the extraordinary Virtues of Tar-water in the Cure of a great Number of Negroes in the Small-pox, on board the *Little Fofter* of *Liverpool*, Captain *Drape*, Commander, on the Coaft of *Guinea*, I fhall here mention the Particulars of my Information. The Reverend Mr. *Thomas Hayward*, of *Warrington* in *Lancafhire*, in a Letter dated the 18th of *October*, 1744, writes, that having received from a Friend an account of this furprifing Cure of the Negroes, he made a Journey, on purpofe, to *Liverpool*, to be fully informed of the Particulars of the Fact; and there was thoroughly fatisfied of the Truth thereof, by Mr. *Conliff*, Mr. *Armitage*, Mr. *Reed*, and Mr. *John Atherton*, Perfons of the beft Credit, and the moft confiderable Merchants of the Place, the three firft Owners of the faid Ship; and they all affured him, that they received the Account from Captain *Drape* himfelf, who was ready and willing to make an *Affidavit* of the Truth thereof, at any Time when defired. And as fo new and extraordinary a Cure, in a diftant Country, required the beft Proof and Evidence, which the Nature of the Cafe could afford, to fupport the Credit thereof, Mr. *Atherton* was afterwards pleafed to tranfmit to me, at my Requeft, Captain *Drape*'s Narrative, and his *Affidavit* fworn before

before the Mayor of *Liverpool*, at the public Sessions, where Mr. *Conliff*, and the other Gentlemen were present, and who were satisfied of the Truth of the Particulars, before it was confirmed by Oath, which *Narrative* and *Affidavit* I here publish, for the Satisfaction of the Public, in the Words of the Original, now in my Possession, which are as follow:

42. " The *Little Foster*, of *Liverpool*, Captain *Drape*, Master, in the Year 1742, made a Voyage to *Guinea*, and having taken in 216 Negroes, before he left the Coast, he had the Misfortune to see the Small-pox break out amongst them: In a very short Time there were no less than One hundred and seventy ill of that Distemper all at once.

43. The Captain was under great Concern, and fully expected, that, for want of Room, and other Necessaries, he must infallibly lose the greatest Part of them. A Person on board advised the Master to infuse a Quantity of Tar in Water, and give it the Slaves to drink, saying, it was practised in the same Case with good Success: The Tar-water was prepared, but the first to whom it was offered, obstinately refused it, and so did many more; that Man died in two or three Days, which the rest seeing, were more easily brought to Compliance, so that, partly by Persuasion, partly by Force, the rest were all brought to drink. The good Effects followed soon after, and were so plainly perceived, by the poor Creatures themselves, that they came upon Deck, and crouding about a Tub of Tar-water, that was set there for them, drank plentifully of it, from time to time, of their own accord.

44. This had an Effect that could hardly be expected under the most commodious Circumstances; for of those one hundred and seventy (most of them grown Persons) not one died, except that one Man, that could not be brought to drink the Tar-water.

Captain *Drape* says farther, that the Negroes continued drinking Tar-water after their Recovery, which they found so much Relief from, that they could hardly be brought to drink any other; and that from the Time of their Departure from *Guinea*, to their Arrival in *Jamaica*, he verily believes they did not drink above a Hogshead of Water, that was not impregnated with Tar, though the ordinary Consumption of Water for so many Slaves, could not be less than a Hogshead a Day.

I do hereby certify upon Oath, that the Contents of the above Narrative are actually and *bona fide* true.

Liverpool, the 14th of *January*, 1744.

Joseph Drape.

Taken and sworn before me,

Owen Prichard, Mayor of *Liverpool*."

45. The said Mr. *Atherton*, in a Letter dated the Fourth of *February*, 1744, writes in the following Words:

"We have a very high Opinion of the Virtues of Tar-water in my Family; my Wife having drank about a Pint a Day of it for eight Months last past, by which she received surprizing Benefit in an Inflammatory Disorder, in which Physick and Bleeding had brought her very low; neither of which she has made use of since: Doctor *Dickins*, one of the most eminent Physicians in this Part of the Kingdom, had her under his Care, and advised her to Tar-water, as an Alterative. So you see Doctors differ about it! Some asserting it to be inflammatory, the contrary of which, I have the strongest Instances of in my own Family, and for which Mrs. *Atherton* and myself, think ourselves under the greatest Obligations to the Bishop of *Cloyne*. These Instances of the Virtues of Tar-water, so well authenticated, together with many others, which will

will be mentioned hereafter, put it out of all Doubt, that Tar-water is so far from being of an inflammatory Nature, or dangerous in inflammatory Disorders, as has been suggested by some, that it is a most safe and sovereign Medicine in such Cases. And I am very well informed, that it is now become a constant Rule and Practice at *Liverpool*, and other Places, which fit our Ships for the *Guinea* Trade, to provide a sufficient Quantity of Tar, to make Tar-water in order to be administred in Plenty, to such Seamen, as may happen to be seized, in their Voyages, with the Small-pox, Scurvies, and other Distempers, which Seamen are subject to.

46. Mr. *Hayward* writes, in the said Letter, that he had laboured under an Ague of four Months Continuance, which had reduced him to a very low State, but that he very happily recovered his Health by the use of Tar-water only; and in his Letter of the 29th of *June*, 1744, he adds, that he was in no manner of Pain about the Return of his Ague; that he had spent the Winter, thus far, in the most comfortable Manner, and enjoys a more lively and comfortable Flow of Spirits, than ever he did in his Life; which, upon all Occasions, are apt to exert themselves in extolling the Source from whence they are drawn, and giving others as high an Opinion of Tar-water, as he had himself; he also makes this Observation, that the Virtues ascribed, and that very justly, to Tar-water, particularly that of removing the Load, that, at times hang heavenly on the Spirits, and infusing into the Soul, those lucid gladsome Sensations, which many unhappily seek for in Drams and Cordials, would almost incline one to think, the *Egyptians* were not ignorant of Tar-water. If that sovereign Cordial of theirs, described by *Homer* under the Name of *Nepenthes*, was not Tar-water, he is sure it was something very

like it, as, he says, will appear from these and the following Lines in *Homer*'s *Odysses*, 4th Book.

Ἑλένη Διὸς ἐκγεγαῦα
Αὐτίκ' ἄρ' εἰς οἶνον βάλε φάρμακον, ἔνθεν ἔπινον,
Νηπενθές τ' ἄχολόν τε, κακῶν ἐπίληθον ἁπάντων.
Ὃς τὸ καταβρώξειεν. Hom. Odyss. Δ.

Thus translated by Mr. *Pope*:

Mean time with genial Joy to warm the Soul,
Bright *Helen* mix'd a Mirth inspiring Bowl;
Temper'd with Drugs of sov'reign Use, t'assuage
The boiling Bosom of tumultuous Rage;
To clear the cloudy Front of wrinkled Care,
And dry the tearful Sluices of Despair;
Charm'd with that virtuous Draught, th' exalted Mind
All Sense of Woe delivers to the Wind:
These Drugs so friendly to the Joys of Life,
Bright *Helen* learn'd from *Thone*'s imperial Wife,
Who sway'd the Scepter, where prolific *Nile*
With various Simples cloaths the fatten'd Soil.

Milton *mentions this* Nepenthes *in his Mask of* Comus.

Behold this Cordial Julep here,
That flames and dances in his crystal Bounds;
Not that *Nepenthes*, which the Wife of *Thone*
In *Ægypt* gave to *Jove*-born *Helena*,
Is of such Pow'r as this, to stir up Joy
To Life so friendly, or so cool to Thirst.

A Letter from the Reverend Mr. *James Menteath*, from *Adderbury* in *Oxfordshire*, dated the 12th of *February*, 1744.

47. " As soon as I heard of the Treatise on Tar-war, and of the Directions therein mentioned, I made the Water with different Proportions of Tar, and drank between two and three Gallons of it; but felt

felt no other Effect, but that it increased a good Appetite to a stronger, from which Time I gave it over; having, I thank God, no need of that, or any other Medicine. As to myself, I was by no Means a fair Subject to make an Experiment of its Virtues upon, being young, of a robust Constitution, which I have kept so, by drinking only common Water and Tea, and eating little Animal Food; and I only drank the Tar-water to convince others, that it could do them no Harm. On the Second of *May* last, being Curate of this Place, I was sent for to pray by a young Woman, who, I was told, lay at the Point of Death: When I came, I found her no better than was represented; speechless, so weak, that she could scarcely open her Eyes; her Parents told me, that a Physician of this Country, a Man of much Knowledge, and great Integrity, had just been with her, and said, there was no Hopes of a Recovery, for that she could not live above three Days. The young Woman was about Twenty, born of poor Parents; she had, for some Months, been troubled with a Cough, and a Swelling in her Legs and Arms, which was now become a Dropsy, and, was seemingly, in the last Stage of a Consumption. After performing my Duty, as a Clergyman, I told the Mother, that as the Doctor said her Case was so desperate, if she would give Leave, I would try a Medicine, which I believed might possibly do her Service; she readily consented, and I gave her two Quarts of the Water, and gave Directions, that she should drink Half a Pint of it at a Time, Twice, or if she could bear it, Three times a Day, and that warm; as the Case was desperate, the greater Quantity I thought necessary. After two Days, she was able to sit up, in four or five was brought down Stairs, had some Appetite, her Cough abated, and the Swellings of her Legs and Arms much sunk; in six Weeks she seemed so well, that I advised her to let alone the Tar-water for some Time. I did not see her again till the beginning of *August*; when her Mother came and told me that her Daughter was again out of Order. I went to see her, and found her a little swelled, with a Cough, her Appetite in some Measure lost, and a pale Look; upon this I sent her more of the Water, made according to the printed Directions, which she drank for a Month, and which intirely recovered her; insomuch, that she went out to Service at *Michaelmas* Term, and, I understand, has been well ever since. As she was going to some Distance from this, I gave her Directions how to make the Water and advised her to drink it, whenever she felt the least Complaint.

48. This is the most extraordinary Cure that has come to my Knowledge, though I had many Patients, who have found great Benefit from it. But I had particular Success with young Girls, who have been troubled with that destructive Disorder, the Green Sickness; though I could not inquire into such Complaints, I can easily discover them from the Complexion; indeed of the almost innumerable Experiments that have been made of it, many of which were by my Recommendation, I am fully satisfied, that there is no Proof of its ever doing hurt; so far from it, that, when properly taken, I have never found that it failed of Success."

49. Thus far Mr. *Menteath*, on which I shall make the following Observation. That since it is always allowed, in Cases where all Hopes of Recovery are lost, to make Trials of any Kind which may give the least Hopes of preserving Life, it is humbly submitted, whether it is not adviseable in such desperate Cases, when every thing else has failed, to make Use of Tar-water, which may possibly recover the Patient from the Brink of Death; as it has done in this and many other Instances men-

tioned in the Course of this Narrative, to the great Surprize of all, Physicians and others, who knew the Disorders of those Patients.

An Extract of a Letter from Mr. *John Berry* of *Manchester* in *Lancashire*, dated the 30th of *May* 1744.

50. "I have taken Tar-water twenty-four Mornings, and sometimes in the Afternoon, for a Dizziness in my Head, which I have had at Times for twelve Months past, and since I began taking it, am as well (blessed be God) as ever I was in my Life."

Part of a Letter from a Physician in *York*, to one at *Bath*, dated *August* 25, 1744.

51. "The Bishop of *Cloyne* is no better treated here than at other Places; but for your Satisfaction, I can inform you, that a Lady, tho' reduced to nigh a Skeleton by a bleeding Cancer, and thought only fit for *Guy*'s Hospital of Incurables, by the Use of Tar-water is so much better, as to be thought in a fair Way of enjoying a comfortable State of Health. She has recovered her Appetite and Flesh, and all bad Symptoms are almost overcome, and her Breast is become soft and easy. This I think will stand as a Sort of Balance to the Hospital Account from *Dublin*."

Part of a Letter from one in *Lisbon*, to his Correspondent at *Bath*, dated the 21st of *January*, 1744.

52. "In respect to Tar-water, I am sure it has been of great Service here in many Cases. It is in Vogue in the *Portugal* Hospital, and they gave it the Princess *De Bocra* in the Small-pox, and she has done very well. I am not a Friend to Quack Medicines,

dicines, but there is nothing to be ſaid againſt Proof."

53. I ſhall here add ſome Pieces printed in the *Engliſh* News-papers on the Subject of Tar-water.

A Letter to the Author of the *General-Evening-Poſt*, *June* the 4th, 1744.

SIR,

54. While Thouſands daily experience the Benefit of the Biſhop of *Cloyne*'s Tar-water, give me Leave to teſtify my Thanks for the Pleaſure I have received from his Diſcourſe upon it. I little expected on ſo low a Subject, to have met with ſuch Variety of Matter, ſuch Penetration of Thought, or that it was poſſible to have expreſſed either in Language ſo clear, and eaſy. Where ſhall we ſee a more accurate Theory of various Diſtempers, or of the Operations of the moſt prevailing Medicines upon them? How beautiful his Anatomy of Trees and Plants? How rational his Principles of Vegetation? How refined his Doctrine of Metals, and of their being tranſformed into each other? How learned his Hiſtory of the Opinions and Syſtems of the Antients? While he gradually leads me on from the ſimpleſt Operations of Nature, through the animal and vegetable World, up to the great Author of both, I am charmed with my Progreſs, and think I ſee in this *Chain* of his, that golden one, which hung down to Earth from Heaven, as this by ſeveral Links carries us up thither. Whether he teaches, reaſons, preſcribes, or analyzes, he does all with the Knowledge of a Profeſſor, the Humanity of a Gentleman, and, to crown all, with a good Biſhop's Piety; and leaves us uncertain whether to admire in him moſt, the Chemiſt, Phyſician, Philoſopher, or Divine. Somewhat like that fine ſubtile Spirit, which, he tells us, operates through the Univerſe, diſtinguiſhes his Writings; a Principle of pure Light,

which you feel in him, as in other Systems nothing but Gravitation. I am, Sir, *&c.*

A Pindarique by the Right Honourable, *L. C. J. M.* inscribed to the Author of *Siris.*

55. Majestick thus great *Nilus* shrowds
His sacred Head in Darkness and the Clouds,
His Birth divine from vulgar Eyes conceals,
But to the Wise by Miracles reveals.
Homage to him ten thousand Torrents pay
Replete with Æther's vital Flame,
While thro' the burning Zone he wings his Way,
While *Siris* is his mystick Name.
Parch'd *Afric* courts him to the *Libyan* Plain,
And strives to intercept his Course;
But marble Mountains are oppos'd in vain,
Resistless his as Ocean's Force.
From the steep Cataracts impetuous as he bounds,
Earth trembles at his Voice, each distant Rock resounds:
Then smooth o'er *Egypt's* Plain his welcome Deluge flows,
And smiling Plenty brings, and chearful Health bestows:
Hail *Egypt*, happy Realm, thy Monarchs were the Gods,
There Arts, and Wisdom there first fix'd their blest Abodes.

On the Disputes about Tar-water.

56. To drink, or not to drink, that is the Doubt,
With *Pro* and *Con*, the Learn'd would make it out.
Britons, drink on, the jolly Prelate cries:
What the Prelate persuades the Doctor denies.
But why need the Parties so learnedly fight,
Or Choleric * *I—r—n* so fiercely indite?
Sure the Senses can tell, if the Liquor be right.

* A Physician and Writer against Tar-water.

What

What agrees with his Stomach, and what with his
Head,
The Drinker may feel, tho' he can't write or read.
Then Authority's nothing, the Doctors are Men;
And who drinks Tar-water will drink it again.

57. On the Enemies of *Siris*, by a Drinker of Tar-water.

How can devoted *Siris* stand
Such dire Attacks? The licens'd Band
With up cast Eyes and Visage sad
Proclaim, alas! "The World's run mad.
"The Prelate's Book hath turn'd their Brains,
"To set them right will cost us Pains.
"His Drug too makes our Patients sick,
"And this doth vex us to the Quick."
And vex'd they must be, to be sure,
To find Tar-water cannot cure,
But makes Men sicker still and sicker,
And Fees come thicker still and thicker,
Bursting with Pity for Mankind,
But to his own Advantage blind,
Full many a Wight with Face of Funeral,
From Mortar, Still, and Urinal,
Hastes to throw in his scurvy Mite
Of Spleen, of Dulness, and of Spight.
To furnish the revolving Moons
With Pamphlets, Epigrams, Lampoons
Against this *Siris*, you'd know why?
Think who they are; you'll soon discry,
What means each angry doleful Ditty,
Whether themselves, or us they pity?

From the *Daily Gazetteer*, published in *London*, *April* 4, 1745.

To the Right Reverend the Bishop of *Cloyne*.

My Lord,

58. Upon the Foundation of some Hints I took from the 29th and 49th Sections of your *Siris*, I resolved

resolved to attempt a Solution of Myrrh, by a low, aqueous Menstruum; and considering the Affinity, and similar Properties that are in Tar, and in Myrrh, I was led to think, that as all homogeneous Bodies attract more strongly than those of different Classes; so possibly the native Vegetable, or acid Spirit of Tar, when gently fermented, might invite the like Principle from Myrrh. Accordingly I put a Drachm of coarse Myrrh, without any Delicacy of Choice, into half a Pint of Tar-water, and set it in a Pint Bottle, in a Degree of Heat of my Fire, equal to that of a hot Sun: In two or three Days I obtained so perfect a Solution, that, upon filtring, I found no other Residuum, than such as is apt to stick to gummy Bodies.

Of this Infusion, I mix about half an Ounce in each Half-pint of Tar-water, which I daily drink; and take them so mixed, with good Success. It makes the Tar-water much more pleasant, giving it an agreeable sub-acid bitter Taste.

59. The second Process I used, after having spent my first Preparation, was very inaccurate; for I threw in an indeterminate Quantity (but as near as I can guess) four Drachms of fine pick'd Myrrh to a Pint of Tar-water. Upon filtring off this Infusion, I had Cause to think the Tar-water was more than saturated with Myrrh, because, among the Residuum, I found a kind of *Stacte*, or fine, transparent, liquid Myrrh, of the Consistency of the best Turpentine; which, however, might perhaps have yielded to a longer Infusion.

60. To you, my Lord, we owe the Tar-water; and to you, how nearly had we owed the Solution of Myrrh? since you furnished the only aqueous Menstruum that will dissolve, and render it fit for internal use: As your Lordship suggested the first Hint, so I know no Person so capable of improving, and so willing to apply this Discovery (if it be one)

to the Good of Mankind as your Lordſhip. To you, therefore, I addreſs it, with all its Virtues, all its Honours. For my Part, I have not Skill enough in any Branch of medical Knowledge, to aſſure whether there be any thing new or valuable in this Experiment of mine, only I conjecture, that at leaſt, it muſt be a good vulnerary Water; but were the Secret as rich as the Treaſures of *Loretto*, both my Fortune and my Love to Mankind forbid me to make any private Advantage of it; therefore I freely give it to the Public under your Lordſhip's Patronage. I am, with great Duty and Eſteem,

Your Lordſhip's moſt obedient humble Servant,

Philanthropos.

61. I ſhall now proceed to give a Narrative of ſuch Caſes, which happened in *Ireland*, as they were communicated to me by Letters from Gentlemen of known Character and Integrity, in this Kingdom, giving a particular Detail of their own Diſorders, or of thoſe of their Neighbours and Acquaintance, and of the Relief they received, together with ſuch farther Accounts as I had from ſeveral Patients from their own Mouths, in and near *Dublin*, with their Names and Places of Abode.

A Letter from the Reverend Mr. *Nat. France*, of *Youghall*, in the County of *Cork*, dated *July* 6, 1744, to *Thomas Prior*, Eſq;

SIR,

62. Reading an Advertiſement in the *Dublin Courant*, dated *July* the 3d, I thought myſelf bound by the ſtrongeſt Obligation, Gratitude for an ineſtimable Benefit received, as well as for the good of Mankind, which every Man ought to have at Heart, to give Teſtimony to the Truth. Upwards of 20 Years I have laboured under a very dreadful Diſorder, occaſioned, as I am fully perſuaded, by a prevailing

prevailing Acid in my Stomach. Frequently for many Weeks together, I never rose from sleep, without violent vomiting, and a continual Sickness in my Stomach; rarely free from a Heart-burn, and that commonly ending in a violent Cholick; nervous Discorders, frightful Spasms, a frequent Palpitation of the Heart in Bed, were the sure unhappy Consequences; my Disorder baffled the Art of Physick, the whole Power of Medicine. The *Pyrmont* and *German* Spaw-water, with the constant Use of Gum-pills for the nervous Complaint, gave some little Relief, but were very far from rooting out the Cause of my Disorder. I industriously shun'd every Acid; my Drink for many Years was Wine and Water, not daring to touch Malt-liquor or Cyder. I have drank Tar-water these three Years past, and, I bless God for it, have no Complaint to make; no Heart-burn; no vomiting in the Morning, which almost deprived me of my Sight; no Return of any nervous Disorder, unless occasioned by a violent Cold, from which I am quickly relieved, by taking a plentiful Draught of Tar-water. Last Summer I laid a-side Tar-water for three Months, believing, I did not any longer stand in need of it; and that the Medicine would cease to be efficacious by the constant Use of it; my Colick, Heart-burn, and nervous Spasms return'd upon me as violent as ever. I again had recourse to Tar-water; its happy Effects was beyond Expectation, in a few Days it perfectly relieved me. I do now, and shall, for the Remainder of my Life, make it my Morning Draught; having no other Complaint against it, but this one; that by creating an Appetite, which it never fails to do; by strengthning the Stomach, and causing a good Digestion, it renders me more corpulent, than I could wish to be.

I am, Sir, your very humble Servant,

Nat. France.

63. A

63. A Letter from the Corporation of *Augher*, in the County of *Tyrone*, dated *July* 7, 1744.

SIR,

Agreeably to your Instructions in the last Newspaper, we the under-written, Inhabitants of *Augher*, take this Opportunity of informing the Public, that most of us, having for many Years been greatly afflicted with chronical Diseases, such as the Gout, inveterate Scurvy, and rheumatic Pains, *&c.* were induced, from the high Character given to the Tarwater, to make Trial thereof.

That those of us, who had any out-breaking, found, after a Fortnight's Trial, the Spots rather more inflamed and painful, but afterwards daily growing easier and better. That some of us who were seized with the Rheumatism found after the like Time a sensible Remission of the Pains; how far it may answer in the Gout we cannot yet pretend to say, but, from the surprizing Recovery of most of us, we in the Gout, resolve to continue the regular and constant Use of that most excellent Remedy; and all of us do, in the most affectionate Manner, return our publick Thanks to the Author of the Tar-water.

Edmund Mac Girr.	*Robert Thompson.*
Revd. Mac Quigan.	*Adam Smyth.*
Dudly Harvey.	*Uri. Mac Dowall.*

64. A Letter from the Reverend Mr. *Thomas Squire*, from *Tallow* in the County of *Waterford*, dated *July* 11, 1744.

SIR,

The Enemies of Tar-water, I find, are greatly provoked, seeing they endeavoured to have it sworn out of Credit and Practice; however, I make no doubt, but that for the six Affidavits against it, you will soon have many Hundreds of creditable Vouchers for

for it; I send you some Cases: First my own. Turned of Sixty, my Stomach began to fail me, and what little I did eat, lay heavy there for two or three Hours after Dinner; my Flesh wasted so that my Cloaths were much too big for me, the Calves of my Legs became soft, and hung from the Bones, and the red in my Cheeks grew dark and livid; I look'd on these, and some other bad Symptoms, as Warnings from my Creator to prepare for my appearing before him in another State.

I had the Honour of being known to the Bishop of *Cloyne*, who advised me to drink Tar-water; which I did for fifteen Months, in which Time I found my Appetite restored, my Food sat easy on my Stomach, I grew up to my former Dimensions, my Flesh became firm, as it had been twenty Years before, and the Blood in my Cheeks of a good Red, so that I reckoned myself in as fair a way of living as any Man of my Age, in the Neighbourhood.

65. A Gentlewoman in my House far advanced in Years, of a tender Constitution, and in a bad State of Health, has for near two Years taken a small Glass of Tar-water every Morning, and often another about Noon; the Physician who has attended her for eight Years, and consented to the Tar-water, has frequently for this last Year expressed his great Surprize at her being so much better, than at any Time since she was first under his Care. I must observe to you, that she takes several other kinds of Physick by the Doctor's Directions; it may not be amiss likewise to observe, that her Apothecary's Bill was last Year reduced to less than half of what it has formerly been, and I am sure, when it comes in next, will fall very short of that.

66. A Servant of mine was so ill of a Cold and violent Cough, that he was going to take to his Bed. I ordered him to drink about half a Pint of Tar-water warm'd; he then set about his Business, and I

have not heard him complain ſince, tho' I forgot to make him repeat the Medicine. I could give Inſtances of many in this Neighbourhood, who have received great Benefit by Tar-water. This Morning a Gentleman, who, by a Cold taken in *February* laſt, was apprehenſive of a Decay, told me that his Fears were over by drinking Tar-water for three Weeks; and Yeſterday a Phyſician, who ſtudied under the great *Boerhaave*, told me that he had preſcribed the Courſe of Tar-water to five of his Patients lately; of thoſe it is probable I may give you an Account hereafter, as well as of two more, whoſe Caſes were very deſperate, and recovered, but I am not fully informed in the Particulars as yet.

I am your moſt humble Servant,

T. S.

67. A Letter from the ſaid Mr. *Squire* from *Curryglaſs* in the County of *Cork*, dated *November* 30, 1744.

SIR,

When I wrote to you formerly, I propoſed to ſend you ſome farther Accounts of the Cures effected by Tar-water; one of which was on a Gentlewoman near *Limerick*, (whom I have not leave to name.) Her Huſband was in this Village laſt *Chriſtmas*, who deſcribed his Wife's Diſtemper in ſuch a manner, that ſhe ſeemed to have ſuffered more by the Scurvy, than Mr. *Connor* of *Bandon*; ſhe was, as the Expreſſion was, juſt flayed alive, and had almoſt loſt the Uſe of her Limbs. I adviſed Tar-water, which a Phyſician approving, ſhe drank for ſome Time; ſo that the Scurvy-ſplotches are perfectly healed, and ſhe is recovering daily the Uſe of her Limbs. This I had from her Huſband's Brother.

68. The following Account I had from Mr. *Robert Atkins* near *Mallow*. A young Gentlewoman related to him had been long ill; ſhe had a great hard Swel-

ling

ling in her Side, lost her Stomach, was extremely thin and pale; some Physicians, who had attended for a considerable Time, at length gave her up. She earnestly entreated one of them, Doctor *Connell*, for Advice, who recommended Tar-water; she drank it for some Months and perfectly recovered.

69. In *Curryglass*, Fourteen, as I find, have drank Tar-water, every one of them have received Benefit thereby, but the most remarkable, after those in my former Letter, were *Hannah Evans*, Wife to *Henry Evans*, Mason, cured of an hereditary Asthma, under which she laboured for two Years, and could not lie down in Bed; but now goes to Bed as formerly, and adds to her nightly Devotion, GOD *bless the good Bishop*.

70. *Henry Evans* in the great Frost took a violent Cold, and every Winter since, has kept his Head and Jaws tied up in Handkerchiefs; he drank Tar-water, the Pain in his Jaws is gone, and he bears Cold as well as ever he did. *Lawrence Linehan*, a Paper-maker, had taken so great Cold as his Work, that he wasted away, had a most deadly Cough, and was thought by all to be in a Decay; he drank Tar-water, and is now as well as ever.

71. Mr. *Crips* drinks Tar-water for an hereditary Asthma; when he is regular in it, some Splotches break out in several Parts of his Body, and the Asthma quite gone; but when he is careless the Splotches disappear, and the difficulty of breathing returns.

72. Mrs. *Rolleston*, who nurses her Child, had some Occasion to drink Tar-water, which succeeded well with her; she had a vast Flow of Milk, when she drank it, and her Child was extremely well; our Physicians here prescribed Tar-water frequently, and all own that no Medicine has ever made so great a Progress in so short a Time.

I am your most obedient humble Servant,

Thom. Squire.

73. A Letter from Mr. *Henry Parsons*, Attorney, dated from *William-street*, *Dublin*, *July* 26, 1744.

SIR,

I lately read an Advertisement in Mr. *Faulkner's Weekly Journal*, desiring, that Persons who had received Benefit from drinking Tar-water, would send you an Account thereof, with the Nature of their several Disorders. As that Advertisement was chiefly intended for the Benefit of Mankind, I think every one ought readily to comply therewith. I therefore send you the following Account:

I have been these twenty Years past, and upwards, grievously afflicted with violent Pains and Swellings in my Limbs; and for want of my natural Rest, which they frequently prevented, I was reduced to a very great Weakness; and I had lost my Stomach to that Degree, that I may say, *My Soul abhorred all manner of Meat, and I was even hard at Death's Door.* I was reduced to that unhappy State, which the Bishop of *Cloyne*, in his Treatise on Tar-water, calls *Tædium Vitæ*, a Weariness of Life, that I could have blest the Means that would have finish'd my Days; and if any one was to have bought an Annuity on my Life, I am sure no one would have given six Months Purchase for it. I am certain that every one, who has known me these twenty Years past, can and will readily vouch the Truth hereof; and not above five Months ago, a Gentleman falling into a groundless Passion with me, for no other Reason, but because he was losing a Game at Backgammon, declared to some Gentlemen, who afterwards informed me thereof, that he would certainly have been the Death of me, but that he was well satisfied I would soon dye by the Course of Nature.

74. I was also afflicted with a violent scorbutic Humour, which broke out to a great Degree in my Face; and about the Beginning of *May* last, on my

first hearing the Virtue of Tar-water so greatly recommended, and on reading the Magazine for the Month of *March*, wherein it is set forth, I resolved on drinking it, and tho' I have only drank about five Gallons thereof, it has not only perfectly cured me of the Scurvy, but has also intirely eased me of all my Pains; restored me to my former Strength, a good Stomach, and a great Flow of Spirits; that now (I thank God) I may justly say, I am a Man again.

I am, Sir, your humble Servant,

Henry Parsons.

Mr. *Parsons*, who may be seen every Day in the Streets of *Dublin*, continues in a perfect State of Health, and Flow of Spirits, and constantly drinks Tar-water.

75. A Letter from the Reverend Mr. *Bernard Ward*, dated from *Belfast*, *July* 23, 1744.

SIR,

Inclosed I send you the Cases of three Persons, who have received Benefit by the Use of Tar-water. In the first I prescribed it myself; the 2d, I had from the Mother of the young Lady, and her Permission to send it to you; the 3d I had from the Father of the Child, who perused and approved of the Account which I send you. I think it the Duty of every Person, as far as he can, to make the World acquainted with the Cases of such as receive Benefit from the Use of new Medicines, especially if they be such as are safe in the Application, and cheap, so as to render them of Use to the Poor: Tar-water, I am persuaded, is of this Kind, and I dare say it will give the good and most ingenious Author of *Siris* a very sensible Pleasure, to find that his Medicine is likely to answer the End, which he had in publishing it, that is, to become of universal Use, and to remove most of the Disorders to which Men are subject.

I venture to send you the inclosed without any Apology, the Truth of the Facts you may depend upon. I am, Sir,

Your most obedient humble Servant,

Bernard Ward.

The Honourable *Arthur Hill*, Esq; adds by way of Postscript, that though these Instances are but three, yet Tar-water is in great and universal Repute here, and I have no Doubt, but, in a little time, abundance more may be given.

76. N° 1. *William Gawdy* of the Parish of *Kirdonnell*, and County of *Down*, Farmer, aged about forty Years, had been many Years afflicted with the Rheumatism. About two Years ago he applied to me, when by the Use of *Ætherial* Oil of Turpentine, his Complaint was removed for that Time: In *May* last I met him near his own House, most grievously tormented with the same Disorder which had then fixed itself in his Loins, and had for some Weeks entirely disabled him from doing any Work; he told me he had used the Turpentine, but without Success; that for some Weeks he had scarce been able to walk. I recommended the Use of Tar-water, four Quarts of which did so effectually remove his Disorder, that, to use his own Words, he was able to lift a Hogshead Sack full of Corn, and to put it upon his Horse, and, in short, was as well as he ever had been.

77. N° 2. Miss *Small*, of the Parish of *Knockbreda*, in the County of *Down*, a young Lady of about sixteen Years of Age, had for some Time been troubled with a Pain in her Side, Shortness of Breath, a Palpitation of the Heart upon the least Motion, and an entire Loss of Appetite; her Mother was apprehensive of a Consumption; yet by drinking Tar-

water

water about a Fortnight, all the above Symptoms were removed, and ſhe can now walk a Mile or two without giving her the leaſt Uneaſineſs, and is in perfect Health.

78. N° 3. *John*, the Son of the Reverend *Anneſley Baile*, Curate of *Comber* in the County of *Down*, at the Age of two Years, was active and ſprightly, and could walk as well as any Child of his Age; he was then ſeized with a Fever, which deprived him of the Uſe of his Limbs; his Joints grew large, and his Belly hard, like a ricketty Child; he continued in this Condition about two Years, till, upon the Publication of *Siris*, his Father made him drink Tar-water, a Wine Glaſs full three Times a Day, and in three Weeks time, he recovered the Uſe of his Limbs, and has been ever ſince in the higheſt Spirits, and very good Health.

79. A Letter from the Reverend Mr. *Uſher*, of *Maryborough*, dated *Auguſt* 23, 1744.

Margaret Large, of the Pariſh of *Coolbonagher* near *Mountmelick* in the *Queen's* County, being about forty-three Years old, laboured under a violent Cough and Oppreſſion on her Stomach for ten Years, which afflicted her without Intermiſſion to that Degree, that ſhe loſt her Appetite, her Body was emaciated, and her Spirits low and depreſſed; but by drinking Tar-water conſtantly every Morning ſince the Beginning of *June* laſt, the Cough and Oppreſſion on her Stomach were entirely removed, her loſt Appetite reſtored, her Spirits became briſk and lively, and her whole Conſtitution and Habit of Body wonderfully improved, and this Change evidently appeared in about ſix Weeks after ſhe began to drink the Tar-water. This Account, he ſays, he had from the Patient herſelf.

80. A Letter from Mr. *Henry Gervais*, of *Lismore* in the County of *Waterford*, dated the 15th of *September*, 1744, to *Thomas Prior* Esq;

Pursuant to your Desire, signified in the public Prints, I take the Liberty of communicating to you the Case of Mr. *William Bryen*, which may not be unworthy your Notice. Mr. *Bryen*, who is an Attorney in Lord *Burlington*'s Manor-courts, after riding five Miles, about two Years since, without a great Coat, in a Winter's Night of very heavy Rain, and so fuddled, that, when he came home he could not put off his Cloaths, threw himself on his Bed, where he slept about six Hours, and, when he awoke, was in an high Inflammation, and not able to speak. A Physician of no small Repute in this Country, came to his Aid, and by the common Process in such Cases, by bleeding, blistering, *&c.* brought some present Relief; but in a little Time a violent Cough ensued, attended with a grievous Pain in his Side, spitting of Blood, and large Sweats; so that having suffered much, and gone through the Apothecary's Shop for a Course of six Months, and exhausted his little Substance, the Physicians, in a Consultation, pronounced that he would die tabid. The Patient not being able to purchase costly Medicines, in Despair had recourse to Tar-water, which he has ever since continued the Use of, with the greatest Benefit; insomuch, that when I talk'd with him, some little Time ago, he told me that he had recovered his Appetite and Rest, and was free from the Pain in his Side, and as well in Health as he could wish, saving a light Cough which remained, but was, in his Opinion, gradually wearing off.

81. Mr. *Gervais* mentions in his own Case in the following Words: "I was under great Apprehensions from the Reliques of the Influenza, which in its Course seized me in a most heavy Manner, and left an acute Pain in my Head, violent Palpitations in the Heart,

Heart, a conſtant Pulſation in the Brain, and Spaſms through my whole Body. *Flagherty cum Sociis* had me in hand for Months; Gum-pills and Spirits of Vitriol I almoſt lived upon, and to no Purpoſe; but now, by the Uſe of Tar-water, I am (God be praiſed) reſtored to good Spirits and Health."

82. He alſo mentions the Caſe of Mrs. *C*——— of *Limerick*, who was, many Years, afflicted with a Scurvy in the higheſt Degree; that he had been informed, by a near Relation of hers, that ſhe had been quite flay'd from Head to Foot, ſo that for many Months, ſhe lay in Cere-cloths, and could not turn in her Bed, but as ſhe was helped by the Sheets: When all Remedies prov'd ineffectual, Tar-water was the *dernier Reſort*, by the Uſe whereof, for ten Weeks, ſhe has got a new Skin, her Sores have ceaſed to run, and her Health is thoroughly retrieved.

83. Mr. *Gervais*, ſoon after, ſent me the following Caſe, drawn up by Doctor *William C*——, of *Mallow*, in the Words following:

Carrol Daly, of *Ardprior* in the County of *Cork*, aged about 28, on exerciſing ſeverely in the Year 1742, was ſeized with a violent Cough, Streightneſs in his Cheſt, difficulty of Reſpiration, and had large Quantities of Blood diſcharged from his Lungs; in which State he remained near ſix Months, without other Aſſiſtance than what his poor Neighbours could adminiſter; till at length (quite emaciated, and in a hectic State, with Fluſhings in his Face, ſucceeded by Rigors and conſtant Night-ſweats) he applied to the neighbouring Phyſicians, who recommended a Courſe of pectoral and balſamic Medicines, with Tincture of Jeſuits Bark, and a Milk-diet, which Regimen he ſtrictly obſerved ten Months and better, when finding little Amendment, and no Hopes of Recovery, he applied to me; I recommended his continuing the ſame Method for ſome time longer, which he ſubmitted to, without further Benefit than that his Sweats somewhat abated; he was now set down as incurable, and, at most, not likely to survive the following Spring; when hearing so much of the Virtues of Tar-water, published by the Bishop of *Cloyne*, and willing to try the Success, as every Thing else failed; I recommended earnestly the constant Use of it to him, and prepared it for him according to the Bishop's Directions. At first it disagreed prodigiously, inducing frequent Nausea's, Sickness in the Stomach, and a Lax, which, in his Condition, I was very apprehensive of; notwithstanding, I made some lighter, which, in a few Days, was so reconcileable to his Stomach, that he took it in large Quantities after, and is now perfectly recovered from all his Symptoms, only a small Cough, which he is subject to, on taking Cold, or any Irregularity.

84. *A Letter from Mr.* William Peacocke, *Merchant, in* Abbey-street, Dublin, *dated* Sept. 22, 1744.

SIR,

My Brother, *Marmaduke Peacocke*, Merchant in *Abbey-street*, was, for several Months, very unwell, he had a great Cough, little or no Appetite, and a great Lowness of Spirits; he cold not walk the Length of a Street, without being in a violent Sweat, and was very much emaciated; he applied to some Physicians here, and to no Purpose. He, by Accident, heard of the Virtues of Tar-water; he made some, drank of it Morning and Evening, and in less than three Weeks, he was as heal as ever, in great Spirits, and as well as he could wish; this I aver for Truth.

85. Last Spring I had a Fit of the Gout coming on me; the Reason I say so, is, because I was seized with the Cramp in my Legs, most violently, for several Nights, I had a great Loss of Appetite, and my Stomach faint and weak, with great Tenderness in my Feet; this is always a Forerunner of a Fit of the Gout with me. I was prevailed upon, by my Brother,

Brother, *Marmaduke Peacocke*, to drink Tar-water, which I did Morning and Evening: The doing ſo occaſioned great Perſpiration in my Feet, and in three Nights after, I had no Cramps, no Tenderneſs in my Feet, I had a good Appetite and Digeſtion, and was every other Way very well. I continued drinking this Water for two Months; afterwards I left it off for a Week, and drank of it only every Morning. I ſtill do the ſame, and am now (thank GOD) as well as any one. Given under my Hand this 22d of *September* 1744.

William Peacocke.

Mr. *Peacocke*, who may be ſeen every Day at *Lucas*'s Coffee-houſe, informs me now in *June* 1745, that he has all along, and now continues to drink Tar-water every Day, and that with Pleaſure; that he has by Means thereof a great Perſpiration in his Feet, and Strength in his Limbs, and is free from all Symptoms and Apprehenſions of the Gout, which ſo long troubled him.

86. *A Letter from* Stephen Bernard, *Eſq*; *Member of Parliament from* Youghall, October 2, 1744.

SIR,

As ſoon as I could completely, and with certainty, I was determined to communicate and acknowledge the Services I had received from the Uſe of Tar-water; which I have taken for three Months, Morning, Noon, and Night, half a Pint each time warm; and which I can now with certainty ſay, has relieved me from a Sickneſs in my Stomach, that ever attended me, but more ſevere for ſix Years laſt paſt, and ſo much more for the two laſt, that it was very rare to have a Day paſs without being troubled with violent Heavings, at leaſt twice, and a Loathing of all Suſtenance; which reduced me to ſo low a Condition, as utterly diſabled me from uſing any Exerciſe. I was alſo ſubject to a frequent Giddineſs, which

which remained, and was encreasing, notwithstanding a long Course of Vomits; in less than a Week after I drank the Tar-water, I not only found my Stomach relieved, but I had really an Appetite, which, I thank GOD, still continues, and, I think, strengthens, and the Giddiness is almost gone; these are the Particulars I can with Truth and Certainty aver. As to my other Complaints which are a flatulent Colick, a Numbness in my Hands, and Obstructions, the Relief not being very sensible, I would not presume troubling you with an Account of it; tho', with GOD's Permission, I have the utmost Confidence, I shall be able to give you an Account of a complete Cure; and make all the Acknowledgments in my Power for the Good received from the most ingenious learned Labour of the excellent Author of *Siris*. I am, Sir, your most obedient humble Servant,

Ste. Barnard.

P. S. A Servant of mine, for Years was troubled with a consumptive Cough, and is quite recovered by Tar-water.

87. *An Extract of a Letter from* Charles Coote, *Esq; Member of Parliament for* Cootehill, October 6, 1744.

SIR,

I am to inform you, that I drink Tar-water constantly; besides the Disorders, I have always been subject to, which are called nervous, I have the Gravel to a great Degree, but without Pain. I discharge great Quantities, by Urine, and my Stomach, Digestion, and whole Frame, used to be greatly disordered, when I was loaded with it; the Use of this Water, not only discharges it, but I believe alters that Disposition in my Constitution, and I have always found myself better in Spirits, Digestion, and the Enjoyment of myself since I drank it.

88. By

88. By the Teſtimonies of *Samuel Moore*, and *John Maxwell*, Eſqs; the Reverend Mr. *Handcock*, Curate of *Cavan*, and many others of this County, Mr. *Donaldſon* of *Cavan*, late Sub-Sheriff of this County, has been long afflicted with the Gout in an extreme Degree; he has drank the Tar-water, ſome Months, and from a cloſe Confinement to his Bed and Chair, to his great Loſs while he was Sub-Sheriff, he is now walking about the Streets, and does not remember when he was able to do ſo for many Years paſt, and refers it wholly to that ſingle Medicine.

89. Mr. *Waren*, within two Miles of me, is Agent to Alderman *Dawſon*; he was Aſtmatic, and ſeemed to be conſumptive to the laſt Degree. I have not ſeen him lately, but Mr. *Richardſon*, our Rector, aſſures me, that he is recovered of all his Complaints to a wonderful Degree, ſolely by the Tar-water, and that he confeſſes he never knew tolerable Comfort, ſince his Illneſs, till he took it.

90. A poor Fellow, in ſome Under-Office about the Church of this Town, was alſo Aſthmatic, and almoſt incapable of any Action, and is now reſtored by it, as our Rector aſſures me. I am, dear Sir,

Your moſt affectionate Servant,

Charles Coote.

91. *P. S.* My Brother-in-law, Mr. *Prat*, who has been extremely ill, many Years, of ſcorbutick Diſorders, and has, in vain drank all the Waters in *Europe*, drank the Tar-water a good while, and I believe continues to do ſo; he is now active, in Spirits, and able to do Buſineſs, and, indeed, appeared to me, not long ago, to be quite recovered; he made it but of half the Strength, the full Strength diſagreeing with him, and he declared, he thought his Amendment was entirely owing to it.

92. *A Letter from* William Ryves, *Esq*; *from* Castel-jane *near* Tipperary, *dated* October 11, 1744.

SIR,

I shall always take Pleasure in any Thing for the publick Good, therefore with Pleasure sit down to answer your's, and to give you the Account you desire, of the Benefit my Tenant, *John Cornick*, received from the Use of Tar-water.

This Man has been, for many Years past, a Mower and a Plowman, in the Occupation of which, by Heats and Colds, he acquired a Cough, which continued on him for several Months, and which sometimes, especially in the Spring, disabled him from following the Plow; but about *March* last, he was obliged to keep his Bed, notwithstanding he had the Advice and Directions of two Physicians, at different times; and being worn away to perfect Skin and Bone, the Physicians pronounced him very near his End. About *July* last, I got, and read *Siris*, and immediately directed this poor Fellow to drink Tar-water, which he did constantly, twice or three times a Day: For the first Week, or ten Days, he coughed prodigiously, and brought up great Quantities of fetid Corruption; every Day after his Cough abated, and his Stomach increased, and at the End of three Weeks drinking, he was able to walk half a Mile with Pleasure, which he did, every Morning, between his first Draught and Breakfast; and, in five Week's time, had gathered a good deal of Strength; his Tar being then out, and he thinking himself pretty well, he omitted drinking since; but I have now ordered him a fresh Parcel of Tar, and do not doubt but he will be as well able to hold his Plow, next Spring, as ever, and mow the following Summer: In short, his Cough is gone, and he finds himself hearty; I this Day examined him.

93. *Edward*

93. *Edward Moore*, Esq; of *Moore*'s *Fort* in the County of *Tipperary*, a Gentleman of Fortune, was extremely out of Order, and, by all the Physicians that attended him, was judged to have an Ulcer in his Bladder, and was preparing to go to some Waters proper for him; he had quite lost his Stomach and Complexion, but by the Use of Tar-water, for five or six Weeks, is not only quite well of his Disorder, but has recovered his Stomach and Complexion; and, I do believe, still continues to drink it. I can also assure you, my Wife has drank it, for some time, for a little barking Cough, which she has had these three Years past, which afflicts her most, just as she gets up in the Morning; and she has found such an Abatement of it, that I do not doubt, but, in a little time, she will be quite free from it. If these Accounts be of any Use to the Publick, and a satisfactory Answer to your Letter, it will fully answer the Design of, Sir,

Your very humble Servant,

William Ryves,

94. *A Letter from* William Connor, *Esq*; *from* Bandon *in the County of* Cork, *dated* October 23. 1744.

SIR,

I am favour'd with your's of the Sixth Instant, and have since communicated the same to my Brother *George Connor*, who is the Person, you heard, had been relieved, in a scorbutick Disorder, by the Use of Tar-water; for which he is full of Acknowledgments to the Author of *Siris*; and (had not the Badness of the Weather, and some other Accidents in his Family, hitherto prevented) he designed, e'er now, to have paid his Compliments personally to the Bishop of *Cloyne*, and have acquainted him with the whole Progress of his Disorder, and almost incredible Benefit he had received in

less

less than a Month, by the Use of that most sovereign and universal Remedy; for which Purpose, he desired me to let you know, that he intends waiting on his Lordship as soon as he can conveniently leave Home; there are several other Instances in this Neighbourhood, of Persons benefited by the same Means, but none more so (that I have heard of) than one of my Daughters, who had laboured under a kind of hysterick and nervous Disorder for some Months, which afflicted her with a Palpitation and Difficulty of Breathing, insomuch, that she frequently imagined she was expiring; of which Complaint, she is now (God be praised) quite free, and attributes her Cure solely to that most excellent Remedy, Tar-water, having received little or no Benefit from any Thing else; tho' she had been under a Course of Medicines, for some Months, before she took to the drinking Tar-water, for the Discovery of which she is infinitely obliged to the good Bishop, and so is, Sir,

Your most obedient Servant,
William Connor.

95. Mr. *George Connor*, whose Name is mentioned in the precedent Letter, having been pleased himself to communicate his own Case, and Relief, in *November*, 1744, I shall here insert the Particulars thereof, which shew the wonderful Powers of Tar-water.

Mr. *Connor* had been several Years afflicted with a scorbutick Disorder, and finding no Relief here, from the Prescriptions of Physicians, he went to *England*, where he made use of the *Bath*, and other Waters, without receiving any Benefit; upon his Return to *Ireland*, his Distemper became so violent, and increased to such a Degree, that his Physicians, not knowing what to do else, were for sending him to *Bath* again, when, by Chance, he met with *Siris*, which

which put him upon the making and drinking Tar-water, which quite recovered him in a Month or six Weeks Time; his Case was wonderful, his Body was all over one continual Sore, he was obliged to shift himself four times a Day, and his Shirts stood on End, stiffened by Corruption; his Limbs and Body were wrapped up in Linen spread with Suet, to keep any Thing from touching him.

The sharp Humours used to run through his Cloaths on the Ground. He could neither digest, sleep, nor rest. The first Effect of the Tar-water was, that an incredible Number of blind Boils appeared in the Skin over his whole Body, and very sore, by which the morbifick Humour was driven to the outward Parts, and by constant drinking Tar-water, these Boils grew milder, and by Degrees healed and dried away, so that in less than six Weeks, he was quite easy, and he attributes his Cure solely to Tar-water. Upon first taking the Water, he was very costive for several Days, which frightened him, and made him take some gentle opening Purge. But this rather retarded his Cure, for where the Tar-water throws out the Venom into the Skin, it should not be disturbed by the Revulsion of a Purgative, howsoever such casting out may naturally produced a Costiveness. Such Costiveness is not to be reckoned a bad Effect, but a good Symptom; it shews that Nature is throwing out the bad Humours through the Skin, and not by Stool, and when it has sufficiently done that Service, in which it ought not to be disturbed, the Body will naturally return to its usual Discharges; as many have experienced.

96. *A Letter from* Cornelius Townsend *of* Betsborough *near* Mallow *in the County of* Cork, *Esq*; *dated the* 30*th of* October, 1744.

SIR,

I received the Favour of yours, but a Hurry of Business prevented my answering it sooner; I assure you, I never had it in my Inclination to conceal any Thing that I thought may be of general Use to Mankind. Before I enter on the Particulars of my complicated Disorders, I must beg leave to observe to you, that I am thoroughly convinced, from my own Experience, and my Observations on others, that nothing yet discovered stands fairer for being considered as an universal Medicine for all Disorders, than Tar-water, taken as lately directed by that great good Man, the Bishop of *Cloyne*, in his Treatise on the Virtues thereof. As to my own Experience, about fifteen Years ago, and about the 32d of my Age, after a most remarkable good Stock of Health from my Infancy, I was first seized with a violent Heart burn, and soon after had slight Fits of the Rheumatism, which in a few Years became very violent, and then getting the better of my often envied good Constitution, a most inveterate Scurvy appeared, particularly on my Temples, and Forehead; my Fits of the Rheumatism were in the Beginning irregular, and did not hold above a Month or six Weeks at a Time; but about eight Years ago, they became regular, and used to confine me to my Bed during the whole Winter and Spring, and always began with a light Fever and terrible Head-ach, which generally held for the first nine or ten Days. I have been likewise subject to a Scurvy in my Gums, and in spight of all my Care, apt to get old, which frequently afflicted my Lungs and Glands, and occasioned a Deafness; till about three Years ago by the Advice of the present Bishop of *Killaloe*, I began the Use of Tar-water, which

which within a Month carryed off the Heart burn; and soon after the Scurvy in my Gums, Temples, &c. began to lessen, and about that time twelve Month, was quite gone; it has also carryed off the Inflammation of my Glands, and I am not so apt to get cold, or be very deaf as formerly; and when, through Carelesness of myself, it happens I get either, I am under no Apprehension about any ill Consequences, finding that honest Tar-water does the Business. My Fits of the Rheumatism, since the Use of Tar-water, have indeed been as tedious, with as great a Weakness in my Knees and Ancles as ever, so that I am not able to stand, but not near so painful, and almost free from the Fever and Head-ach I have mentioned. I am now under a Course of bathing my Legs in warm Tar-water, by Direction of the Bishop of *Cloyne*, and hope in some Time to be able to give you an Account of its Success. I fear I have tired your Patience, but as you desired I should be particular in the Account of my Ailments, I must farther let you know, that from the Beginning of my Disorders, I have had such a costive Constitution, that I seldom had the Benefit of Nature, without the Help of Electuaries, or some other Openers; my Fundament was so inflamed with Piles, that I was very apprehensive of a Fistula, my Flesh was bloated and very tender every where; I was subject to a Palpitation of the Heart, Cramps, Meagrims, &c. from all which (I thank God) I am quite free by the constant Use of Tar-water only.

The famous Doctor *Barry* several Years ago, put me under a Course of Rhubarb and Sulphur, to which I regulary stuck for upwards of two Years; and other Physicians since put me under different Courses of Physick for my Rheumatick and other Disorders, but all to no manner of Purpose.

97. As to my Obſervations on others, a Gentlewoman in my Family, who had a paralytick Diſorder, and the Scurvy to a great Degree, with many Diſorders in her Stomach, for which ſhe ſtuck to the *Mallow* Waters for ſeveral Seaſons, and was only for the Preſent relieved thereby, and my Wife, who has been tormented with the Scurvy, Hiſtericks, *&c.* are both recovered, and very well by the Uſe of Tar-water.

98. One Mrs. *Buſtid*, who lives near *Killmallock*, having had a Heart-burn for ſome Years to ſuch a Degree, that in her Strainings, ſhe would frequently diſcharge Blood out of her Stomach; ſhe was ſubject to a racking Pain in her Bowels, had a Ganger in her Mouth, and her Teeth were all looſe; ſhe was given over by all the ſkilful Perſons in her Neighbourhood; but, hearing of the great Benefits I received by the Uſe of Tar-water, began to drink it, and ſoon found herſelf much better. Of which an Apothecary in *Killmallock* having had an Account, ſent her word, that ſhe was ill adviſed to take it that way, and ordered her by all Means to mix her Tar with hot Water, and then drink it; which ſhe accordingly did; but it operated ſo violently by purging up and down, that ſhe was at Death's Door; however, ſhe afterwards found, that taking it even that way, did her vaſt Service; ſhe is now perfectly recovered, and firmly reſolved never to take the Advice of an Apothecary again. I could mention ſeveral more, who, by my Advice, in various Diſorders, received very great Benefit, or were perfectly cured by drinking Tar-water; in ſhort, I make it my Buſineſs to recommend it to all my Acquaintance, and whatever your Diſorders are, you may ſafely take it; if you do, I don't at all doubt but you will ſoon join in the Praiſe of Tar-water, with, Sir,

Your moſt obedient humble Servant,

Corn. Townſend.

99. *An Extract of a Letter from a Physician, whose Name I am not at Liberty to mention; communicated to me in* November, 1744.

" A Man of about thirty-five Years of Age consulted me, who from a pleuritic Disorder imperfectly cured, fell into an hectic Fever, attended with a desperate Cough, with this dreadful Symptom, an Ulcer in the left Lobe of his Lungs; which plainly appeared, first from his being at first attacked by the Pleurisy in the left Side. Secondly, from almost an impossibility of lying on the right Side. Thirdly, from a vast Heaviness and suffocating Burthen he complained of in the left Part of his Thorax; till relieved in some Measure by throwing up a vast Quantity of fetid purulent Matter, intermixed with pure Blood, and (I may say) *sanguine spumoso*, so justly called by the great *Hippocrates*; which Excretion generally happened to him once a Month or thereabouts, and which, as he informed me, had always like to have suffocated him. This evacuated Pus must have been gathered in its proper Vesicula, which being external in the Lobe was usually broke by a strong Fit of Coughing, or some other violent Shock of Nature. Upon further Examination, I found he had cold nocturnal Sweats, and almost all the Signs of the *Facies Hippocratica*. You may easily judge, that the Prognostic I formed, was very doubtful, as his Case was both dangerous and difficult. However, I ordered him immediately to drink Tar-water, and, as the Indication required, I prescribed some balsamic and detergent Pills, besides some Stomachic Medicines, as he almost entirely lost his Appetite; I have also ordered him to take a Ride, Morning and Evening constantly. I can now with great Truth and Pleasure assure you, that he is quite recovered; which I must in Justice attribute to the Tar-water, as the last Medi-

 cines,

cines, though prescribed before Tar-water, had little or no Effect. I have tried this Medicine of Tar-water in two Cases of the asthmatic Kind, and in three acute ones, in all which it has had wonderful Success."

100. *An Extract of a Letter from* Henry Edgworth *of* Lizard *in the County of* Longford, *Esq;* *Member of Parliament, dated the* 10*th of* November, 1744.

"I shall soon be able to send you some very remarkable good Effects of Tar-water, which has been taken both by myself and two others of my particular Friends, and those of Judgment and good Sense, who have given this innocent, useful, and cheap Medicine, fair Play. I can't have their Leave to mention their Names; but as to myself, I must do it the Justice as to say, that few Men of my Age and temperate Way of Life, I believe, have been more afflicted with the Rheumatism; more especially in the Winter Season, and in changeable Weather; and after the Violence of the Fits abated, it frequently and almost these fourteen Years past, (about which Period of Time I was first attacked by that inveterate Enemy) left me in a worse Condition, even Pain cannot in my Apprehensions in any Sort be compared to the excessive Lowness and Dejection of Spirits, I laboured under for certain Times, more or less, till I took Tar-water; and though my Affairs would not permit me to have Recourse to it as regularly as I ought, yet even as I took it, it has pleased God, not only in a great Measure to mitigate the Violence of the Fits of the Rheumatism, but I have in no Sort had the least Return of any Dejection of Spirits this whole Winter. I am no Bigot of my Sort, I assure you; but I am fully persuaded this most excellent Remedy, if properly prepared and taken, would work more miraculous Cures, than

than ever were pretended to have been wrought at the Tomb of *Thomas a Becket*; and has more real Virtue in it, than the Touch or Blood of any of the Line of the *Stuarts* whatever; and this Account you may publish whenever you think fit, as Truth and Matter of Fact."

101. *A Letter from* Charles Tottenham *of* Tottenham-Green *in the County of* Wexford, *Esq*; *Member of Parliament*, November 18, 1744.

"For the good of the Publick, and in Honour of the Bishop of *Cloyne*, I inform you, that *William Cooper*, my Servant, on *Tuesday* the 9th of last *October*, fell ill of a violent Fever, Stitch and Pleurisy; on *Wednesday* and *Thursday* was bled, his Blood very bad each Time, on *Wednesday* Evening he began to drink warm Tar-water, and by *Thursday* at Noon, had drank above two Quarts; at which Time his Stitch and Fever left him; he sweated greatly; a blistering Plaister was sent for on *Thursday* Morning, which was brought to the Patient that Evening, but finding himself easy would not suffer it to be applyed; he continued free from Pain till *Saturday* Morning, at which Time his Stitch returned, his Lungs so greatly oppressed, that he could scarce breath, his Inside very sore, and his Head very painful. On *Saturday* Evening a blistering Plaister was put on between his Shoulders; he continued very ill till *Sunday* Evening, at which Time his Blister began to run, on which he had immediate Ease, and continuing to drink Tar-water, by Eleven o'Clock that Night his Head was free from Pain, his Stitch and Cough gone, slept well that Night, and on the 20th of the same Month, was as hearty and as heal as ever. Said *William Cooper* is between fifty and sixty Years old, has had a violent Cough and bad Lungs these thirty Years past, until now, not having any Cough, Pain withinſide, or Oppreſſion on his Lungs: This ſhould have been ſooner ſent, but that I thought it proper to wait, and know whether any of his old Diſorders returned; they did not, he never was better nor ſo full of Spirits.

P. S. It is to be obſerved that the Patient drank Tar-water the whole Time."

102. *A Letter from Mr.* George Johnſon, *a young Officer in the Army, to* Thomas Prior, *Eſq; dated the 25th of* November, 1744.

"I was great afflicted with the Bloody-flux from *February* 1742-3, to the Beginning of *May* 1744, the greateſt Part of which Time, I was ſo ill, that I was not expected to live, nor could I eat or drink any Thing that would ſtay upon my Stomach; nor had I any Eaſe during the whole Time, but when I uſed to ride, which I did three or four Weeks ſucceſſively, three or four Times during my Illneſs, on Buſineſs; a Week or ſix Days after which, I was tolerably eaſy, and could eat pretty hearty, after which, tho' I took ſeveral Things, and by the beſt Advice, I ſtill grew worſe. I was adviſed to take Tar-water, which I did once a Day for near a Week in the Beginning of *April*, 1744, but it would not ſtay on my Stomach, and made me ſick, ſo I left it off for about three Weeks; but continuing to grow worſe, I was adviſed to take it *May* following, which I did (I thank God) with Succeſs, for by taking regularly twice a Day, with a Doſe or two of Rhubarb during the Time, which was about three Weeks, (I thank God) I was perfectly well.

N. B. I ſeveral Times before took Rhubarb during my Illneſs in all Shapes, without any Benefit."

103. *An-*

103. *An Extract of a Letter from the Reverend Mr.* Thomas Collier *of* Aunfield *near* Ross *in the County of* Wexford, *to* Thomas Prior, *Esq*; *dated* January 24, 1744.

SIR,

I have had it often in my Thoughts to communicate to you a particular Account of the Case of the Woman mentioned in your Letter, and of some others, in regard to the Effects of Tar-water. The poor Woman had for three Years before she drank the Tar-water, been troubled every Summer with very ugly Blotches and Ulcers, especially on her Face; and as the poor People about me generally apply for some Cure or other for their Disorders, I advised her to a Course of Marsh, or wild Celery-Tea. This gave some Relief for the Present, but she grew worse in the main, that is, every Summer the Ulcers increased in Number and Size, so that I advised her to the Hospital in *Waterford*. Just as I had read *Siris*, she came to my Door, her Face swelled to a monstrous Size, hardly any Eyes to be seen, and in as loathsome a Way as ever I saw one in the worst and most dismal Stage of the Small-pox. She told me she was dying, and begged a little Charity from me: I had some Tar-water just made for myself, and I made her take along with her two Quarts, and desired her to drink them off, and come to me again; I did not see her for a Week, and then she told me, she had tried to take the Water, and it was so cold on her Stomach, that it almost killed her; that instead of comforting her, it threw her into a cold Sweat, all mortal Symptoms. I then advised her to go home and take it as warm as she could possibly bear it; she did so, and in a Week came to me for more Water. By that Time, the Swelling had much subsided, and she could see with both her Eyes. I then gave her a Gallon of Water

ter more, and in about a Month after ſhe came to me quite well, no Swelling in any Part of her Body, and only a Redneſs in her Face juſt as after the Small-pox. I forgot to mention, that, when ſhe firſt came to me, her whole Body was greatly ſwelled; ſhe continued well till laſt Summer, when ſhe had a ſmall Return of the Diſorder, which was cured the ſame Way, and is at this Time ſeemingly well. In this Caſe the Cure was prodigious, and what I eſteemed almoſt miraculous, becauſe I had known the Woman's Ailment a long Time before ſhe took the Tar-water, and as it was inveterate and of a long ſtanding, I thought it would take up a good deal of Time and Water, if ſhe could be cured at all. As far as I am able to judge, her Diſorder was a Scurvy occaſioned by poor Living in every Senſe, and this in its laſt Stage attended by a Dropſy. Her Name is *Catherine Dobbin*.

104. The next Caſe I tried was for a violent Pain in the Stomach, which had greatly troubled a young Gentlewoman of my Acquaintance for about a Twelve-month, and for removing which, ſhe had taken ſeveral Things, but to no Purpoſe; one Gallon of Water cured her, and ſhe has had no Complaint of the Kind theſe fourteen Months paſt.

105. A third Patient who received Benefit by drinking Tar-water, was an old labouring Man, who was ſo weakened by a long dry Cough, that when I ſaw him I took him to be on the extreme Verge of Life. He was ſo weak, that he was aſſiſted in coming a Quarter of a Mile to my Houſe, and was obliged to ſtop at every third or fourth Step: I gave this Man a Pitcher of Tar-water, and in about a Month he came to me to know if I had any Work for him, his Cough quite removed, and with a ruddy healthy Countenance; he has been ſince labouring conſtantly, and is in a better State of Health this Moment, than he was for any time

during three Years before he took the Water. His Name is *Edmund Dunfy*.

106. Within this Month paſt a very extraordinary Cure has been owing to Tar-water: A Servant-Maid in this Pariſh, was ſeized about a Month paſt with a violent Itching all over her Body, which in three or four Days broke out all over her in watery Puſtules, which as they broke, threw out a ſcalding ſharp corroding Liquor, which burnt the Skin wherever it touched it; ſo that the poor Creature was almoſt diſtracted: But prepoſſeſſed violently againſt Tar-water. At laſt, with great Perſuaſion, ſhe was prevailed on to take it, and by the time ſhe had finiſhed two Bottles the Puſtules diſappeared, and ſhe is now free from all the Symptoms, and in very good Health: The common People called it the St. *Anthony*'s Fire, but I can't pretend to ſay what the true Name of the Diſorder was. If any thing elſe remarkable ſhould occur, I ſhall make bold to let you know it, and am,

Sir, Your moſt obedient humble Servant,

Tho. Collier.

107. *A Letter from Col.* Nicholas Loftus, *of* Loftus-hall *in the County of* Wexford, *Eſq*; *Member of Parliament, to* Thomas Prior, *Eſq*; *dated* Feb. *the 1ſt*, 1744.

I have your Favour of the 29th of laſt Month: I have drank Tar-water theſe three Months paſt, half a Pint Morning and Evening, with great Succeſs: My Diſorder was ſevere Pains in all my Bones, and particularly in my Joints, which I believe were Rheumatick, and was very apprehenſive of a Return of the 'Sciatica, having had a ſevere Fit of it laſt Spring. I had a Stiffneſs in my Limbs, which made walking very uneaſy to me: Which Exerciſe I uſed a great deal of before. My Pains are now

all

all vaniſhed, and I can walk ſome Miles in a Morning as well as I ever did. Some in my Neighbourhood have taken it, for a Year paſt, in the Gout, and the Fits of it have been much lighter than they had been many Years before.

108. I have a Servant who had a very violent Aſthma, who I made drink it, and he hath been ſince ſurprizingly relieved: I am convinced that it is very good for many Diſorders; I have found it very diuretick. I am told, that you are about publiſhing ſomething about it, for the Good of the Publick: As you deſerve their Thanks in many Inſtances, pray accept of theſe, particularly from, Dear Sir,

Your moſt obedient humble Servant,

Nicholas Loftus.

109. *A Letter from* Peyton Fox, *Eſq*; *of* Weſtmeath, *to* Thomas Prior, *Eſq*; *dated* Feb. *the* 15th, 1744.

Dear SIR,

I had Yeſterday the Favour of your's of the 29th of laſt Month; and according to your Deſire acquaint you, that for theſe ſeveral Years paſt, I have been ſubject to great Colds; but laſt Winter I had ſuch a violent Cold and Cough, as confined me within Doors for five Months, and found not the leaſt Benefit from Remedies, of which I took a vaſt Quantity: But when I got the good Biſhop's *Siris*, I took the Tar-water, which perfectly recovered me, and do not find I am ſo apt to get cold as I was. My Stomach is not extraordinary good, but much better than it was. Within theſe three Months I got, by venturing too much in my Garden in cold Weather, two Colds; but the Tar-water, in a few Days, carried them off without ſevere coughing. Since I firſt took the Tar-water, I have not had the leaſt Touch of the Gout, and my Spirits are more lively: I look on my Cure to be the more extraordinary, conſidering my great Age, being ſeventy-four.

I hear

I hear of many who have received Benefit by the Tar-water, bu can't be particular: If I hear of any worth acquainting you with, I will; and assure yourself, I am,

Dear Sir, Your most humble Servant,

Pey. Fox.

110. *A Letter from the Rev. Mr.* Roger Lyndon, *of* Ballysax *in the County of* Kildare, March 26, 1744.

Dear SIR,

I had the Favour of your Letter by last Post, desiring I would inform you concerning my drinking Tar-water, and the good Effect it hath had on me.

Last Summer, and sometimes before, I found myself under several Disorders, a Gravel, Pains in my Back, confining me some short Times to my Bed; great want of Appetite, frequent Dizziness in my Head, unseasonable Sleepiness, Soreness in my Gums, and the loosening and falling of some of my Teeth, insomuch that I could scarcely chew my Meat; and by such great Uneasiness in my Mouth, I was often reduced to Broths, and other soft Aliments. All these Disorders, I was informed, proceeded from the Scurvy; and therefore I was resolved to try the Benefit of the so much talk'd of Tar-water. I began to drink it, pursuant to all the Rules, last *Michaelmas*; and have continued it to the middle of this Month, without Intermission: I was from the beginning very exact in keeping up to Discipline, and therefore soon found the Benefit; and, I bless God, have not, in the least Degree, felt any of the Disorders before-mention: I can walk great lengths; have a constant and good Appetite; can eat my Meat, with Teeth as well-fastened and easy in my Mouth, as I could for some Years past. This, Sir, is in Fact all I have to acquaint you with, the Arguings I leave to better Judgments; and if you think this Account may be of any Service to others, you

may

may (as you have desired) communicate it, in what manner you please, to so good an End. I am, Sir,

Your affectionate humble Servant,

Roger Lyndon.

111. *A Letter from* John Usher, *of* Lismore *in the County of* Waterford, *Esq; dated from* Lismore, Feb. *the* 4*th*, 1744, *to* Thomas Prior, *Esq;*

In Performance of my Promise, I send you the two following Cases, which happened lately, and may be relied upon. A Soldier in Capt. *Burston's* Company, in General *Frampton's* Regiment, whose Name I cannot learn, tho' he was some time in this Town, being afflicted with a spitting of Blood and purulent Matter, for a considerable Time (which Disorder was occasioned by a Peripneumony or Pleurisy, tho' he could not tell which, having had it before he came to Quarters to *Dungarvan*, about two Years ago) and having also a violent Cough and strong Night-sweats, Symptoms of a deep Decay, which quite emaciated him, Mr. *Charles Smith*, Apothecary in that Town, ordered him to drink Tar-water, which was made with Lime-water, instead of common Water, knowing Lime-water to be a great Dryer of Ulcers: He had not used it long, when he found his Cough and other Symptoms left him entirely, and in a short time he grew surprizing fat and healthy.

112. *Richard Kearney*, Servant to Mr. *Thomas Barbon* in *Dungarvan*, was for many Years afflicted with a Cough and Difficulty of Breathing, which arrived at length to a confirmed and violent Asthma, so that upon the least Pressure of the Atmosphere he was constantly visited with his Disorder, and disabled from rendering his Master any Service: About four Months since, by the Persuasion of his Master, he began to drink Tar-water; and had not used it above a Fortnight, when, to his Surprize, he found a great

a great Heat and Scalding in his Urine, and a *Gonorrhœa* of a most virulent Colour ensued, which so frighted him, that he left off drinking the Tar-water, attributing these Symptoms to the Use of it; but upon his Master's urging him to it, he again took to the Use of it, when, in about a Month, not only these Symptoms left him entirely, but in a great measure, his Cough and Asthma. He still uses the Tar-water, and is much recruited in both his Strength and Flesh, insomuch that last Week he walked up a steep Hill at the Back of the Castle here, nimbly and in a few Minutes, which, he assured me, before he took the Tar-water, he could not crawl up in an Hour. The above *Charles Smith* enquired of him, whether formerly he had not some venereal Taint, which he did not deny, and he attributes the above Symptoms to some Remains of that Distemper, which the Tar-water carried off; it wrought him and still doth much by Urine. These two shall suffice for this time; in my next you shall have more on the same Subject, from

Your most humble Servant,

John Usher.

113. The said Mr. *Usher* having also communicated the Effects and Virtues of Spruce-beer, which he justly reckons to be a Kind of Tar-water, both proceeding from the Juices of the Fir Kind: I shall beg Leave to insert in this Place, the Particulars thereof: He writes "That having an Estate on the Coast in the County of *Waterford*, from whence many of his Tenants go yearly to the Fishery of *Newfoundland*, he frequently observed, that such of them as went out meagre and pale, like Skeletons, and troubled with Itch and Scurvy, always returned fat, with ruddy Complexions and great Health, notwithstanding their great Fatigues there; and on Enquiry into the Cause thereof, he found that they all attributed their Recovery to their constantly drinking

ing of Spruce-beer while they are there; that as ſoon as they arrive there, they cut the Branches of the black Spruce Fir, which is the only Fir made uſe of there for Spruce-beer, and therewith make their Beer in the manner mentioned hereafter; and this Practice of making and drinking Spruce-beer, they continue during the Time they ſtay there, and in their Return, and bring great Quantities of the Branches with them to make Spruce-beer, after their Arrival, which they are very fond of; and notwithſtanding they live on ſalt Proviſions many Months, and have frequently thick Fogs on the Banks, yet they are no way troubled with Scurvy, Itch, or any Eruptions whatſoever, owing, as they ſay, to the conſtant drinking Spruce-beer. They ſay farther, that the People are very prolific, and that no Part of the World has ſo many Children as St. *John*'s in *Newfoundland*, conſidering the Number of the Inhabitants; probably this may be owing to the conſtant Uſe of Spruce-beer, or their living ſo much on Fiſh, or both."

114. *The Way of making Spruce-beer in* Newfoundland, *as communicated from the Fiſhermen to Mr.* Uſher.

Let ſixteen Gallons of Water be well boiled in a Pot, along with a good Quantity of the Branches of the Black Spruce Fir cut into ſhort Pieces, as much as will fill the Pot; it will take three or four Hours boiling, and the Method to know when it is boiled enough, is when the Bark of the Spruce ſlips readily off the Sticks between your Fingers. The Spruce is then taken out, and a Gallon of Molaſſes put to the Water, which is ſufficient to make a ſixty Gallon Caſk, and proportionably a greater Quantity of Molaſſes for a larger Caſk. The Water is then to be well ſtirred and well boiled once after the Molaſſes is put to it; it muſt then be put into a Caſk, which

is

is to be filled up with cold Water, and to be very well ſtirred with a Stick at the Bung, and, by the Help of the Grounds remaining in the Caſk from a former Brewing, will immediately ferment, and the next Day the Bung is to be cloſed up, and the Day following it will be fit for Uſe. But if you have no Grounds of a former Brewing, then put a ſmall Quantity of Barm to it, which will in one Night's Time ſufficiently ferment it; next Morning cloſe it up, and it will be fit for Uſe the Day following, and will hold good a Fortnight. But if you would make Spruce-beer to laſt ſeveral Months, then you muſt add a greater Quantity of Molaſſes two or three, or more Gallons, and more Spruce to give it a ſtronger Body.

115. *A Letter from* John Uſher *of* Liſmore, *in the County of* Waterford, *Eſq; dated* April *the 6th* 1745, *to* Thomas Prior, *Eſq;*

The conſtant Employment, I have here, has hindred me from collecting Caſes relating to Tar-water; however, you ſhall have ſome in a Poſt or two: My own is worth taking Notice of, and is as follows. I have been, for twelve or fourteen Years, troubled with a Diſorder in my Nerves; it came on gradually, but at laſt to ſuch a Pitch, that there was ſeldom a Night that I have not been obliged to get out of my Bed, and walk about the Room for ſome Minutes, before I could compoſe myſelf to Reſt; eſpecially on the leaſt Exceſs in Drinking, or the leaſt Cold. As I was ready to drop aſleep, my Mind uſed to be extremely agitated, in a manner not to be deſcribed: I uſed to feel at the ſame time a Thrilling down my Thighs, and a Deſire to ſtretch, as in an Ague-fit, which relieved me for that Moment: The Bed was then intolerable to me, nor could I find any Relief but by getting up and walking about tho' I have bore it with the utmoſt Pain for above an hour. I was at *Spa*, and took all the nervous medicines from divers Physicians to no Purpose. Doctor *Lacky*'s Advice concurred with my own Inclinations, to induce me to drink Tar-water; and I solemnly affirm, that in a Fortnight's drinking it, I never had a single return of it from that Day to this, which has made my Life comfortable, as I used before to dread the Approach of Night. This I the rather insist on, as I am very sure I never drank a drop of good Tar-water: For a Cask of Tar I had from *Cork*, I am now confident, had been all used before; and I am now, to my great Concern obliged to discontinue it for want of good Tar; for there is not a drop to be had in *Cork* that is good; and I have had Complaints from the good Bishop on that Head: However I have had no Return of my Disorder.

116. *P. S.* I am not at Liberty to mention the Names to you of two Women that have been cured of an inveterate *Fluor albus*, even by bad Tar-water, and in a short Time; in such Disorders Names are not to be mentioned, but I am thoroughly convinced of the facts, and have as much Evidence as the Nature of them will admit. I shall for the present conclude this long Letter with assuring you, that I am yours, &c.

117. *A Letter from Mr.* Lewis Lloyd *of* Kinsale, *dated* March *the 8th*, 1744. 10

A poor Labourer of this Town, rendered incapable to get his Bread, by a most violent Itch that siezed both Legs; after the Advice of Doctors, Surgeons and Apothecaries, and the last Expedient, Salivation, proved ineffectual, being advised to rub the Sores with Tar-water, was in three or four Days perfectly cured, to the great Surprize of those who had before administred to him.

118. *A Letter from the Revered Dean* Isaac Gervais *of* Lismore *in the County of* Waterford, *dated* May *the 8th*, 1745.

I have, for a considerable Time, been prevented by many incidental Avocations, from communicating a Case, as much to the Honour of Tar-water, as perhaps any yet publickly known, and the more so, in that it is the only Instance of that Nature I have heard of.

Being in *Waterford*, some time in *July* last, I advised a Sister of mine, now in Years, who had been long afflicted with an inveterate Rheumatism, to the Use of Tar-water, which she readily complied with; so that, having a Call there about seven Weeks since, I had the Pleasure of seeing her strong enough to meet me on the Stairs without Stick, without which, for a long time, she was not able to walk across her Room.

119. That is not all, but an usual Effect of it; for besides, she had, for near two Years before, been grievously tormented with a cruel and unquenchable Thirst, to which the other Disorder was nothing, in Comparison. It was become the Plague of her Life. She had by scrupulous Care, and Choice of Diet, the Advice of Neighbours and Acquaintance, and others, pretending to more Skill, done all that could possibly be devised to get the better of it; but all in vain, till, by the Blessing of GOD on the Use of Tar-water, her Thirst gradually lessened; so that at present, she is perfectly easy, and so effectually cured, as she seems almost to have lost her Appetite to Drink itself; though not yet quite relieved from the other Disorder, yet she bears it patiently, it being easy in Comparison of the Torment she has got rid of. I am yours,

If. Gervais.

June 18, 1745.

SIR,

In Compliance with your Request, I send you the following Account of certain Persons in my Neighbourhood, who have received Benefit by drinking Tar-water. Many others, about me, have taken it to good Effect; but I mention none but such whose Maladies and Cures fell within my own Knowledge. I am,

Sir, your very affectionate humble Servant,

Benj. Everard.

An Account of certain Persons, near Blessington *in the County of* Wicklow, *who have received Benefit by drinking Tar-water, to wit:*

120. *Catherine Cardy*, forty-one Years of Age, troubled with a Cough, Stuffing in her Chest, and Shortness of Breath, all the Winter of 1742, not free from these Complaints in the Summer of 1743, and feeling them all more severely in the following Winter; but in the Spring of 1744, affected with them all in the highest Degree, labouring under a Difficulty of Breathing, without Appetite, not being able to work or walk, or lie down at Night, getting little or no Sleep, her Body emaciated, her Breast, Neck and Face swelled; and her Lips black, and scarce able to speak. She began with Tar-water the 4th of *April* 1744, and thought herself recovered with drinking six Bottles; but finding a Streightness in her Breast, after leaving it off four Days, she took two Bottles more, and became quite well.

The first Morning after taking it, she spit a Quart of tough Phlegm and ropy Matter, after much Coughing. She coughed for ten Mornings after with less and less spitting: In this time her Complaints wore off; in three Days she could lye down in her Bed, and sleep all Night; her Stomach

mach came to her, and she recovered her Strength and Freedom of Breathing; so that, on the eighth Day, she walked a Mile up Hill, and back again, without being disordered, and towards the latter End of *May*, was able to bear the Fatigue of nursing a Foundling Child, left at her Door, and walked with it seven times in that Month, to and from *Blessington*, which is a Journey of more than three Miles. She passed the last Winter and Spring without any other Disorder than a Cough, at odd times, upon catching Cold; which was always removed by a Bottle or two of Tar-water.

121. *James Dooling*, Labourer, aged about thirty-five Years, taken with a Fever in the Spring of 1744. which increased with threatening Symptoms, particularly a Looseness, so that his Life was despaired of: On the 9th Day Tar-water was given him, and on the 13th the Fever turned; in a Week after he got out of Bed, and walked about his Cabbin; in about another Week he went abroad, and soon after fell to his Work, looking clear and ruddy, and of a healthful Countenance.

122. *Anne Osborn*, about fifty Years old, troubled with Stitches at times, for four or five Years, kept her Bed for three Months in the Winter of 1743, labouring under Stitches, a Cough, and Shortness of Breath, without Appetite or Sleep, and worn away to Skin and Bone, drank Tar-water, Night and Morning, the Beginning of *April* 1744, and with eight Bottles was perfectly recovered. At first, she threw up a great deal of foul Stuff from her Stomach: In three Takings her Stitches left her; she soon recovered her Appetite and Rest, and was able to lye down in Bed; her Cough ceased, she gained Flesh and Strength, and walked abroad in three Weeks Time.

123. *Eleanor Dowling*, aged about thirty-five Years, troubled with a hard dry Cough for ten

Years together, worn away by it greatly, and troubled with a Wheezing and Shortneſs of Breath, by drinking Tar-water in the Summer of 1744, all the above Complaints wore off equally to her Surprize and Joy; which ſhe expreſſed by ſaying; "That "if ſhe had twenty Cows, inſtead of two, ſhe "would have parted with them all, to have become "as well as a few Gallons of Tar-water had made "her."

124. *Joan Ardle*, a Gatherer of Ruſhes for Candles, ſtuffed up and choaked with a Cough, without Stomach or Sleep, and her Huſband affected much the ſame way, both cured by two Bottles of Tar-water: They are aged Perſons.

125. *Lawrence Kane*, Pedlar, about fifty Years old, laboured under an Ague, about *Holland-tide* 1743, which was followed by a ſevere Cough, that held him for ſix Months; he drank but two Bottles of Tar-water in *May* 1744, and found himſelf perfectly recovered.

126. *Bryan Mee*, troubled with a Pain in his Stomach, and Loſs of Appetite, cured with one Bottle of Tar-water.

127. Three Children, in one Family, between ſix and eight Years old, took the Small-pox in the Summer of 1744, and came very ſafe and well through the Diſtemper, without any other Preparation or Medicine than Tar-water, which they had drank conſtantly from *April* foregoing, and continued to drink it during the whole Time of their Illneſs, except about two Days, when the Pock in their Mouths and Throats became ſore, and broke, and ſmarted by the Tar-water; they have gone on drinking Tar-water ever ſince without any Reluctance to, or Miſchief from it; on the contrary, they fall a crying, if by any Accident, they do not get it at the uſual Times; and by the conſtant Uſe thereof, one of them hath been kept from the Re-

I turns

turns of a threatening Fever, to which he was subject, and had been seized by it three Times in the space of six Months. Another was troubled with Lumps under his Jaw, and other glandular Swellings, which have abated since his drinking Tar-water, and are now almost gone; and all the three since their drinking Tar-water, have better Stomach, and more Spirits and are much freer from Coughs and Colds than formerly.

128. *A Letter from a Gentleman of Character and Integrity, who desires his Name might not be mentioned, dated* June *the 18th,* 1745, *to* Thomas Prior, *Esq*;

What Mr. *Arthur Hill* told you, of the Benefit I have received by Tar-water, is so much Fact, that I now enjoy a very good State of Health, compared with what I had for several Years past, owing entirely, under GOD, to that easy, useful Medicine, as I have Reason to believe.

As you desire a particular Account of my Disorder and the Relief I have had from it, I think it is but imitating the Benevolence of the Author, to give you that as distinctly as I can, in hopes the same may prove useful to others in the like Circumstances.

129. You must know then, that about twenty-five Years ago, I had the first regular Fit of the Gout, which used to lay me up frequently after, in Autumn and Spring especially; but never affected me higher than my Feet or Ancles, until 1738, when I was seized with a most violent Fever, which occasioned my being severely blister'd on my Legs, which gave the Humours a Course that Way, and being mixed with gouty Matter, prevented the Sores, made by the Blisters, from healing, though all Care was taken by the Physicians for that End:

After I recovered from my Fever, it was thought that this prevented the regular Fits of the Gout, which I used to have, and made it fly about my Body and Head, from whence Indigestion, Lowness of Spirts and Sweatings followed; and at length I used to be frequently seized with a Giddiness or Swimming in my Head, especially after eating, which would continue until I had lighten'd my Stomach by puking: In hopes to get better Relief for these Disorders from the Physicians in Town, I went to *Dublin* in 1742, and by the Directions of two there, justly esteemed for their Knowledge, I went through a continued Course of gentle Physick, and was forbid every Thing of Nourishment, but light, white Meats, and a little Port Wine, until Summer 1743, when they ordered me a Course of *Spa* Water with Exercise. These Rules I observed pretty carefully, and found myself a good deal reliev'd from my Lowness of Spirits, and the Giddiness in my Head, until the Autumn following, when I had a severe Return of both, to which, I believe, my great Hurry and Fatigue contributed not a little. This put me under a Necessity of returning to my Course of Physick during the Winter 1743, and until *May* 1744, when I read the worthy Bishop's elaborate Treatise on Tar-water, of which (tho' in many Parts too refined for my Knowledge) I understood so much, as convinced me of its Usefulness, and the kind Design of the Author; whereupon I altered my Intention from *Spa*, to Tar-water, and drank about Half a Pint in the Morning, and as much in the Evening, with due Regard to the Rules prescribed, as to not eating before or after for two Hours; which produced a regular and pretty sharp Fit of the Gout in my Feet and Ancles, soon after I began the Course, and seem'd to warm me and increase my Sweatings. In about two Months after I had a Return of the Gout, but much gentler

gentler, and my Sweatings abated. Then I had a violent Itchiness over all my Body and Limbs, which was followed by Blotches and Eruptions on the Skin. In Autumn I got some Cold, and I believe had lived too freely for an Invalid, which was attended with a little of the Swimming in my Head, and Disorder in my Stomach; but I had so much Faith in Tar-water, that I made use of it air'd, instead of Sack-whey, or Tanzey and Sack, which I formerly used to take, with Intention to repel the Gout; and through this last severe Winter, I have continued in very good Spirits, freed from the Disorder of my Head and Stomach, tho' I have not confined myself to any regular Diet; and notwithstanding I am much thinner in Flesh, I find myself much stronger and abler to undergo Fatigue than at any Time since my Fever. The Benefit I have received, makes me recommend and prepare it for several of my poor Neighbours, who generally receive Benefit by it, if they will continue to use it.

130. A Collier, that was forced to quit his Labour by an asthmatic Disorder, is wonderfully recovered, tho' he used it but about a Fortnight.

131. And my Master *Salter* was often seized with a violent Palpitation in his Heart, and had taken several Medicines for it, but it was rather increasing; when he made use of Tar-water about three Weeks he recovered from a violent Fit, and was so well that he quitted the Water, and then had a Return; upon which he was again relieved by the same Means, which he now continues to use, and enjoys better Health than for some Years past.

132. We have many Instances in this Neighbourhood of Persons being relieved by Tar-water, under very different Disorders, tho' I am surprized they should, for if the common People do not immediately receive all the Relief they wish and promise to themselves upon once or twice drinking of it, like a

Charm,

Charm, they give it up, not confidering what the Bishop has so plainly urged; that in all chronical Cases it is an alterative, that requires Time to change the Mass of Blood. I find I am going out of my Depth, and I am sure I have trespassed too long upon your Time, if any Enthusiast in Praise of Tar-water can do so; therefore I will now release you with only this Observation, that if these Hints can afford you any Matter, to be reduced into more useful Form for the Benefit of others, I shall be highly pleased.

133. *The Case of Mr.* John Brooks *Engraver, living at the Sign of Sir* Isaac Newton's *Head, on* Cork-Hill, Dublin; *communicated by him to* Thomas Prior, *Esq; on the 22d of* June, 1745.

The said Mr. *Brooks* was, in *November* 1744, seized with Stitches, and a pleuritic Fever which continued eight or ten Days; he was blooded once and became better, but going abroad too soon, caught Cold and relapsed, and was much worse than before, being seized with more violent Stitches, Oppression on his Chest, Difficulty of Breathing, with most profuse Sweatings so as to wet his Bed-cloaths twice a Night, which so weakened him in some Time, that he was reduced to Skin and Bone, without any Appetite or Rest, so that it was thought he could not live an Hour, as he could hardly draw his Breath; he was advised to go out of Town to the Park, and drink Tar-water, which he did at the Rate of three Pints a Day, for ten Days, warm, going to Bed, and getting up, and cold at other Times, at eight different Times a Day; along with which he only took thin Gruel, or Chicken-broth; at the End of Ten Days as he was able to go abroad, mending every Day, the Tar-water having removed his Stitches, Sweatings, and made him breathe as free as ever. He was advised

vised to ride, which he did, and on the first Day of riding an Imposthume broke, which lay upon his Lungs; the first thing thrown up was a Bag which contained the impostumated Matter, which was followed by a great Discharge of corrupted Stuff mixed with Blood: He was immediately seized with a violent Spitting of Blood, which continued several Days, and was blooded, but still continued to drink the Tar-water as before, which he found to heal his Lungs, and stop his Spitting of Blood, and in a Fortnight's Time got into so good a State of Health as to be able to pursue his Business; he is now as well as ever he was, his Spirits and Appetite rather better than at any Time before, and he still continues to drink Half a Pint every Morning.

134. Mr. *Benjamin Prince*, of *Great-Britain-Street*, an Officer in the Excise, came to me, on the 7th of *August* 1745, out of a strong Sense of the Benefit he received by the Use of Tar-water, and communicated his Case, which I took from his own Mouth, as follows: He said, that for four Years he had been troubled with violent Pains in his Back and Kidneys, and frequent Colics; that he used to have two or three sharp Fits of the Gout every Year, and, after a Fever, had a fixed Pain in one of his Arms, so that he was not able to lift it up; he had lost his Appetite, Spirits, and Rest: But being advised to drink Tar-water to get him a Stomach, he began to drink it in *June* 1744, at the Rate of half a Pint every Morning, and no more. In a Fortnight's time the Pain in his Arm abated, and soon after went off; so that he got the full Use of it; in less than a Month's drinking he voided by Urine, a great deal of slimy Matter, and in two or three Months, after frequent Stoppages of Urine, he had great Pains in his Reins, and at last discharged a Stone as large as an Olive-stone, which was

nine

nine Days passing; after which he voided, from time to time, twenty-five Gravel-stones, of different Sizes, nine at once, and frequently discharges small Gravel or Sand all jagged and pointed, which seem to be broken off from a larger Body of Stone: He is now at ease as to his Gravel, and but seldom troubled with Colics, and what Pain he has that way, he imputes to the Remainder of the Gravel not yet discharged; he had no Apprehension or Suspicion, before he drank Tar-water, and discharged Gravel, that his Pains arose from the Stone or Gravel; he thought his Disorder was nothing but a Colic, for which he took many things to no Purpose. He also says, that he has not had the least Fit or Symptom of the Gout since he drank Tar-water, which is near fifteen Months ago; and he never fails to drink it constantly every Day, finding that he has thereby got a good Stomach, high Spirits, and good Sleep, and imputes all his Relief to Tar-water only.

August the 15th 1745.

135. This Day Mr. *John Powell*, living at the Glass-ware-house in *Crow-street*, Merchant, was pleased to come to me, and gave the following Account of his Case and Relief, which I took down in Writing, from his own Mouth, as follows: Mr. *Powell* had the Gout for near twenty Years, off and on, but in the Winter 1743, he had a violent Fit which lasted twelve Weeks. He was also troubled with violent Pains in his Bowels, for two Years before that time, which he thought was a Colic, had no Appetite, a bad Digestion, and little Sleep; He had those Fits of the Colic twice or thrice a Week, each Fit lasting twenty-four Hours, with racking Pains, so that it was thought that his Life was in great Danger. In the beginning of the Year 1744,

on

on reading the Treatise on Tar-water, he was advised by his Physician to drink the Water, which he did regularly for six Weeks at the Rate of a Pint a Day, taken in the Morning and Evening; and in three Weeks time his Pains began to abate, and in six Weeks all his Colic Pains went off, and he has not had the least Fit ever since: He seldom fails to drink the Water every Morning, and resolves to continue the constant Use of it, having got a very good Stomach and Digestion, and sleeps very well; nor has he had the least Fit of the Gout ever since he began to drink Tar-water, being perfectly free from all Symptoms of it; he has the full Use of his Limbs, and walks as well as ever he did, and he imputes all his Cures to Tar-water only.

136. *James Brown*, about ten Years old, to whom the late Earl of *Kildare* left an Annuity of twenty Pounds a Year, for his Father's long and faithful Services under him, was miserably afflicted with the King's Evil for four Years, and being long under the Care of Surgeons in *Dublin*, was sent in *August* 1744, to his Relations in the County of *Cork* to take care of him, as there were no Hopes of his Recovery in *Dublin*. When he came there, he had many running Sores in his Arms, Hands and Feet, and Swellings on each side of his Throat without Appetite or Digestion. In this Condition he was immediately put into a Course of Tar-water; he drank about a Quart a Day, a Naggin at a time, and after some Days drinking the Water, they washed his Sores with strong Tar-water, and for a Plaister used the Oil of Tar, which was skimmed off the Water, spread on Lint or Linen: The Effect was, that in a Fortnight's Time most of his Sores were healed up, and Swellings gone, and in less than six Weeks Time he was perfectly recovered, and now continues very well, with good Appetite and Spirits. This Account the Author had from the

young

young Man himself, and from his Relations; and though he is very well, yet he continues to drink Tar-water, by which he received so much Benefit, but in smaller Quantities.

137. *Another Instance of the Efficacy of Tar-water in the Cure of the King's Evil, is as follows.*

Michael Carney of *Protestant Row* in *Cavan-street*, about sixteen Years old, was troubled with the King's Evil six Years, having running Sores in his Arms, Neck, Legs and Body, and had been in *Mercer's* Hospital a Year without Benefit, and had almost lost one of his Eyes by the Evil; the Author being informed that this Boy was in Danger of having his Eye rotted out of his Head by the Evil, directed the Wrist Plaister to be applied to him, which was attended with such Success, that in a Fortnight's Time, in the latter End of the Year 1743, the Evil was quite driven from his Eye; but the Boy continuing full of running Sores, and great Pain in one of his Arms, of which he had little Use, in *April* 1744, I gave him Tar-water to drink, a Pint a Day; in a little Time he discharged two Splinters of Bone, black and carious, from his Arm, whereby he had immediate Ease there, and continuing to drink Tar-water, and washing his Sores with it also, in two Months Time all his Sores healed up, his Appetite and Strength returned, and he was perfectly recovered, and continues very well, and now lives with Mr. *Barry Colles*, Attorney, at *Stephen's Green.* These Instances, and many more come to my Knowledge, convince me, that the King's Evil, hitherto reckoned incurable, may, in a short Time, by the Method before mentioned, be perfectly cured.

The

The Rev. Dean Madden, *of* Molesworth-street, Dublin, *was pleased to give me, in* July 1745, *the following Instances of Cures by Tar-water, which came to his Knowledge.*

138. The Rev. Mr. *George Philips*, of *Anne-street, Dublin*, was seized last Summer with a violent Pleuritick Stitch: He was then in the Country, three Miles from *Dublin*. He sent for a Surgeon to bleed him; as he was long a coming, his Pain increased. He drank freely of Tar-water warm, and in a few Hours his Pain so far abated and the Height of his Pulse lessened, that when the Surgeon came, it was resolved not to bleed him. He continued to drink Tar-water; the Disorder abated, and in a few Days went entirely off.

139. *John Waller*, of the Parish of St. *Anne, Dublin*, aged sixty seven Years, had in Spring 1745, a violent Cough, and a general Failure of Nature. He was reduce so low, that all who saw him gave him over. He was persuaded to drink Tar-water in his extream low Condition, and in five Weeks, he was able to go about his Business, and continues hearty and well.

140. Mrs. *Stear* of *Ginnets* in the County of *Meath* near *Trim*, had the worst Symptoms of the most violent Scurvy, her Hands and Arms black in some Parts, so that a Mortification was sometime apprehended. She drank Tar-water for several Months; it struck the most virulent Humour out on her Face and Arms, so that no one could know her: She was not discouraged, but continued to drink Tar-water, and in a few Months her Skin was intirely clean. Before she drank Tar-water, she was often sick and low spirited; while she drank it, she was hearty and well every way, and has continued well many Months.

141. Mrs.

141. Mrs. *Woodrof*, who lives near *Cork*, was troubled with a Rheumatiſm in her Head, Dropſy in her Legs, and an Aſthma, from which ſhe was relieved in two Months Time by drinking Tar-water. Her Son Mr. *Woodrof*, a Clergyman who gave this Account, ſays, that above two Years are paſſed ſince ſhe was relieved.

142. The Reverend Mr. *Thomas Goodwin*, of *Dawſon-ſtreet*, *Dublin*, was relieved of a Megrim and a Sleepineſs by the Uſe of Tar-water, and continues well, *June* 29, 1745.

143. Mr. *Palma* the Muſician, was troubled with a Rheumatiſm, his Limbs ſo ſwollen, that he could not walk, but was cured in a Month's Time by drinking Tar-water, and continues well.

144. The Reverend Mr. *Edmond White* of the County of *Wexford*, was in like manner relieved of violent Pains in his Limbs, and a Colic of a long ſtanding.

145. Mr. *Jones* of *Grafton-ſtreet*, between ſixty and ſeventy Years old, had for ſeveral Years a violent Aſthma, attended with a great Cough and frequent ſpitting of Blood and Corruption in great Quantities, finds himſelf greatly relieved in every Reſpect, by the Uſe of Tar-water; and he neither ſpit Corruption, nor Blood laſt Winter.

146. Mr. *Wollaſton* of *Trim*, Clerk to Mr. Juſtice *York*, was aſthmatic for a long Time, and not able to live in *Dublin*, was relieved by Tar-water in ſix Weeks Time, and is an altered Man, and continues well, *June* 20, 1745. Thus far Dean *Madden*.

147. Mrs. *Ann Fitzgerald*, Wife of Mr. *Will. Fitzgerald* of *Ballyrone* in the *Queen*'s County, was for ſeven Years afflicted with violent Hyſtericks, Pain and Wind in her Bowels, which threw her frequently into ſuch Diſtractions as deprived her of the Uſe of her Underſtanding, ſo that ſhe was utterly

unca-

uncapable of minding the Affairs of her Family, and a Servant was conſtantly employed to take care of her, and ſometimes to prevent her laying violent Hands on herſelf. Many Phyſicians in *Dublin* and the Country, had her under their Care, and preſcribed many Medicines, which had no Effect; at laſt ſhe was prevailed upon to drink Tar-water, and in a few Days, found ſome Benefit, and by continuing to drink it for a conſiderable Time, ſhe is now perfectly recovered, and free from all her Ailments; and the only Inconvenience ſhe had from Tar-water is, that as it gave her a good Appetite, ſhe is grown much fatter and more corpulent than ſhe was before, or deſires, and ſhe ſtill continues to drink the Water in ſmall Quantities by way of Prevention. This Account I had from herſelf and her Husband.

148. The ſaid Mrs. *Fitzgerald* alſo informed me, that ſome Years ago, one of her Sons was grievouſly troubled with a running Sore in one of his Arms, that the Humour which iſſued out was ſo corroſive, that it eat into the Fleſh, and ſpread all over his Arm, notwithſtanding all the Pains taken, and Plaiſters applied to ſtop the Progreſs of it, whether it was a Tettar or Cancer, or what elſe ſhe could not tell; ſhe then recollected what ſhe had formerly been told, that a Plaiſter of Tar had been uſed with Succeſs on ſuch Occaſions; accordingly, ſhe put ſome Tar into a Pot over the Fire, and added ſome Mutton Suet to it, and having gently boiled and mixed them well together, ſhe made a Plaiſter and ſpread it thin on Linen, and applied it to the running Sore as hot as the Child could bear; the Effect was, that in ten Day's Time, all the Sores were healed up, and the Arm entirely cured, and continued ſo ever after.

149. *A Letter from the Reverend Mr.* Robert Brereton, *of* Burton *in the County of* Cork, *dated* November 9, 1745.

I here ſend you an Account of the Benefit received by me from drinking Tar-water.

I had been greatly afflicted with a Jaundice for two or three Years, which returned on me ſeveral Times in that Period, and was always attended with exceeding lowneſs and dejection of Spirits. I was adviſed by my Phyſicians to enter on a Courſe of Steel Preparations; but unwilling to undergo a tedious Courſe of Phyſick, I had Recourſe to Tar-water, from which in five or ſix Weeks I found great Relief, and at length a perfect State of Health, and good Spirits, which I now enjoy.

150. I am farther to inform you that Mr. *Ralph Crofts* of *Liſcarrol* in the County of *Cork*, my Neighbour, above ſeventy Years old, was greatly emaciated, and worn out with lowneſs of Spirits and want of Appetite, and, did not expect to live out the Winter 1744. He was adviſed to drink Tar-water, from which in leſs than a Month, he was much better, and in two or three Months perfectly recovered to as good a State of Health and Spirits as he had in any Part of his Life.

I am, Sir, your moſt humble Servant,
Robert Brereton.

151. Mr. *Jocelyne Daviſon*, of the Town of *Carlow*, came to me on the 19th of *November* 1745, and gave me the following Account of his Diſorder and Relief, which I took down in writing from his own Mouth, and is as follows:

In Winter 1744, he got a great Cold, which cauſed a violent Cough, and an Inflammation in his Lungs, attended with very great Spitting and Diſcharges; he continued in this miserable State for near four Months, without receiving any Benefit by the Medicines he took, so that it was thought he could not live; his Father advised him to drink Tar-water, which he neglected to do for some Time, but finding his Disorder increase, he took to Tar-water, and drank about half a Pint warm every Day in the Morning as soon as he got up, and in six Days Time, he found himself much easier; he then observed, that the Tar-water had thrown out a great Rash, like an Itch or Scurf on the Surface of his Body, which alarmed him at first, and inclined him to lay aside the Water, but finding himself still better, and that the Venom of the Distemper was cast off that Way, he continued the Use of it, and in six Weeks perfectly recovered from all his Ailments, and now continues very well.

152. He also informed me, that Mr. *David Simms* the Presbyterian Minister at *Carlow*, was long troubled with an Asthma and Difficulty of breathing and speaking, so that it was thought by all who saw him that he could not live long; but by drinking Tar-water a considerable Time, he is quite recovered from all those Disorders, and as well as can be expected of one of his Age.

The Reverend Doctor *Bacon* of *Lemavaddy* in the County of *Derry*, communicated to me in *November* 1745, the three following Cases:

153. *James Crowders*, Postillion to Colonel *Forward* of the County of *Donnegal*, Member of Parliament, was seized with a violent asthmatick Cough, swelled all over his Body, and no Appetite, so that it was thought it was impossible he could live: He drank Tar-water about a Month, Morning and Evening, a large Glass, which purged him violently, and perfectly cured him: This happened about a

Year and half ago, and he continues perfectly well ever ſince. This was confirmed to me by Mr. *Forward* himſelf.

154. Mrs. *Ann G——e*, a Widow Lady of the County of *Derry*, had been troubled with an aſthmatick Diſorder for about ſeven Years; her Caſe was, that ſhe breathed freely in a ſmoaky or foggy Air, but was ready to expire in thin ſharp Air. After trying many Medicines, and eſpecially Goat-whey in vain, ſhe drank Tar-water, of which ſhe took only a Wine Glaſs full at Night, when a-bed, and in the Morning before ſhe got up, (for it made her very ſick, when ſhe took it in the Day, and was obliged to go to Bed immediately.) The Effect was, that ſhe grew better upon her taking the Tar-water, and was quite cured upon drinking it three Months; ſhe has continued well ever ſince, which is ſix Months, and has begun to drink a little lately, by way of Precaution.

155. The Reverend Mr. *S——t* of the Dioceſe of *Derry*, was troubled with an Aſthma of the oppoſite Kind, could not live in foggy Air, and was obliged to remove from his own Houſe, which was in a low Situation, to a Friend's Houſe, ſituated upon a Hill, where he found himſelf better; at length he drank Tar-water, which recovered him ſo much that he returned to his Dwelling quite well, and has continued ſo for a Twelve-month paſt.

156. Mr. *Cunningham*, Collector of *Portpatrick* in *Scotland*, arrived in *Dublin* in *June* 1744, and then declared to me and ſeveral others his Caſe and Relief, which I had from his own Mouth, and is as follows. He had been troubled with the Gout for many Years, but the laſt two Years he was ſo miſerably afflicted with it, that he was confined to his Bed and Chamber for many Months, not being able to go abroad or walk at home, having ſuch a Stiffneſs

Stiffneſs in his Knees after the Fits were over, that he had not the Uſe of his Limbs; but in *May* 1743, he was adviſed by Mr. *Makenny* a Surgeon, to drink Tar-water, which he did for four or five Months, the firſt Effect was, that in a little Time he was freed from a Difficulty of breathing he laboured under, and finding his Limbs grew eaſier and ſtronger by Degrees, he drank the Water till Winter following, by means whereof he recovered the Strength of his Limbs ſo much, that in the Spring following he had the full Uſe of them. Whereas for ſeveral Years before, he never failed to have a Fit in the Beginning of Winter, and another in Spring; ſince that Time he has had no Symptom of the Gout; and he told me that he could then mount the higheſt Horſe in *Ireland* with Eaſe, and could walk as well as ever he did, and was reſolved to drink Tar-water three Months in every Year of his Life.

157. Mr. *John Milton*, Confectioner in *Caple-ſtreet*, *Dublin*, gave me in *November* 1745, the following Account of the Benefit he received by Tar-water. He was afflicted with the Gout ever ſince he was ſixteen Years old, frequently attended with very violent Pains, ſometimes he was laid up three or four times in a Year, and laſt Spring was laid up for eight Weeks; and it left ſuch a Weakneſs after it, that he was hardly able to crawl for a long Time, till he had recourſe to Tar-water, to which he was adviſed by one who received Benefit by it. He began to drink it in *July* 1745, and continued the Uſe of it to the middle of *November* following, taking a Pint each Day, half a Pint in the Morning, and the ſame at Night; which has fully reſtored him to the Uſe and Strength of his Limbs, and removed all his other Complaints: He has got a good Appetite and Digeſtion, which he had not for many Years before, and tho' he uſed to be

laid up at this Seaſon of the Year, yet he has not the leaſt Symptom of the Gout, and is as ſtrong, and can walk as well as ever he did. He had alſo great Pains and Swellings in his Bowels, and Hardneſs in his Belly, which were quite carried off in a Week or ten Days Time by drinking Tar-water only.

158. Mr. *Cavanaugh*, Hatter, at the Raven in *Skinner-row*, *Dublin*, was long afflicted with Rheumatick Pain, great Swellings and Stiffneſs in his Loyns, Thighs and Knees, inſomuch that he could not walk abroad, or ſtir at home without Difficulty and Pain; to remove which Ailments, he tryed every Thing that was preſcribed by Phyſicians and Surgeons, but to no Effect. In the Summer 1744, when Tar-water began to be in Vogue, he drank near a Pint a Day for ſix Week, without any ſenſible Benefit as to the Weakneſs and Pains in his Limbs, but got much better Appetite and Spirits. However he ſtill perſiſted in drinking the Water, and in three Months Time he found his Swellings abate, his Limbs grew ſtronger every Day, and in a few Months after all the Swellings, Stiffneſs, Hardneſs and Pains in his Limbs went off, and he recovered the Uſe of them; and continuing ſtill to drink Tar-water, he can walk without Difficulty or Pain, and is in great Spirits. This Account I had from himſelf in *July* 1745, and now in *December* 1745, he continues perfectly well.

159. Mrs. *Duggan*, Midwife, living at the Cradle in *Great-Britain-ſtreet*, *Dublin*, gave me the following Account of her Caſe, That ſhe had been long troubled with a violent inveterate Scurvy, attended with a great Oppreſſion in her Cheſt and Heart, and Difficulty of breathing, that ſhe had loſt all Appetite, and was in a miſerable Way, that ſhe took many Things for her Relief to no manner of Advantage, that at laſt ſhe had Recourſe to Tar-

water,

water, which he took at the Rate of half a Pint a Day every Morning, and before ſhe drank three Gallons, all the ſcorbutic Heat and groſs Humours were driven out on the Surface of her Body, and continuing ſtill to drink it, all the aforeſaid Symptoms went off, ſhe breaths freely without the leaſt Oppreſſion, recovered her Appetite, and ſhe never knew herſelf in better Health or Spirits, and reſolves never to be without Tar-water, finding it always relieves her when ſhe catches Cold, or is out of Order.

160. *A Letter from Mr.* James Hanning, *of* Cloyne *in the County of* Cork, *to* Thomas Prior, *Eſq*;

My Daughter, *Mary Hanning*, about eleven Years old, was laſt *May* taken ill of a Fever, after which, ſhe came by Degrees to be entirely deprived of the Uſe of her Tongue and Limbs, being unable to ſpeak, ſtand, or put her Hand to her Mouth, and all her Joints ſhaking with the Palſy. She took Medicines preſcribed by a Phyſician, and was often exerciſed in open Air, while the Weather permitted, but all to no Purpoſe. Whereupon we put her into a Courſe of Tar-water about the beginning of *November* laſt, and ſhe has ever ſince drank a Quart a Day, which in five Weeks has ſo far recovered her, that ſhe can ſpeak and read plain, feed herſelf, ſtand and walk without Help, and even go up and down Stairs, to the Amazement of all thoſe, who had ſeen her lately carried about dumb and helpleſs like an Infant. She has taken no other Medicine ſince ſhe began to drink Tar-water, nor had ſhe the Benefit of Air and Exerciſe from that Time, the Weather not permitting. One of her Arms continues ſomewhat weak, and ſhe has a Weakneſs too in one of her Legs, but as ſhe daily grows better, I hope Tar-water, with GOD's

Bleſſing, will perfect her Cure. *December* 17, 1745.

James Hanning.

161. *A Letter from a Gentleman of Character and Credit, giving a particular Detail of an extraordinary Fever cured by Tar-water, dated* December 20, 1745.

A Youth about fifteen Years of Age, being ſeized with a Fever in *April* 1745, an old *French* Woman of the Family, who was appointed to attend him, with Directions to give him Tar-water (the only Medicine preſcribed) about a Pint every Hour, gave him a much ſmaller Quantity, and indulging his Appetite, fed him ſecretly, five Days together, with Roaſt-Beef, ſeaſoned Pye, Cheeſe, Ale, and ſuch like Diet inſtead of Water-gruel, which alone had been ordered.

162. This unnatural Diet terribly inflamed his Fever, and produced ſuch an intire Proſtration of Appetite, that for thirteen Days together, he took no Nouriſhment of any Kind but Tar-water, whereof he drank about a Gallon every Day, which made him ſleep at Night and kept up his Spirits by Day in a ſurprizing Manner. Having ſo long faſted, he at length took a little *Naples*-Biſcuit, with two or three Spoonfuls of Sack and Water, which increaſed his Fever and diſordered his Head, but he was ſoon quieted by Tar-water. While he regularly took this wholeſome Draught he ſlept ſound every Night. But one Day being diſguſted at the Tar-water, it was judged proper to change it for Sage and Baulm Tea, which he drank plentifully though not with equal Succeſs. For his Spirits ſunk, he loſt his Colour and Look, he paſſed the Night reſtleſs and anxious: All which Symptoms were removed next Day by Tar-water.

163. After this, his Diſtemper took ſeveral ſtrange and violent Turns, being ſometimes attended with the

the worst Symptoms. He was at Times speechless convulsed, dilirious, and his Blisters would not rise. In the Dilirium Tar-water could not be given; he was then blistered, and the Blisters not rising, he was brought with some Difficulty to drink his Tar-water again, which had a speedy good Effect, when nothing else gave him Relief. And in general, it was observed, that upon neglecting to give him Tar-water, the feverish Symptoms of Heat, Anxiety and difficult Respiration became very troublesome, being constantly heightened by omitting, and as constantly allayed by returning to drink it.

164. It were tedious to relate all the surprizing Changes in the Course of this Illness, which lasted ten Weeks. Probably such a Case was never known before, as it is probable, that no Fever ever happened to be inflamed and heightened by the same Cause. For I believe no Patient was ever known to have been dieted in the first Days of a Fever on such extraordinary Food, which Nature is accustomed to loath at those Seasons. But Tar-water gives an Appetite even in Fevers.

165. Tar-water, during its long and obstinate Conflict with the Venom of the Disease, operated in divers Manners, as a cardiac, diaphoretic, sudorific, emetic, carminative and paregoric, seeming to adapt itself to the several Symptoms and Stages of his Malady, and for the most Part gave him a great Flow of Spirits, a florid lively Look, a clean well-coloured Tongue, with such Vigour in his Voice and Eyes, as astonished all who saw him, and knew how long he had been ill, and how little Nourishment he had taken. It is to be observed, that on some Days he drank greedily, even so far as ten or twelve Quarts of Tar-water, calling for it with great Impatience, even though it wrought him as an Emetic; whereas both before and after his Illness, he shewed the greatest dislike and loathing of it.

166. In

166. In the laſt Stage of the Fever, his Face and Body ſwelled, and a general Eruption appeared all over both, ſomewhat like an Eriſipelas or cohæring Small-pox, which laſted a Week. For two or three Days of this Period he drank ſparingly of Tar-water, perhaps not more than a Quart a Day; but during all that Time he conſtantly, by his own Choice, held his Mouth to the Spout of a Tea-pot, half filled with hot Tar-water, ſucking the Vapour, which, he ſaid, he found very chearing and comfortable.

167. At the Cloſe of this tenth Week, he fell into a moſt copious Sweat and the next Day his Puſtules were quite gone, and his Fever left him, not ſpiritleſs, puny and pale, but as lively and hail, in appearance, as ever he had been known, though after an Illneſs, that for Length of Time, and Variety of deſperate Symptoms, ſurpaſſed any I remember to have heard of, or met with in the Hiſtory of Fevers.

168. But he did not continue in this healthy State; for the very ſame Day, he expreſſed ſuch an earneſt longing Deſire to change his Bed and ſhift his Linnen, that it was thought proper to indulge him, and although this Step was made with the utmoſt Caution, yet it gave him a freſh Cold, which ſeized upon his Head, and produced a new Fever with a Raving or Frenzy, that continued many Weeks, in all which time, he could not be prevailed on to take one Glaſs of Tar-water. But at length by a proper Uſe of Aſſes-milk, and Ground-ivy, with a careful Regimen, he was recovered ſo far, as that he might be perſuaded to drink daily four Glaſſes of Tar-water, which, with GOD's Bleſſing, reſtored his Strength and completed his Recovery.

I have here given the general Sum and Subſtance rather than a regular and complete Diary, containing all the particular Circumſtances of this extraordinary Caſe, which it had been impoſſible to recollect at the Diſtance of ſo many Months.

169. *An Extract of a Letter from the Honourable Colonel* John Custis, *of* Williamsburgh *in* Virginia, *and one of the Council of that Province. Dated from* Williamsburgh, July 10, 1745.

Mr. *Custis* writes, that he unfortunately got a great Cold, which threw him into the Chin or Hooping Cough, which caused cruel Fevers; that when the Cough was gone, he was troubled with a prodigious Spitting; that he took great Doses of Elixir Vitriol to allay his intense Thirst in his burning Fever, which so relaxed his salival Glands, that he feared they would never come to their due Tone again, nor perform their proper Offices; they are the Sluices that cast off the vitiated Lympha: That he had studied and read Physic more than forty Years; that he had the Opinion of Doctor *Brown*, of *Maryland*, deemed the greatest Physician in *America*, that the Seat of this Distemper lay in his salivary Glands, and that it was dangerous to stop the Spitting, which he well knew by woful Experience, having stopt it by taking an Ounce of Diacodium going to Bed, which flung him into Fevers, Faintings, and many other Disorders, so that he was obliged to procure the Spitting again; he was once so reduced, that he could not get up when down, nor was able to put on his Cloaths, and had no Appetite to any Sort of Food. But, to use his own Words, he writes, that reading one Day in the *Magazine*, I found the Virtues of Tar-water, which I verily believe saved my Life; I had not taken it a Week, before I began to have an Appetite to Victuals, and continued taking it three Months, Night and Morning, which miraculously restored me, so that I can now eat heartily any Thing my Palate has a Mind to, tho' I cannot taste any Thing, but what is salt, sweet or sour, and I bless God, I am much mended. But my Spitting continues with a great Discharge, but eating supports that

that Discharge, and I resolve to take nothing that may lessen my Stomach, the Saliva not performing its due Office, keeps my Palate and Throat always hot and dry, tho' I have not any Fever, which the Doctors tell me I must bear; but I hope Time and Tar-water will entirely free me from that Uneasiness.

This Letter was sent from *Virginia*, to Mr. *Peter Collinson* of *Grace-church-street*, *London*, who was pleased to transmit the same hither, giving this Reason for doing so, That he was persuaded, that the reading some Parts of this Letter would not be disagreeable to the good Bishop to find that his laudable Endeavours to benefit Mankind, are attended with such great Success, and perhaps not more remarkably so, than in the uncommon Case of the said Colonel *Custis*.

170. The Reverend Mr. *Sion Hill*, Chaplain to the Work-house in *Dublin*, having had great Opportunities of trying and knowing the Effects of Tar-water, both in the said House, and all over the City, where he had dispersed above a thousand Gallons of the Water to those who had occasion to call upon him for it, and having set down in writing the Particulars thereof, as the Facts came to his Knowledge he has been pleased to communicate the same to me in the following Narrative, entitled,

A short Account of some remarkable Cases, with their Success, by GOD's *Blessing, on Tar-water.*

171. In *April* 1744, after reading the Treatise on Tar-water, Curiosity as well as Humanity, prompted me to make tryal of the Effects of the Water, and if I should find it answer the Character given of it in *Siris*, to make use of it on several Occasions that offered; having it greatly in my Power, as Chaplain to the Work-house, to make Experiments on a great many Subjects, who, since I came there, were long troubled

troubled with cutaneous, ſcrophulous, and chronical Diſorders.

172. For this End, I picked out of the many in the Work-houſe, four of the moſt afflicted, to whom, for four Days, I adminiſtred Tar-water: And indeed the Succeſs ſo ſurprized me, that being at that Time, ſeverely attacked with an Hoarſeneſs, and ſore Throat, I ventured to take it alſo; and with ſome Pain (my Throat being inflamed) I got down about the Quantity of a Naggin; after which, I felt no Pain in that Part, but could ſwallow without the leaſt Difficulty. From this welcome and aſtoniſhing Experiment, I naturally conceived future joyful Hopes of this powerful Medicine; accordingly, I took it for three Days after, twice each Day with Pleaſure; which ſo wrought me the third Day, I was not able to ſit, by Reaſon of the Acrimony of the Diſcharge. Notwithſtanding, I ſtuck to my Medicine, and the fourth Day, I perceived myſelf much better without any Manner of Complaint; and, I thank GOD, have continued ſo ever ſince; whereas, before I took Tar-water, I was ſubject to a Head-ach, Cramps, Pains in ſeveral Parts, more eſpecially in the Kidneys, very acute from any Wheel-carriage; I was tormented alſo with an Heart-burning, all which Diſorders, I now aſſure you are perfectly vaniſhed, and I am reſtored, bleſſed be GOD, as it were, to a new Life, having a keen Appetite, good Digeſtion, Spirits ſufficient to bear me through all Fatigues, with ſound and eaſy Sleep, tho' now on the Borders of Sixty.

173. The great Benefit I received from Tar-water, induced me for the general Good, to make it for other poor People; who had it ſince laſt *April* 1744, and ſhall always have it Gratis, while I make it, to whom I have diſtributed, with others, above a thouſand Gallons, without any Complaint yet, but with great Acknowledgments, as by the Sequel will appear.

appear. Having dispatched my own Case, I beg Leave to lay before you those others, with their Success, which I durst not do till *October* was past, because some predicted frightful Consequences at that Time to all such, who ventured on this Medicine. But now *May* 1745 being past, and still no bad Symptoms appearing on those Adventures, I look now on this Prediction as a *Brutum Fulmen.*

174. I have now been eight Years Chaplain to the City Work-house, in all which Time the Children of that House, have been sorely afflicted with an inflammatory Itch, or Scurvy, of which we could never get them entirely cured. This I have often complained of to the proper Officer, who once assured me, all the Druggs in the Apothecary's Shop would not cure them; nay more, that it was not in his Power to cleanse them, whilst the Children were continued on an Oat-meal Diet: On this frank and helpless Confession, I imagined I might, without Offence, try Tar-water on those poor Incurables, as well for their Relief, as the Good of others; accordingly, I did so, and really I observed the joyful Success exceeded my Expectations: For above a hundred Children variously affected, were for the most Part comfortably relieved in one Month's Time, at my own Expence; each Day administering eight Gallons, often with my own Hands, with three Pounds of Liquorice-ball, cut into little Bits given to the Children, to render the Water agreeable.

175. At this Time, there was a Girl about nine Years old in the Work-house, by Name, *Mary Mac Culla,* confined to her Bed for some Time, with a most violent Scurvy; she had little or no Appetite, full of Pain, because flay'd in several Parts by repeated Rubbings of Brimstone; at last the Girl fell into a most languishing Way, taking neither sufficient Food, nor Rest to support Nature, every Day declining, so look'd on by all who came to see her,

as

as paſt all Hope. Nevertheleſs, by taking Tar-water a Week, the Girl recovered wonderfully; and by continuing the Uſe of the Water her Sores ſoon dried and ſcaled off, and ſhe looked as one out of the Small-pox, but her Appetite returning, ſhe revived immediately, and is at this Day, *May* the 6th, 1745, one of the ſtrongeſt Children in our Houſe, reads well, and is worth all my Expence and Trouble.

176. The next Subject was *John Hall*, about nine Years old, who in *April* 1744, could neither ſleep, nor eat what was ſufficient to keep the Child alive, as his Mother informed me, ſtill moaning, and complaining of his Belly, which was greatly ſwelled, and in all human Probability, would ſoon have died, had the Child not been relieved ſeaſonably by Tar-water, which cauſed the Child to void a large Quantity of Worms, ſince which Diſcharge, is well, and I hear of no Complaints as formerly: This Child's Mother, *Mary Hall*, then a Nurſe in the Work-houſe, being called on by the Governors for her ſolemn Teſtimony in this Matter, ſwore, that her Son, ſoon after taking Tar-water, voided a Chamber-pot full of Worms, ſome of which, ſhe obſerved to be alive; and further ſwore, that ſhe herſelf was relieved from a violent Pain in her Side and Stomach, by a wonderful Diſcharge both Ways, cauſed by two Quarts of Tar-water taken in four Days, and from no Appetite before, ſhe then, *May* the 10th, 1744, enjoyed a very good one.

177. The next was *James Ellis*, now in the Work-houſe, a Lad of above thirteen Years old, whoſe Hands for a long Time were in a manner uſeleſs by a running Evil, but are now perfectly cured by this Medicine. Nay, there is another Boy in the ſame Houſe, by Name, *George Dorton*, whoſe Glands beneath the Chin, were greatly ſwelled and inflamed, ever oozing forth putrid Matter, moving a Nauſea in all Beholders. This Boy took Tar-water one Month

Month only, which greatly dried up his Sores, and is now very well.

178. A similar Case like this is that of a young Woman, named *Mary-Ann Empty*, in the Parish of *Glandorkin*, about four Miles from *Dublin*, who was of late frightfully afflicted with an Evil in many Parts, especially her Face; she was some Time ago recommended to me by her Parish Minister, and is greatly relieved, of which I am an Eye-witness: Her Mother gave me the following Account of her Cure: That by drinking Tar-water, her Daughter's Ulcers dried up, which so affected her Face and Jaws, that she could neither eat nor swallow, but the Ulcers in the Girl's Face burst as she slept, making a large Discharge. The Mother overjoyed at her Daughter's unexpected Relief, was curious to examine the Filth which lately tormented her Daughter, and she assured me, she found in the Filth that was discharged, a flat Bone about an Inch long, not quite so broad, both black and jagged: This I suppose stopt the Vent of the Ulcers in the Face, because, when removed, the Discharges for some Time were very large, after which the Maid grew well, and is very little disfigured, and by continuing to drink Tar-water, the Girl is now, in *December* 1745, perfectly cured of the Evil.

179. Another Cure like this was performed on a Lad, Son to a Servant of Alderman *Kane*. This Lad received a Contusion in one of his Hands; the Cure not perfected, the Sore broke out again on the Back of the same Hand; moreover, another Ulcer broke out at the same Time in the Lad's Heel, both Ulcers submitted to this Medicine, tho' for a long Time obstinate, and before the Lad took Tar-water thought incurable.

180. *Ann Maddin*, Sister to Woman who nurses for Mr. *Putland*, had a very sore Hand so swelled and inflamed, that the Surgeons believed it mortified,

 and

and so doomed it to be cut off; yet the Doctor that attended, as I am informed, advised, before taking this last Extremity, to try Tar-water, which she did; and when I viewed the young Woman's Hand some Time ago, it looked kindly from a shapeless black Lump; and I am informed by a Relation of the young Woman, that she is in a manner well, having no Pain in that Part, and can use it like the other Hand.

181. *Peter Evard*, Stocking-weaver, to be heard of at the Ship, in *Old Corn-market*, was so ulcerated all over his Body, and in many Parts eat away with the Scurvy, that he could not work: Tho' all Methods were used by the Infirmary several Months, but in vain; so reckoned amongst the Incurables; on this he took this Medicine, and immediately recovered, now follows his Trade, and comfortably provides for himself and others. His Mother, an aged Woman, long afflicted with an Asthma, took with her Son part of his Medicine, which relieved her of her Asthma, though an old Disorder.

182. A Gentleman bred an Apothecary, (and therefore will not mention his Name) came one Evening into our Hall in a very melancholy Way with an inflamed sore Throat; he said he could not swallow his Spittle, and that he had a great Lump in his Throat, which he must get launched immediately, or it would choak him; with much a-do, I prevailed on the young Man to take a little Tar-water, which relieved him immediately, and he felt no more of his frightful Lump, but continues both easy and well. From this, and many other Instances, I find nothing ever relieved a sore Throat so soon and so effectually as this Medicine.

183. Mrs. *Catharine Williams*, who sells Earthen-ware near the End of *Dirty lane*, *Thomas-street*, had one of her Legs so long ulcerated, that it was doomed to be cut off, after great Expence and most

acute Pain; yet that very Leg was restored to Ease and perfect Soundness by this powerful Medicine in a short Time without any external Application.

184. *Mary Philips*, now in the Work-house, for a long Time had lost in a manner, the Use of a Leg, with a constant Numbness or Tingling, as if it were asleep; she could not walk on it but with Difficulty; but if she stirred quick ever so little, she then felt most acute Pain, and in frosty Weather, would often be forced to sit up in Bed many an Hour by Night, moaning and rubbing it; but by Tar-water that Numbness is entirely gone, and tho' she walks ever so quick or long, she feels no manner of Pain in that Part, the sure Consequence (before Tar-water) of such Motion.

185. A Son of Mr. *B——y*, Iron-monger, in *Thomas-street*, was infected with a dry Scurf in the Scarf-skin, for some time, much like a Leprosy; no Expence, no Advice, was either with-held or wanting, yet the Youth found no Relief: On this the tender Mother asked the Doctor, if she might venture to give the Child Tar-water, so much in vogue about that Time; "Ay, ay," says the Doctor, "if you have a mind to kill your Son." To demonstrate which, he gave this Reason, "what "Nature kindly throws out," says he, "you will "certainly cork up by the searing Quality of Tar-"water, and so your Son must inevitably perish." Nevertheless, Tar-water was ventured upon, with the utmost Dread; but behold in a short Time the Lad became perfectly clean and healthy, and still continues so. Of this I am both an Eye and Ear-witness, because the Lady and the Lad paid me a Visit, and acknowledged thankfully this great Blessing, and related the above Story.

186. *Robert Scot*, Tape-weaver, to be heard of at *Paul Johnston's* in *James-street*, was cured suddently by this powerful Medicine, of an old Ulcer

in

in the Thigh, and relieved from a consumptive Cough, which so weakened the poor Man, that he was not able to work; but now looks brisk, and gets his Bread comfortably; and, to use his own Words, he makes his Paws maintain his Jaws.

187. Mrs. *Birmingham*, then living at Mrs. *Becks* in *James's-street*, labouring for many Years under an acute Pain in her Side, supposed to be an Imposthume, by this Medicine was suddenly reliev-ed by a Discharge of an incredible Quantity of Filth and Matter upwards; since which Time, the Woman, tho' much in Years, enjoys the Comforts of Life, being now both vigorous and easy.

188. *Elizabeth Wood*, at Mr. *Mac Guires*, the Corner of *Meath-street*, was relieved by Tar-water from an old Asthma and Dropsy, with both which the poor Woman seemed every Moment to be ready to expire; both her Ailments are cured by this Water, and she now thinks of living as long as any of her Neighbours, being both hearty and strong.

189. *William Billingsly*, formerly of the Work-house, now living on *Crooked-staff*, was troubled with Swellings and violent Pains in both his Legs and Feet, which suffered him neither to work, nor walk; but after taking this Medicine only one Month, all his Disorders vanished, he grew so strong and hearty that he wove in the Work-house four Yards of Check-linnen each Day; I spoke to him *February* 7, 1744, at which time Time he was very well.

190. *John Rose*, now in the Work-house, was a long Time bed-rid, with Cramps all over him, from whence the Pain was so acute and constant, that his piteous Moans both Night and Day, disturbed all about him; but by taking Tar-water one Month, his Disorder vanished, as it were, without the least Return since *May* 1744, and now enjoys his Limbs, tho' not able to stir one Foot before.

191. *Robert Turnbowl*, a Boy of the ſame Houſe, was brought on a Boy's Back, and laid down at my Chamber-door, not being able to ſtir one Step, yet by uſing this powerful Medicine one Month, recovered his Legs, and now goes tolerably.

192. *John Warburghs*, of the ſame Family, was frightfully afflicted with an Inflammation in his Head, his Eye-lids were ſo ſwelled, that the Boy was led to my Apartment, being as dark as one Stone-blind, and there ſupplicated very ſolemnly and fervently for Tar-water; he obtained his Requeſt, tho' I was then doubtful of Succeſs; yet on taking this Medicine three Days, the Inflammation ſo cooled, that the Boy's Eyes were perfectly reſtored; however, his Forehead, Chin, and the Back of his Head, were covered with a large and ſtrange Eryſipelas; all which in three Days Time ſcaled off, the whole Inflammation cooled, and the Boy continues very well, and free from that Diſorder now upwards of twelve Months.

193. *Richard Keeves*, of this Family, had two bleeding Ulcers in his Thigh, which did not permit him to ſleep, work, or walk, both which were cured in a ſhort Time by this Medicine without any outward Application.

194. There is a Gentlewoman on *Arbour-hill*, who ſuffered a great deal a long Time by an Ulcer in her Leg, and after many coſtly Experiments, and painful ones too, was injoined Patience, as being incurable. Then, as her laſt Shift, ſhe fell to Tar-water, by which ſhe is ſo well recovered, that ſhe is now able to go to Church, to return Thanks for ſo great a Bleſſing; nay, walks without Pain or Difficulty any where, though before ſhe could not ſtir a Foot without both.

195. There is an Officer in the Barracks, who, for a long Time felt, after walking a little Way, a grievous Pain in the Back-ſinews of his Legs, but on

on drinking Tar-water, all Complaints there are perfectly vanished, tho' he walks ever so much and fast, having made the Experiment; and this I had from his own Mouth.

196. *Matthew Lynch*, an old Man, seventy Years at least, now living at Mr. *Floyd*'s in *Kilmainham*, was lately asthmatic to a great Degree, and so afflicted with the Piles, that he was always scared to Death whenever he had a Call that Way, the Pain was so great; but now by the powerful Help of this Medicine, he can do every natural Office with Ease, and is not only relieved from all his old Disorders, but seems to have regained new Life and Vigour.

197. The present Reader in *Christ Church*, was attacked with an Hoarseness a considerable Time, and assured me he was frightened at its Continuance, but is now so cleared up by Tar-water, that he is able now to sing, *O be joyful*.

198. Mr. *John Purcell*, Son to the present Treasurer of the Work-house, seemed for some Time to be in a declining Way, from a consumptive Cough and frequent Stitches; but by taking this Restorative, he revives daily, and no Wonder, for from Time to Time the Lad voided several large Worms, accidentally discovered, and many probably we know nothing of.

199. *Jane Hamilton*, now in the Work-house, *Dublin*, being grievously afflicted with a scald Head, for which she was four Years under Cure in *Mercer*'s Hospital, but without Effect, was after admitted into the Work-house, where for several Years all Methods of Cure were pursued, but to as little Purpose: On which Account, she was sent to me as an obstinate Case, to try what Tar-water would do. I accordingly took the Girl in Hand, and gave her nothing but Tar-water, Morning and Evening for a Month; then I had her Head washed and rubbed twice a Day with a Spunge dipp'd in warm

ſtrong Tar-water, made of a Quart of Tar, and two Quarts of boiling Water, till all the Scurf came off; by which Method, the Girl is now perfectly clean, healthy and ſtrong, with a thick Head of Hair, as if nothing had ever ailed her, to the Admiration of all, who once knew her in a moſt miſerable Condition.

200. One Mrs. *Eager*, now living at *Mullineback*, near *New-row*, *Thomas ſtreet*, threw up from time to time, ſuch vaſt Quantities of Blood that ſhe was as pale as a Ghoſt, and ſo feeble that ſhe could ſcarce ſtand: But after taking Tar-water, the bloody Diſcharge ceaſed, and ſhe improved daily, till now ſhe is become a hearty ſtrong Woman.

201. Mr. *William Dickiſon*, oppoſite *James*'s Church, was for ſome Time very Deaf; he took Tar-water, on which his Chin broke out, after which he could hear as well as ever, and continues to do ſo, though upwards of two Years ago.

There are a great many more Caſes, very aſtoniſhing for their Succeſs, which I muſt paſs by in Silence, not being permitted for ſome Reaſons to mention the Names of the Parties concerned; yet there is one ſo remarkably true and aſtoniſhing, that I cannot omit it, without Detriment to the Publick: On which Account, I hope the Perſons concerned will take no Offence, ſince deſigned only for the Benefit of others.

A moſt remarkable Caſe.

202. The Third of *November* laſt, a Surgeon of this City paid me a viſit, in order (as he ſaid) to thank me for a moſt wonderful Cure performed by my Tar-water: This made me curious to know the Caſe: He aſſured me, a Perſon in this Town had laboured for ſome Time under the foul Diſorder, which had ſo infected the whole Maſs, that Part of

the unhappy Creature's Nose was lost, before he was called in; so that the Infection by that Time was spread from Top to Toe; for in one of the Calves of the poor Creature's Leg, he could thrust his Fist, and the whole Back was as bare as a cased Rabbet; as also the Head and Glands were so inflamed, he often spent two Hours about this one Subject; but, says he, to shorten my Story, having some Time tried in vain all Methods in Practice for such a Disorder, I then gave my Patient your Tar-water; the sensible and sudden Effects of which astonished me; all the Ulcers appearing more cool and kindly; I then began (continues he) to conceive some Hope of my Patient, though before in good Truth, I had none at all. After my Patient had taken a Gallon of your Tar-water, as I came in one Morning, I found my Patient full of Complaints, seemingly very fretful, and uneasy; on asking the Cause, my Patient protested very solemnly, never to touch one Drop more of Tar-water, because the last Night's Operation caused by Tar-water, was so violent and searching; I strove to get the better of this rash Dislike, by shewing plainly the true Reason and future Benefit of this strong Operation, but to no Purpose; so Tar-water was omitted forty-eight Hours, at the End of which Time, all the Sores and Ulcers became once more putrid, and inflamed very sensibly, plainly demonstrating an absolute Necessity of returning to our old Medicine; after some Struggle with my Patient's obstinate Prejudice, we did so, and now I am able to assure you, Sir, says the Surgeon, my Patient is perfectly recovered, the Nose excepted; and this whole Cure, strange as it is, was accomplished by your Tar-water, and no other Medicine. Now, Sir, continues he, I must confess, that a Principle of Gratitude is not the only Motive of this Visit and frank Confession, but also to intreat you, to inform me of your Sort of Tar; and how you make your Water: Which I imagine, says he, will be of great Service to the most wretched of Mankind: Accordingly I informed him of the Sort of *Norway* Tar I made use of, and how I prepared the Water.

203. A Gentleman, now lodging on *Arbour hill*, was so afflicted with inward Pains, and emaciated to such a Degree, that he was obliged to part with an honourable and profitable Commission, when commanded lately abroad. When all other Medicines and Advice failed, he drank for some time Tar-water of his own making, which he assured me had almost poisoned him, without any manner of Ease or Relief. On this Disappointment, by Advice of a Friend, he sent to me for some of my Tar-water: On taking which, for some time, his Pains immediately vanished, and never returned, though upwards of four Months, he still continuing the Use of the Water. Moreover the Night passes now insensibly, whereas before he drank my Tar-water, he generally reckoned, by the Clock, every Hour of the Night, from which comfortable Composure, his natural Appetite returned, and he is now become an hail brisk strong Man.

204. Mrs. *Dickson*, now living at Mrs. *Ford*'s at *Island-bridge*, laboured a long time under a Complication of Disorders, but more especially, a frequent Colic, and inveterate Scurvy, which affected her whole Body, and her Face particularly, which are now all cured by this Medicine only.

205. Miss *Martha Dowers*, living opposite to the Cock and Bowl in *Plunket-street*, was long afflicted with an inveterate Scurvy over her whole Body, and for Years continued incurable, tho' all Methods were tryed, that the young Woman could either purchase, or think of; at last she took Tar-water, which effectually cured her; of which I am

an

an Eye-witneſs, being with me at the Work-houſe the 26th of *November* 1745, to acknowledge the Bleſſing ſhe received, and to return Thanks, not having the leaſt Speck or Spot, and looking healthy and well.

206. Mr. *William Foſter*, Brother to Mr. *Foſter*, Brewer in *James's-ſtreet*, *Dublin*, came to Town the Beginning of *November* 1745, ſorely afflicted with a Swelling in both his Legs, together with a ſevere Cough, for which he took but one Gallon of Tar-water, and this Day, *Navember* 26, I am aſſured by his Nephew, that the Swelling is gone, and alſo the Cough, and he who ſeemed to be in a languiſhing Condition when he came to Town lately, revives daily, and ſeems to be reſtored to a new State of Health.

207. Meſſieurs *Maſſy* and *Boucher*, of the County of *Limerick*, from long Confinement, and other Misfortunes, contracted ſuch ill Habits of Body, that their Phyſicians gave Teſtimony that they could not live, if confined in the Place where they were, ſo were brought into my Neighbourhood to preſerve their Lives: by which happy Accident, hearing of Tar-water, they immediately ſent for ſome, which they drank, and were reſtored ſurprizingly in a ſhort time, after every other Method, preſcribed by the beſt Phyſicians, had failed. The 5th of this Inſtant *November* 1745, I ſpoke to them both, and they aſſured me, that they have been well ever ſince they took Tar-water, now upwards of ſix Months.

208. A Gentlewoman of my Acquaintance, was attacked *September* laſt 1745, with a ſevere Ague-fit, about Three in the Morning, which ſhook her upwards of two Hours. On this I gave her about a Naggin of Tar-water, which compoſed her immediately, and ſhe took a refreſhing Nap for ſome time; at Nine the ſame Morning preparing to riſe, ſhe

could not stir her Left Leg, being very stiff and sore, and greatly swelled and inflamed. On this a Surgeon was called in, who assured it was a most violent Disorder, nor could he foresee the Consequence; being thus alarmed, she kept her Bed for some time, and stuped her Leg with Spirits of Wine, but took no Medicine inwardly but Tar-water, by which Means, she had no other Ague-fit, and her Leg is now neither swelled nor inflamed, but in all Appearance, and by its easy natural Use, as well and as sound as the other.

209. *A most remarkable Cure of a Gentleman's Daughter about nine Years old, lately in the Small-pox.*

Miss *Hannah Hartnell*, now living at Mrs. *Green*'s in *Rainsford-street*, the 6th of *November* 1745, fell ill of the Small-pox, her Parents having, from reading *Siris*, a good Opinion of Tar-water, were willing to make use of it; accordingly I ordered the Quantity of a Naggin of Tar-water to be given to the Child warm every sixth Hour; the Child took it, and it sat easy on her Stomach, till the third Day, but then she threw it up in a short time after it was down with a Load of Filth and Phlegm; by which Means all Oppression and Pain in the Child's Stomach ceased, of which she continually complained before. Moreover, on that Day, (*viz.* the third) she had a violent Lax, which continued about twenty Hours, still she took her Tar-water as before, but observing she threw up all or most of it, I then ordered a third of warm Water to be mixt with it, to make it weaker, which caused it to sit, for she never threw it up after, nay was not so much as sick, or made the least Complaint, until *Monday* the 17th of *November*, being the 13th Day; at which Time when I payed my Visit in the Morning, I found the Child in a most hopeless Way;

the

the Discharge at her Nose and Eyes was stopt, which before that time was very large (the Disorder on the Child's Face being confluent, and never filled, the *Pus* discharging itself that way) the Small-pox on her Hands appeared black or livid; the Child grew cold, with little or no Pulse, together with an hard Hoarseness, and a continual Cough. Those deadly Symptoms and sudden Alteration astonished me greatly, having left the Child the Evening before in a very promising Way. I then strictly examined how this frightful Alteration happened, and found, that by Accident, Water was spilt in the Child's Bed, out of which she was taken, tho' in a cold frosty Day, and continued so for some considerable Time, because she was not put into Bed till all the wet Things were dried and adjusted. From that Instant, all our former Hopes of the Child's Recovery vanished, and as for my Part, I did not imagine she could struggle twelve Hours, from the Obstructions in both Head and Throat, which appeared most stubborn and obstinate, the Child being able neither to speak, swallow, or breathe freely: However, tho' my Hope was indeed but very small, immediately I warm'd a Naggin of Tar-water, without any Mixture, and obliged the poor Child with some Difficulty to sip it, little by little, till in some considerable Time, she got all down, and it staid with her. On this I ordered some healthy careful Person to be put into Bed, and to take the Child into their Arms, to infuse Heat if possible. The tender Mother readily obeyed, in some time the Child grew warm and easy, fell into a fine Sweat, and slept for about two Hours, after which, the former Discharge from both Nose and Eyes burst forth a-new, and appeared as large, if not larger for some time than ever; which greatly promoted the Child's speedy Recovery from this most imminent Danger. Being now up and well, with a keen Appetite, good

Digestion

Digestion, and what is most astonishing in the whole Process, for the Space of twenty-one Days, she was not once sick, or made the least Complaint, the 3d and 13th Days excepted. Now I beg Leave to assure the Publick, that this Child took no manner of Medicine, but only Tar-water, not one Drop of Sack or Sack-whey, her common drink was two-milk Whey, or boiled Milk and Water, of which she took plentifully, and always warm: By a Blessing on which Method, she is now livelier and heartier than before she lay down, being only the 23d Day, this 28th of *November* 1745.

210. Mr. *William Charleton*, in *November* 1745, was attacked with a violent Fever, of which he seem'd to get the better, but relapsed immediately, under which he languished for some Time, and seem'd past Hope; as an Addition to his Disorder, an inflamed Ulcer so affected his Throat inwardly, that he could not swallow; upon this he sent to me for Tar-water; on taking which his Ulcer vanished, his Appetite returned, his Fever entirely left him, without any bad Symptom, and the young Gentleman is now, I thank God, both lively and strong, from a very languishing dangerous State: All which, this Morning *December* 24, he thankfully acknowledged in my Room, where he took with me a Cup of Tar-water with the greatest Alacrity. He lodges at Mr. *Silk*'s opposite the Work-house.

211. *John Mac Donald*, now in the Work-house, was miserably eat away with the King's-evil in many Parts of his Body, it consumed half his Face, so that he was nauseous both to himself and others. This first happened to him in the Country: In Hopes of Relief, he set out for this City, and by Accident met the Bishop of *Cloyne*, who advised him to Tar-water, and gave him some Money to provide it. The Lad neglected this good Advice, but obtained Admission into one of the Infirmaries, where

where being twice salivated, but nothing better, he was turned out as incurable; being in great Distress, he came into the Work-house as a Vagabond, where he was salivated also, but his Evil still continued obstinate, without the least Sign of Relief, tho' reduced in a manner to a Shadow; as he was crawling about, I took notice of him, and advised him to Tar-water, he complied, and in the Space of a Fortnight, he found most sensible Relief, so continued taking Tar-water about six Weeks longer, which cured all the Ulcers of his Body; but where the Sores were, the Skin is drawn up in Wrinkles, tho' without any Weakness or Pain. Thus far Mr. *Hill.*

212. *An Extract of a Letter from a Gentleman of Veracity and Credit, relating to his own Case; dated the 10th of* December 1745.

It is somewhat more than a Year ago I first meddled with Tar-water, only playing with it. I found it good for a slow Digestion, and a Strengthner of a weak Stomach. At Times I was wont to be troubled with the Piles, and with a Pain in the lower Part of my Back, in both which Cases it befriended me. But afterward being pretty well at Ease, I thought but little of Tar-water, till the Beginning of *July* last, when the same Pain in the lower Part of my Back afflicted me so violently, as to cause me to apply to a Physician, from whom I gathered that what I had deemed to be of the Gravel-kind, was gouty. However I determined with myself to go into the Use of Tar-water in earnest; which I have regularly done since that Time, only with short Intermissions now and then; and, by the divine Blessing, with much Advantage to my Health and Strength; Freedom of Spirits and Chearfulness. When I came into the regular Use of it, I took a Resolution to oblige myself to as cool and mild Diet as I could well bear, and to deal less than formerly in Flesh-meat, and Malt-liquor, or Wine, or Cyder: And many Times, I believe, much less than a Pound of Flesh, and a Quart of those Liquors put together, had served me a Week. This I did on Account of its being warm, as I supposed, and Cordial in its Nature, concluding it would sufficiently support the Constitution, as the Effect has proved. Indeed, I find little or no Inclination to drink except at Meals, and then less than formerly, nor find the want of Cordials, whilst in the Uses of Tar-water.

I was near thirty Years old, when an ulcerous Ailment came upon me in my Seat; and 'tis now somewhat more than thirty Years, that it hath been a running Grief or Issue, more or less, to be sure some time in every Moon pretty plentifully discharging a purulent Matter; but this Discharge is now stopped by the Means of Tar-water.

This Gentleman, though perfectly freed from all his Ailments, yet is apprehensive, that the stopping and healing up his Ulcer may be attended with bad Consequences, under the Notion, that the want of such a Discharge, which he has been so long accustomed to, may occasion some Disorder else-where, and therefore would be advised about continuing the Use of Tar-water; and at the same time, says, that having found it so friendly, he is afraid of being advised to forbear the Use of it, as long as the Benefit received is manifest in the Enjoyment of a better State of Health and Ease, unattended with any present Inconvenience. It is pleasant to see how this Patient is frighted at his being cured of a running Ulcer, which had infested him for thirty Years: He could not be perfectly cured, unless his Ulcer was healed, and there is nothing to fear from thence, as the peccant Humour was not repelled, or driven to other Parts, but corrected and mended; such is the wonderful Force of Tar-water in sweetening the Blood and Juices.

213. *In*

213. *In* September 1745, *the two following Gentlemen gave me, at their respective Houses in* Cloyne, *an Account of the Benefits they received by the Use of Tar-water.*

Mr. *James Hanning*, by catching cold, was seized with a violent Fever in *November* 1743, his Feet and Legs were at first extreamly cold, his Head much disturbed, and he lost all Appetite, being judged by all to be in a dangerous Condition by the Height of his Fever; he had recourse to Tar-water, which he drank in Plenty, and took nothing else; in ten Days drinking, his Fever, and all other bad Symptoms went off, and in a Fortnight's Time he was perfectly recovered.

214. Mr. *Clement Forster*, who deals much there in the Worsted-trade, was in Summer 1744, seized with a Fever, which greatly affected him, and made him incapable to do any Business: He was advised to drink Tar-water, which had such an Effect, that in ten Days his Fever turned to an Ague, which was so easy, that on the first taking the Bark, he was perfectly cured; he informed me also, that he used to be troubled with one or two Fits of the Gout every Year for several Years past, but that he had no Return of it, since he began to drink Tar-water.

215. *Robert Dillon* of *Clonbrock* in the County of *Galway*, Esq; Member of Parliament, was pleased to give me the following Account in *January* 1745; that he had been afflicted with the Gout above fifteen Years, which became more violent every Year; that he used to be confined in the Fits for many Months together, with great Pain, and such Weakness in his Limbs, that he could hardly walk; that when he was out of the Fits, he was troubled, in the Morning especially, with a great Uneasiness and Loathing in his Stomach, and a Discharge of a great deal of Phlegm; that he had no Relief from

any Medicine he took; but that in Summer 1744, he began to drink Tar-water, which he has continued for a Year and half without Intermiſſion, taking conſtantly half a Pint in the Morning, and as much every Night, which he was encouraged to do by the Benefit he received by it; all the Loathing in his Stomach is quite gone, and though he has now and then ſome Fits of the Gout, yet they happen but ſeldom, and laſt but a ſhort time with little or no Pain, and he now enjoys good Appetite and Spirits, though his Limbs are ſtill weak, and he thinks himſelf happy in compariſon of his former Condition.

216. *Henry Leſtrange* of the *King*'s *County* Eſq; Member of Parliament, informed me in *January* 1745; that he had been troubled with the Gout for ten Years paſt, that about four Years ago he was ſeized with the Small-pox, from which he recovered with great Difficulty, that for a Year after he had no Return of the Gout, but that for the laſt three Years, the Gout returned upon him with more Violence, ſo that he had a Fit every Autumn and Spring; that the Fit in the laſt Spring laſted three Months, which deprived him of Reſt, Appetite, and Spirits; that being adviſed to drink Tar-water, he began to drink it in Summer 1745, which he has continued the Uſe of ever ſince, with ſuch good Effect, that he has had no Return of the Gout in the uſual Seaſon, nor any Symptom of it, and now enjoys a good Appetite, Flow of Spirits, and Freedom from all Uneaſineſs, and has the full Uſe and Strength of his Limbs as much as ever, and reſolves to drink Tar-water conſtantly, to which he imputes all his Recovery.

217. Colonel *Charles Tottenham*, of *Tottenham-green*, in the County of *Wexford*, Eſq; Member of Parliament, informed me on the 30th of *January* 1745, that he had been afflicted with a dead Ague for five Years,

Years, and had not any cold Fits, but that his hot Fits were very violent, being constantly attended with prodigious Sweats, which wasted and weakened him greatly; he had lost his Appetite and Spirits, and though he took great Quantities of the Bark, he found himself the worse for it. In this decaying Condition, he consulted the Physicians in *Dublin*, and took their Prescriptions without any Relief. But in Summer, 1744, he had Recourse to Tar-water, which he drank cold, half a Pint in the Morning, and as much at Night, for a Month or six Weeks, and found that the Tar-water griped him very much, and gave him no Relief; upon which he discontinued the Use of it: but finding that his Disorder still grew worse, and hearing that it was advised in Cases of Agues, Colics, and Fevers, to drink Tar-water warm, and in smaller Quantities at a Time, he followed that Advice, and from the Moment he drank it Milk-warm, he found it agree with his Stomach, and got immediate Relief, and continuing to drink it plentifully in that Form, he has entirely got the better of his dead Ague, and is quite free from all Symptoms of it; he has recovered his Appetite, Spirits, and Rest, and attributes his Recovery altogether to Tar-water, which he still drinks, and resolves always to drink, as it is no way disagreeable to him, and so very useful.

218. Mr. *William Willan*, Tape-weaver, in *Thomas-street*, *Dublin*, informed me in *January*, 1745, that for many Years, he had been afflicted with the Gout, which gave him much Pain, and frequently confined him to his Chamber; that being advised to drink Tar-water, he did so in a regular Manner; which gave him Spirits, Appetite, and Ease, by which, he is now able to attend all his Business abroad without Pain from the Gout; and though he has still a Weakness in his Limbs, he imputes that to the Necessity of walking much abroad, which his

Affairs frequently require, and acknowledges the great Benefit he received by drinking Tar-water.

219. Captain *Solomon Debrisay*, of the City of *Dublin*, favoured me with the following Detail of his Case in *January*, 1745. He was troubled with a scorbutical Disorder above twenty Years, for which he took several Medicines in *England*, *France*, and *Ireland*; and though he sometimes had some Abatement of his Disorder, yet at last it grew very violent, breaking out into running Sores, and Scruff, and attended with great Pain, so that he could hardly ride or walk without great Uneasiness. In this Condition in *September*, 1744, he got an Inflammation of the Lungs and violent Cough, by catching cold, for which he was blooded and vomited; and when he had got the better of the Inflammation, he took Tar-water to remove his Cough, at the Rate of a Pint a Day, which in a little Time carried off his Cough; and finding the Water to agree with him, and that it made him easier in the Scurvy, he continued the drinking of it for six Months, by which Means, he was entirely cured of the Scurvy, without the least Sore or Spot remaining, and has had no Return of it since that Time, though he has left off the Use of the Water, as having no farther Occasion for it.

220. Mr. *George Rumford*, aged Seventy-five Years, who lives at the *Black-pits*, *Dublin*, was in the Year 1744, seized with a most violent Cough, attended with a continual Spitting of corrupt Stuff and Phlegm. In this dangerous Condition he made Use of every Thing the Doctors had ordered, without receiving the least Benefit, upon which they gave him up as past all Hopes of Cure. But a Friend of his coming to see him, and finding him given over, begg'd he would drink Tar-water, which he did in the Quantity of a Pint each Day, till he made use of three Gallons of Tar-water; in which

Time,

Time, he was quite recovered, freed from his violent Cough and Spitting, and restored to a good Appetite, and is now in a great Flow of Spirits, and as well as he could wish for one of his Years, and he verily believes, that, had it not been for Tar-water, he would have been dead long ago, and that he owes his Life to the Use of it.

221. *James Reyly*, Servant to Mr. *Phepoe* Brewer in *Millstreet*, was in the Year 1745, afflicted with an Asthma, Shortness of Breath, and great Cough, and at the same Time, his Belly, Thighs, and Legs were swollen to a monstrous Size, so that he could not walk or breath but with great Difficulty, and he lost all Appetite; he made use of many Things prescribed for him without receiving any Benefit, and he continued in this miserable Way for some Time; but hearing of the Effects of Tar-water, and what Relief others had received from it, he began immediately to drink it, about a Pint a Day, until he had made use of a Gallon, by which Time his Breath was restored, his Cough was gone, and all the Swellings in his Body and Limbs fell away, and he recovered a good Appetite, and could eat three Times for once he could before. He had also at the same Time a great Scurvy in his Face, which was also carried off by drinking Tar-water, and he is now hearty and well, and able to go through his Business as well as ever.

222. Mr. *Enoch Mason*, who lives with Mr. *Bursiquot*, Clothier, near *Essex-bridge*, gave me the following Particulars of his Disorder, on the 31st of *January*, 1735. He had been troubled with rheumatic Pains in his Joints for fifteen Years, which he could not remove by any of the Medicines he took; but in 1744, his Disorder appeared in a new Form; he had great Difficulty of breathing, insomuch, that he could not lie down in his Bed for six Weeks, his Belly was drawn up, and he suffered great Pains;

the Physician called it a Contraction of the Bowels; he could not sleep by Reason of his Pains and Difficulty of breathing, and though he took many composing Draughts, which made him doze, yet he got no Refreshment: he went through the common Course of Physic, vomiting and other Prescriptions, which giving him no Relief, his Case was judged to be desperate, and accordingly, he was advised to go into the Country and drink Milk, which might possibly prolong his Life for some Time, but without any Hopes that he could last long. At this Time, he heard much of Tar-water, and was advised to drink it, which he did at the Rate of a Pint a Day; which in a little Time removed the Contraction in his Belly, restored him to a Freedom of breathing, and brought him to a good Appetite, so that he mended every Day, and continuing to drink the Water, obtained a perfect Recovery from his Rheumatism, and all his other Disorders, which he attributes altogether to the Use of Tar-water.

223. Mr. *John Wilkinson*, Clerk in the Surveyor General's Office in the Castle of *Dublin*, informed me the first of *February*, 1745, that he had the Misfortune to break his Leg by a Slip in the Street, which confined him for three Months; that by laying so long on his Back in Bed, he got the Gravel, which gave him great Uneasiness; that at the same Time, by catching cold, he lost his Hearing, and was so deaf, that he could not hear the Drums that beat near his Chamber in the Castle. To ease him of his Gravel, he was advised to drink Tar-water, and he had not drunk above a Gallon, when, to his Surprize, he found his Deafness carried off, and he could hear as well as ever he did, and continuing to drink Tar-water, which he found very diuretick, he voided a small rough craggy Stone, and, by Degrees, a great Deal of Gravel; and he is now entirely

tirely free from all Pains or Symptoms of the Gravel, and hears perfectly well.

224. *Matthew Haynes*, Sword-Cutler, at the *Black-lion* on the *Blind-quay*, opposite to Mr. *Thomas's* Mohogany Ware-house, informed me on the first of *February*, 1745, that he was for fifteen Months ill of a Decay. He was so sore and streightened all over his Body, that he could not bear his Apron or his Cloths on without much Pain; he had lost all Appetite and Rest, and was brought so low, that he was not able to work at his Trade, or even to go up or down Stairs without Help; and though he was oppressed with Phlegm, and could hardly breath, yet he dared not cough or spit, on Account of the great Pain caused thereby in his Breast and Body. Being in this miserable Condition, he was advised by Mr. *Bradish*, who employed him, to drink Tar-water, and being resolved to try any Thing recommended to him, he incautiously drank near a Pint of cold Tar-water at once, which he instantly threw up with great Violence, together with a great deal of Phlegm. He then thought himself a dead Man, and was for sending for a Clergyman to pray with him for the last Time, as he thought; but in a few Minutes after, he found himself much easier in his Stomach and Chest, and mended all the Day. This good Effect reconciled him to Tar-water, and made him resolve to drink it in smaller Quantities, and Milk-warm, which he did twice a Day, half a Pint each Time, and, by continuing to drink it that Way for some Time, all the Sores in his Breast and Body went away, he breathed with Ease, and recovered his Rest and Appetite, and eats a hearty Breakfast, which he never could do before in his best State of Health. He is able to work at his Trade as formerly, and is persuaded that he owes his Life to Tar-water.

225. *An Extract from a Letter of* William Pleasants, *of* Knockbeg *in the County of* Carlow, *Esq*; *to* Thomas Prior, *Esq*; *dated* February 4, 1745.

The Person who received such great Benefit by drinking Tar-water, was a Boy who drove my Plough; he laboured under what was judged, by most who saw him, a scrophulous Disorder, or King's-evil; he had several ulcerous Sores about his Jaws and Neck, which continued running for great Part of some Years. His Mother, who had some Knowledge in Herbs, applied different Kinds to his Sores, which eased a little, but had no other Success.

I recommended him to a Friend in *Dublin*, who prevailed on some Gentlemen of Skill, to endeavour to cure him. They had Compassion on the Creature, and gave him Medicines, but they also proved ineffectual. My Friend then gave him Tar-water; when he had taken a small Quantity, he found more Relief from it, than he had done from all that had been done for him before. He returned to his Mother, and I supplied him with Tar-water; and, as well as I can remember, he had not taken a Gallon of it, when the Ulcers began to dry, and his Face, which was very much swollen with his Distemper, began to re-assume its natural Form. He left me last Spring, and stayed from me till Harvest. At his Return, he told me, that Tar-water had cured him, and that his Disorder had given him no Uneasiness, the Time he was absent from me. I am

Your most humble Servant,
William Pleasants.

226. Mr. *Patrick Butler*, Shoemaker in *Crane-lane*, *Dublin*, informed me on the 5th of *February*, 1745, that he had been afflicted with the Rheuma-

tiſm for ſeveral Years, that about two Years ago, the Fits were ſo violent, that he was laid up three Months together, that for eight Days in that Time, he could not ſtir Hand or Foot, and was turned in his Bed by other People, the rheumatick Pains having ſeized his whole Body; that when the Violence of the Fit abated in 1744, he made uſe of Tar-water, which in a little Time gave him great Relief, which encouraged him to perſiſt in the Uſe of it ever ſince, with ſuch good Effect, that all his rheumatic Pains are gone, and he has had no Return of them ſince he began to drink the Water: he has got the full Strength of his Limbs, Appetite, and Spirits, and reſolves to drink Tar-water conſtantly, finding that if he gets any twitching in his Limbs, by cold or ſharp Weather, Tar-water immediately relieves him.

227. *William Heany*, Shoemaker, Journeyman to the ſaid Mr. *Butler*, was in 1744, ſeized with ſuch violent Pains in his Legs, that he could not walk, reſt, or work at his Trade. He was adviſed to drink Tar-water, which he did, and found in a little Time all his Pains go off, and was reſtored to the full Uſe of his Limbs, and able to get his Bread by his Trade, though before he was apprehenſive that he ſhould not be able to ſubſiſt, having no other Means to ſupport him but his Labour, which the Violence of his Pains diſabled him from performing.

228. Mrs. *Bonvillet*, who lives in *Kings-ſtreet*, near *Stephen's-green*, informed me on the 3d of *February*, 1745, that near twenty-eight Years ago ſhe had the Misfortune to fall down Stairs, and pitched upon her Shoulder, which occaſioned a Contuſion in that Part, but as the Pain ſoon went off, ſhe did not then take any Care about it. She afterwards obſerved a Sort of Pimple in that Part, but finding no Pain in it, ſhe ſtill neglected it.

However, it still increased every Year, without any Manner of Pain; till in the Year 1744, it had formed a Wen of an enormous Size, which spread from her Shoulders to one of her Ears, and under her Arm pit, as large as the Mould of a Hat; so that she was obliged to enlarge her Cloaths to cover it, and hide the Deformity; but as she had no Pain with it, she neglected all Thoughts of preventing its Progress, which might have been easily effected in the Beginning: but in 1744, we found herself troubled with other Ailments, with Vapours, Lowness of Spirits, want of Appetite and Rest, which greatly reduced her; for removing these last Disorders, she was advised to drink Tar-water, which she did regularly for a considerable Time. The first Effect was, that in a little Time she recovered her Appetite, got Rest and Spirits, and was freed from all her Vapours and Disturbance in her Stomach, and has continued well from those Disorders ever since; as she found that Tar-water did her so much Service, she still drank it for several Months, and observed that in some Time, the great Wen on her Shoulders began to grow soft and fall away. This encouraged her to continue the drinking of the Water, and in a few Months after the Wen was reduced to a Fourth of its first Size, and daily grew softer, and seemed to have some floating Roots in it: finding herself easy, and in so good a Way, she laid aside Tar-water for some Months before the Wen was quite dispersed, and then found that it began to grow hard and swell again; upon which she has of late resumed her Tar-water, of which she drinks near a Quart a Day, and finds that the Hardness and Swelling have already greatly abated; and she resolves to persist in the constant Use of it, in full Hopes that in some Time she will quite get rid of her Wen. And her Hopes are the greater, considering the Benefit which a *French* Gentleman received

ceived by it in a parallel Caſe: This Gentleman had, as ſhe informed me, a great Lump, that by Degrees grew on the Crown of his Head, which became at laſt as large as an Egg, inſomuch, that he could hardly keep his Hat on his Head; and though it was not attended with Pain, it was very troubleſome. The Gentleman took Tar-water for ſome other Diſorder, from which he was relieved, and found at the ſame Time, that this Lump or Wen ſoftened and waſted by Degrees, and that at laſt it quite melted away and vaniſhed.

229. Mr. *John Wilme*, Silver-ſmith, who lives in *Coles-alley*, near *Caſtle-ſtreet*, informed me on the 5th of *February* 1745, that by an Accident he got a Hurt in his Shin-bone, which cauſed a Running and Swelling, and being laid open by a Surgeon, was in ſome Time healed; yet he after found, that a Humour flowed to and ſwelled the Part, and gave him great Uneaſineſs. He had at the ſame Time, a Lump or Excreſcence on the Crown of his Head, which grew to the Size of a ſmall Egg, at leaſt an Inch high, and was ſo angry and ſore, that the leaſt Thing that touched it gave him great Pain, and he could hardly bear a Hat on his Head. His Mother had alſo the like Lumps on her Head. He was adviſed to take Tar-water for the firſt Ailment, which he did for three Months, and though he drank ſcarce half a Pint a Day, yet he ſoon found a great Abatement of the Swelling and Uneaſineſs in his Leg; and to his great Surprize the Excreſcence on his Head grew eaſy and melted away, and became as flat as any Part of his Head, and finding ſuch Benefit from the Water, he reſolves to take it in greater Quantity for the future.

230. Mrs. *Morgan*, Wife of Mr. *Morgan*, Patten-maker at *Nicholas-gate*, *Dublin*, informed me on the 3d of *February* 1745, that ſhe had been

troubled

troubled with a paralytic Disorder for some Time; that her Fingers were so drawn up, that she could hardly open them, that she was hardly able to walk in the Streets, her Feet were so tottering and weak, and very cold and stiff; and she was apprehensive that she would quite lose the Use of them, and have a Palsy all over her Body, as nothing that she took gave her any Relief; and hearing that Tar-water was useful in many Distempers, she resolved to try it in her own Case, and soon found a sensible Benefit; in six Weeks drinking she recovered the Use of her Fingers and Hands, got Strength, Warmth, and Supplenefs in her Limbs, and by continuing the drinking of the Water, she has recovered the full Use of them, and now walks with Ease. She laid aside Tar-water for several Months, and if she finds herself out of Order at any Time, she has Recourse to the Tar-water, which always gives her Relief.

231. Mr. *Hewetson*, between Seventy and Eighty Years old, who lives in *School-house-lane*, informed me the 3d of *February* 1745, that he had been for many Years troubled with the Gout, during which Time, he was sure of having a Fit the Beginning of every Winter, which laid him up for several Months; but that in Summer 1744, he drank Tar-water for several Months running, and the Effect was, that he had no Fit of the Gout in the Winter 1744, and got a good Stomach and Spirits, and walked tolerably well without Pain; in Summer 1745, he drank some Tar-water, and then laid it quite aside for six Months together, but in Winter 1745, on catching cold, he had a Return of the Gout, attended with great Weakness in his Limbs, though with little Pain; and it is probable, that, had he continued taking Tar-water all along in sufficient Quantity, and avoided catching cold, he would either have had no Fit at all, or a slight one. In such Cases, Tar-water should be drank warm, before the

the Fit, in the Fit, and after the Fit, at leaſt a Pint a Day, or a Quart, which would be much better, without any Danger from the Quantity, and with great Comfort to the Patient.

232. Mr. *Francis Watſon*, Sadler in *Capel-Street*, informed me on the 4th of *February* 1745, that he had been troubled with a Stuffing, Wind and Oppreſſion in his Stomach for five or ſix Years paſt, attended at Night-time with a Difficulty of breathing, and with a great Cough in the Mornings, which made him ſtrain and heave, and deprived him of his Stomach and Digeſtion; that in 1743, he was firſt ſeized with the Gout, and had another Fit in 1744, which was followed by a Fit of the Gravel. That in *October* 1744, he began to drink Tar-water at about half a Pint a Day, which he continued to do till *Chriſtmas* following, with ſuch good Effect, that in three Weeks Time he found great Benefit, and ſoon after he was free from the Wind and Oppreſſion in his Stomach, breathed freely, recovered his Appetite, loſt his Cough, and diſcharged a great deal of Gravel without Pain, and has had no Return of the Gout ever ſince; and he now continues perfectly well, and free from all his former Diſorders, and at Times ſtill drinks Tar-water.

233. Mr. *Paſqualino*, the Muſician, now in *Dublin*, informed me on the 8th of *February* 1745, that having play'd a Part in Mr. *Handel*'s grand Oratorio of *Deborah*, which was performed on *Thurſday* the 23d of *January* 1745, for the Support of the Charitable Infirmary on the *Inns-quay* and being in a great Heat and Sweat, was after the Performance expoſed to a very cold Air near half an Hour, by the Footmen breaking into the Room where he was; by which he was immediately ſtruck with a cold ſhivering, and was ſo much out of Order that he could not ſleep one Wink that Night. In the Morning, on *Friday*, he had a violent Head-ach, Colic

Colic Pains, and great Heat all over his Body, which obliged him to keep his Bed. By four o' Clock in the Afternoon, his Fever grew so high and violent, that he became a little delirious; his Wife had a mind to send for a Physician, but as he had been cured of a Fever some Time before by drinking Tar-water, he ordered, that Tar-water should be got for him in plenty, and nothing else; which he began to drink about five o'Clock Milk-warm, near half a Pint every Quarter of an Hour, and continued to drink at that Rate till eight o'Clock next Morning, on *Saturday*, bating some little Intermissions, when he got a little Sleep; though he had given Directions to his Servant, to awake him if he should happen to sleep, and make him drink the Water: and he computed, that in the said Space of Time, he drank eight Quarts: And the Effect was, that during the whole Night, he was in high Spirits, had a great Perspiration, and by Eight o'Clock in the Morning, his Heat and Fever had quite left him, and he was perfectly easy, and very hungry. On *Saturday* he kept his Bed by way of Precaution against catching cold, free from all Symptoms of a Fever; and on *Sunday* went abroad, and took the Air, being perfectly recovered.

234. A Gentlewoman near *Sycamore-Alley, Dublin*, informed me on the 12th of *February* 1745, that she had been troubled with Fits for some Time, which came upon her all at once, without any previous Symptom, and deprived her of her Senses for three, four, or five Minutes at a Time; that these Fits became more frequent, and disordered her Spirits and Mind, and she was apprehensive that she would be carried off in one of them. She took several Things to prevent their Return, without any Effect. She was advised to drink Tar-water, and though she had no Opinion of it, yet she complyed

to satisfy the Desires of her Friends in trying every Thing they recommended. She drank near a Pint a Day for five Days, in *July* 1745, and found no Return of her Fits, and got good Appetite and Spirits; at the End of five Days, she observed a great Itching all over her Body, and soon after, a great Number of black Spots appeared all over her Arms, Shoulders, and Body, as black as Ink. She then thought that she was poisoned by Tar-water, and exclaim'd against it; but her Friend, who recommended Tar-water, came to see her in this Condition, and finding that she was in good Spirits, and otherwise very well, told her, that since the Water had driven that Humour out on the Surface of her Body, it was so far from doing her Harm, that it did her all the Service imaginable; and encouraged her to persist in drinking it, since it has so good an Effect, which she continued to do for two or three Months in small Quantities; and she found, in a little Time, that all the black Spots first became yellow, and by Degrees disappeared one after another, so that she became entirely freed from them, and has had no Return of the Fits since she began to drink Tar-water, but found, that, by getting a greater Appetite, she has grown much fatter than she was before.

235. A Captain of a Man of War in 1744, informed me, that he had been troubled with the Scurvy several Years, and had taken many Medicines, and went to *Bath*, and drank the Waters, but all to no Purpose; his Disorder rather increased, and broke out in Sores, and Scurff over his Arms and other Parts of his Body, especially his Head, which he could not suffer to be shaved; but that by taking Tar-water six Weeks, all the Sores, Spots, and Scurff went off, and he became as hail and clean as ever he was, with a great Increase of Appetite.

I shall

I ſhall now give an Account of ſome Caſes communicated to me from Gentlemen of Character and Veracity who aſſured me of the Truth of the Facts, but did not think proper to mention the Names of the Patients, moſt of them being of the female Sex.

236. Two Siſters in this Kingdom, at the ſame Time drank Tar-water, the one for a Strangury, the other for a Diabetes, and both were cured, in a little Time, of thoſe oppoſite Diſorders.

237. A Gentlewoman had a Deafneſs, which daily increaſed, ſo that ſhe was apprehenſive of quite loſing her Hearing; ſhe had drank Tar-water in ſmall Quantities ſeveral Weeks with no Effect; but being adviſed to take double the Quantity of the Water every Day, ſhe did ſo, and was ſoon after cured of her Deafneſs.

238. One Gentleman was cured of an habitual Coſtiveneſs by Tar-water, and another was made coſtive by it.

239. Two Gentlewomen near *Youghall*, were likewiſe affected in different Ways, one was made coſtive, and the other looſe by Tar-water.

240. An old Beggar-woman with a moſt ſhocking cancerated Breaſt, was in a few Days much better by drinking, and waſhing the Sores with Tar-water.

241. A Woman that was twice married, and yet never was with Child, took Tar-water for a Diſorder ſhe laboured under, and conſtantly drank it for a conſiderable Time, which removed her Ailment. She ſoon after became pregnant, and ſhe imputes her Pregnancy to Tar-water. I deſired to know whether her Huſband alſo drank Tar-water, and I was aſſured, that he drank it at the ſame Time. Many other Inſtances have been mentioned to me of Perſons who unexpectedly became with Child, which they verily believe was owing to the Uſe of Tar-water.

242. A young Lady was cured by Tar-water of violent Head-achs, to which ſhe had been long ſubject.

243. A poor Woman, whoſe Legs were monſtrouſly ſwollen, and deformed with Ulcers, was adviſed to apply Tar as a Salve or Poultice, and to drink Tar-water at the ſame Time, which ſhe did, and was ſoon perfectly cured, having before in vain uſed many Things preſcribed for her.

244. A Gentleman's Servant had the Misfortune of having a Coach-wheel run over his Foot, which was thereby terribly bruiſed, and ſwollen to a great Size, with much Pain. A Poultice of Tar was applied to the Part, which ſoon put an End to both the Swelling and the Pain.

245. A Maid Servant, who for many Years had a Tetter in her Arm, conſulted a Country Practitioner, who applied the blue Stone, upon which her Arm ſwelled up to her Shoulder, and was pained to ſuch a Degree, that her Maſter apprehended ſhe might loſe it. He then made her waſh and foment it with hot ſtrong Tar-water, and apply a Plaiſter or Poultice of warm Tar, which ſpeedily cured both the Ulcer and Swelling.

246. A Gentleman in an eminent Station, was troubled with a fixed Pain in his Side for two Years, he took ſeveral Medicines without Benefit. He was adviſed to drink Tar-water, which he did for a conſiderable Time; and he aſſured me of late, that his Pain is quite removed, and that he is at perfect Eaſe from that Diſorder.

247. A Perſon ill of the Ague, was cured in *January* 1745, by drinking two Quarts of Tar-water warm in the cold Fit.

248. Many Parts of the Country have been of late infeſted with ſore Throats, whereby ſeveral Children have died; but thoſe who drank a Gallon of warm Tar-water a Day, immediately recovered

of

of it, without any other Application, as I am assured by a Person of Credit.

249. Many Instances have been communicated to me of the great Success and Efficacy of Tar-water in the Cure of venereal Disorders, Gleets, *&c.* but in such Cases, Names are not to be mentioned. But in Charity to those unhappy Creatures who labour under such Ailments, it may be proper to hint so much, and to recommend to them the sole constant copious drinking of Tar-water, *viz.* one Quart a Day, at six or eight Glasses, which without any other Medicine, but only a prudent Regimen, avoiding the catching of Cold, aud eating of improper Food, has been found in many Instances to work a perfect Cure.

250. A Gentlewoman in the Country had hurt her Leg, which being neglected, grew exceeding bad, a Gangrene was apprehended, she had a Physician and Surgeon from *Cork* to attend her. After some Months physicking, cutting, and tenting, they abandoned her, declaring she must never hope to recover the Use of her Leg, which was wasted and useless, and left her with a running Ulcer, kept open with Tents. Her Son came to the Gentleman who gave me this Information, to know whether she might not take Tar-water with the Bark, which had been prescribed by the Doctor. She was advised to abstain from the Bark, from the Surgeon's Fomentation, and every other Thing but simply Tar-water; whereof she should take three Pints daily, in nine Glasses, which in three Weeks quite cured her, to the Surprize of all the Neighbourhood. She had a House full of Children, who depended on her Care, and who had despaired of her Life.

251. A Maid Servant was seized with a vehement Fever and Stich, on the 19th of *April* 1744, in the Morning; her Face as red as Crimson, her

Pulse

Pulſe exceeding high, ſcarce able to utter a Word for the great Oppreſſion about her Heart, and her Blood and Fleſh hot in an extreme Degree, with other Symptoms declarative of the worſt Kind of Fever and Pleuriſy. Her Caſe was looked upon as deſperate from the Manner of her falling ill; which was, that the Night before, after hard Work in the Houſe, being in a Heat and Sweat, ſhe drank a great Quantity of cold ſmall Liquor, and after that ſat abroad in the open cold Evening Air in her Sweat. In this threatening Caſe, ſhe was ordered to drink five Quarts of Tar-water in ten Hours, which ſhe did with ſuch good Effect, that the next Morning her Fever left her, and ſhe was ſo well recover'd, that ſhe put on her Cloaths, and was ready to go to work, but ſhe was ordered to keep quiet in Bed for a Day or two longer. This laſt Caution is found neceſſary to prevent a Relapſe, which Patients in ſuch Caſes are ſubject to by catching the leaſt Cold; for as they find themſelves in high Spirits, and free from the Fever, they imagine themſelves to be quite recovered before they are out of Danger, and therefore 'tis found neceſſary, that the Patient ſhould keep quiet in Bed for a Day or two longer, in which Time the Danger of a Relapſe may be over. There is nothing ſo much to be apprehended in Fevers cured by Tar-water, as an Opinion of their being relieved and quite out of Danger before they are really ſo.

252. On *Wedneſday*, the 1ſt of *Auguſt*, 1744, a young Boy about nine Years old, was ſeized with a dangerous Illneſs, a Peripneumony or Inflammation of the Lungs, ſhort Coughs, Pain, Soreneſs in the Throat and Thorax, Difficulty of Breathing, glazed Eyes, Scarlet Cheeks, and burning Heat. In this Condition he was put to Bed, and, drank Tar-water five Pints the firſt Day, and about two Quarts the ſecond, at a Glaſs every half Hour. The firſt

Day it produced an extraordinary Diſcharge by Urine; the ſecond, it threw him into moiſt Perſpirations, and ſometimes Sweats; every Glaſs put Life into him, eaſed his Symptoms, and kept him in continual high Spirits and good Appetite; on *Friday*, which was two Days following, he was paſt all Danger. It was remarkable, that on drinking Water coloured with Milk (which he deſired) he conſtantly relapſed, and was as immediately eaſed upon taking a Glaſs of pure Tar-water. The Child was ſo ſenſible of this, that he cried out, "Mamma, "What is this Tar-water made of, that it is ſuch a "ſudden Cure?" It was of this Diſorder that the late Biſhops of *Oſſory* and *Elphin* died: There is no Diſtemper more threatening and ſudden, than a Pleuriſy or an Inflammation of the Lungs. The moſt copious Bleedings are preſcribed by Phyſicians, even to ſeventy or eighty Ounces; but without bleeding, bliſtering, or any other Medicine, Tar-water alone effects the Cure; were the World ſufficiently apprized of its Virtue in acute Caſes, that alone would preſerve a Multitude of Lives. To induce the Child to drink plentifully of Tar-water, they gave him a Groat a Glaſs, and he earn'd half a Guinea in two Days. This is the only Way to prevail on young Children to drink it, and 'tis ſurprizing how ſoon they recover Strength and Spirits, who are recovered from Fevers by the ſole Uſe of Tar-water.

253. A Boy was ſeized with a violent Fever in *September* 1744, having wetted his Shoes and Stockings (a new Thing to him) and ſuffered them to dry on his Feet. The Attack was violent, firſt a ſhivering cold Fit, then blood-ſhot Eyes, wild Look, burning Heat all over his Body; he drank a Gallon of Tar-water, which made him vomit, after that he ſlept and ſweated moſt copiouſly for ſixteen Hours, and when he awoke, was outragiouſly hun-

gry,

gry, and in very high Spirits, every Symptom reduced very low, and the Fever almost gone the third Day; but was kept in Bed two Days longer, to prevent a Relapse.

254. In *October* 1744, a Boy was seized with a violent Fever, and being put to Bed, he drank near two Quarts of Tar-water the first Hour, and continued drinking very copiously. The next Day, he was in Appearance very well, but he was kept quiet from all Company, and confined in Bed one Day longer; after the third Day, he was as well as ever.

255. Another young Lad in *October* 1744, was seized with a violent racking Pain all over his Body, attended with a hot Fever; about Noon he was put to Bed, and at a Groat a Glass, he drank in nine Hours twenty-five Half-pint-glasses of Tar-water; with all which (what is very singular) he did not sweat, but vented it all by Urine; and his Pain and Fever left him at nine a Clock at Night; and next Day was hearty, merry, and in as good a Temper, as ever in his Life. It is wonderful in this Medicine, that it works as an Emetic, Diuretic, Diaphoretic, Sudorific or Cordial, as the Case and Constitution requires, and that this alone should, as one may say, in the twinkling of an Eye, cure all Fevers of different Kinds.

256. In *January* 1744, a young Woman was miserably tormented with a Pain and Swelling in her Side, which threw her into a Feverish Disorder. She drank Tar-water copiously, and in a short time found herself easy and well. It is to be noted, that she applied a Plaister of Tar and Honey to the Part, which ripened, broke, and then healed it, she drinking Tar-water all the Time.

257. A Gentleman in *February* 1744, had the Gout five Days; at first he drank Sack Whey, and his Pain and Fever were violent, so as to pass a

whole Night awake and reſtleſs. From that Time he drank nothing ſtrong, but doubled or trebled his Doſes of Tar-water; this made him ſleep ſound every Night after, and kept up his Appetite and Spirits, ſo that he then reckoned his Gout as good as over, and in a few Days after, was free from it.

258. Mr. *Foulks*, Captain in the Army; Mr. *Philips*, who lodges at the Watch-maker's in *Crane-lane*, and ſeveral others, have informed me, that having had frequent Fits of the Gout, they drank Tar-water; and though they took it but in ſmall Quantities, they found great Benefit from it; their Fits either not returning at the uſual Time they expected them, and when they did, they had leſs Pain and ſhorter Fits.

259. One of my Correſpondents informed me in *February*, 1744, that his Daughter being ſeized with the Small-pox, he gave her no other Medicine than Tar-water, which ſhe drank all the Time, and that ſhe had it very favourably with little or no Sickneſs.

260. A Boy was very ill of a Worm fever in *February*, 1744, when the Small-pox ſeized him; both Evils joined, made his Caſe extremely bad. He was treated as only ill of Worms, the Small-pox not being then apprehended. He was reduced to the loweſt State, without Senſe or Motion, and many Cordials were applied to bring him to himſelf; but all to no Purpoſe, till a few Spoonfuls of Tar-water poured down his Throat without his Knowledge, brought him from Death to Life; and by continuing the drinking Tar-water, the Child recovered daily, and was ſoon perfectly well. My Correſpondent ſays, that they never had a ſtronger Inſtance of the Efficacy of Tar-water, (and its Superiority to all other Cordials) than in this Child's

Child's extreme Illneſs, much heightened by the uncommon and fierce Severity of the Weather.

261. In *March* 1744, a Boy complained heavily of a Stitch about eight a Clock in the Morning; he was immediately put to Bed, and in about an Hour drank eight Glaſſes of Tar-water, at three Glaſſes to a Pint; then fell into a ſound Sleep, and againſt three a Clock in the Afternoon was up, dreſt and well, as if nothing had ailed him.

262. In *April* 1745, a Labourer in the Country, having been taken ill, was bled a little, only one Plate; he afterwards grew very ill of a violent Pleuriſy, attended with ſpitting of Blood; he then betook himſelf to his Bed, and drank copiouſly of Tar-water, which quite recovered him, when his Caſe had been thought deſperate.

263. A Gentlewoman in *April* 1745, took the Air in a cold dry windy Day; that afternoon, ſhe was taken with ſomething like a Palſy, not being able to walk or ſtand upright. She went to Bed, grew feveriſh, and drank immenſely of Tar-water, a moderate Glaſs every Quarter of an Hour, which ſhe continued to drink the next Day in ſmaller Quantity; the Morning following, ſhe could turn eaſily in her Bed (which ſhe could not do before) and her Fever and blunt Pain in her Back and Limbs left her, and the Day following ſhe was quite recovered.

264. A Man Servant had a pleuritic Stitch, which he concealed, and went about the Houſe with it for two Days. After this he was violently ill, went to Bed in a Fever, and ſpit Blood. Then he drank Tar-water plentifully, which threw him into a great Sweat; being impatient under this Sweat, in order to cool and dry himſelf, he flung off his Shirt, and lay almoſt naked, which had like to have killed him. But Tar-water copiouſly taken, recovered him intirely. I have had many Inſtances of Perſons

recovered from pleuretic Fevers, without bleeding, or any Medicine whatsoever, by the sole copious constant drinking of Tar-water warm, one Pint, or even a Quart in an Hour. They cannot drink too much in such Cases; they will be sooner well, and strong without that Weakness, which attends those copious Bleedings, which ruin a Constitution, and entail chronical Diseases.

265. A Lawyer of my Acquaintance in *Dublin*, and two young Ladies, have been cured of Fevers by the copious drinking of Tar-water only.

266. I have had several Instances communicated to me of Persons of both Sexes, who have been cured of the Piles, some by the bare drinking of Tar-water, others by sitting at the same time on a Close-stool filled with very hot strong Tar-water, which with anointing the Parts with the Oil skummed off from the Tar-water, soon healed the Sores, and removed the Disorder.

267. In *December* 1744, a *Prolapsus Uteri*, &c. given over as incurable by the Surgeons, was perfectly cured by Tar-water.

268. My Correspondent informs me of two Persons given over, one ill of a Palsy at *Bath*, and the other of a Cancer at *York*, who were both cured in a short time by Tar-water.

269. A Gentleman's Son in the County of *Limerick*, was cured of a spitting of Blood by Tar-water.

270. An Infant had a Cough from its Birth, and shewed no Sign of Apprehension; those who saw it, thought it could not live, or if it did, that it would be stupid; the Mother was advised to give the Child Tar-water, and to make the Nurse drink it also, which being done, the Child got rid of the Cough, and came to its Apprehension, and is now lively.

271. A Gentleman writes in the following Words from *England*. I know some Instances, where

Tar-

Tar-water has done Wonders, particularly on a Lady, who has long had a Cancer in her Breaſt, and ſuffered greatly; and by taking Tar-water, the only Thing ſhe has found good from, is freed from Pain, and in a fair Way of Recovery.

272. A Gentleman in the County of *Limerick*, as I am informed, was cured by Tar-water of an Impoſthume in his Head, for which he had tried Waters, and conſulted Phyſicians in *England* to no Purpoſe.

273. A Lady was cured of a Megrim and inveterate Head-ach by Tar-water. Several other Perſons have informed me, that they uſed to be ſeized with a Dizzineſs in their Heads on walking in the Streets, ſo that they were obliged to catch hold of the Rails as they went along to prevent falling; and that ſince they took Tar-water, they have had no Uneaſineſs of that Kind.

274. I am well informed, that a Ship being bound from *Portobello* to *Jamaica*, and being detained long in the Paſſage, the Men on board were reduced to great Diſtreſs from the Want of Water, which threw many of them into the bileous or yellow Fever. But to their great Comfort, a heavy Rain fell, which ſet all their Hands to Work to catch all the Water they could; and the Deck of the Ship and Cordage having been new dawbed with Tar to preſerve them againſt the Heat of the Climate, all the Water they got was impregnated with the Tar; notwithſtanding which, they drank plentifully of it, and it had this good Effect, that all thoſe who were ill of the bileous Fever, and drank it, recovered in a ſhort Time from their Fevers, to the great Surprize of them all, as it is reckoned the moſt fatal Diſtemper in that Part of the World.

275. A Boy had a Sore in his Leg, which Leg was alſo inflamed and hard; and being adviſed to waſh it with Tar-water, and apply the Oil of Tar, he was ſoon recovered.

276. A Man of *Youghall*, was deaf for many Years, but by drinking Tar-water for some Time, he is much improved in his Hearing, and though not quite cured, yet has Hopes of Relief by a longer Use of it. Any Relief is an Advantage, and many Reliefs may at last come up to a Cure.

277. A Gentleman who had a Pain in his right Side for fifteen Years, consulted many Physicians, and took a World of Drugs to no Purpose; but on taking Tar-water (and that but a very indifferent Sort) for five Weeks, found himself greatly relieved. At the same time, it caused a Pain a-cross his Diaphragm, and also in his other Side, which he judged to be a Sign of the Efficacy of Tar-water in dislodging the peccant Humour, which being once set a-float, may afterwards be easily worked off.

278. I have an Account of a remarkable Cure performed by Tar-water, on a Woman, who was given over. Her Disorder was owing to the Retention of the After-birth, by the unskilful Management of the Midwife in her Delivery. The Case was attended with the worst Symptoms, and accounted desperate; and when all other Things had failed, some advised Tar-water, rather from not knowing what else to do, than from any Hopes of the Patient's Recovery; she nevertheless recovered by that Medicine, contrary to all Expectation.

279. *Margaret Masterson*, a young Woman, who lives at Doctor *Wynne*'s House at *Harold's-cross*, near *Dublin*, came to me the 21st of *February* 1745, and gave me the following Account of the remarkable Benefit she received by Tar-water in the Cure of an Ulcer in the Bladder. She informed me, that one Day in the Spring, about five Years ago, she walked very fast from *Harold's-cross* to *Crumlin* Church, which is about two Miles, and being in a great Heat and Sweat, she sat on the cold Ground in the Church-yard for above half an Hour, which gave her

her a great Cold, and threw her immediately into Disorders. She grew worse every Day, having great Pains in her Right-side, and lower Parts of her Belly; her Pain was so exquisite, that sometimes, for twenty Days together, she could not get the least Sleep; she lost her Flesh and Appetite, and was reduced to a Skeleton. She could not stand upright, and walked double, nor could she bear any Carriage, every Motion put her to the Rack, and she was forced to confine herself for the most Part to her Bed, and, even there, was not able to stir a Limb, when her Pains came upon her. Nothing that she took did her any Service. She was sent to *Mercers* Hospital, where she stayed three Months, without any Benefit, tho' she had the Advice and Assistance of several Physicians and Surgeons there, who for some time thought she was troubled with a Stone, but they were all of Opinion afterwards, that she had an Ulcer in the Bladder. After she left the Hospital, she was salivated, and took many Things by the Advice of Physicians; but nothing gave her any Relief or Ease, and she was judged to be incurable, She continued in this miserable Condition a long Time, she had also a Sort of Diabetes or involuntary and almost constant Discharge of Water. But in Summer 1744, her Brother hearing that Tar-water had wrought many Cures, advised her to drink it, which she did for two or three Months together. On the first drinking of it, she found it agreed with her Stomach, and gave her some Ease; in a few Days, she received great Benefit, and mended daily, and in a few Weeks, all her Pains and other Ailments went off; she recovered her Appetite, Flesh and Rest, and got the Use of her Limbs, and walked as well as ever, to the great Surprize of the Surgeons, and others, who had her under their Care, and who thought she could never recover. She then laid aside Tar-water, thinking she had no farther Occasion

for

for it, and has continued free from her Pains ever ſince, except now and then ſhe has ſome Twitches on catching cold, which ſhe imputes to her Diſuſe of Tar-water for eight or ten Months paſt; but reſolves to take it again, to remove the Remains of her Ailments. I have obſerved in ſeveral Inſtances, that ſome who had received great Benefit by Tar-water, laid it aſide too ſoon, thinking themſelves quite recovered, before they were really ſo, and that afterwards their Ailments returned upon them in ſome ſmall Degree, which they totally removed by perſiſting longer in the Uſe of it.

280. A Tradeſman in the Earl of *Meath*'s Liberty, was in the Year 1744, greatly afflicted with a Diſcharge of bloody Urine, which was ſometimes ſo violent, that what came from him appeared as clear Blood as any that comes from a Vein on bleeding, and this was attended with great Torture. He could not walk a Quarter of a Mile, but in great Pain, and he waſted away. He continued in this Condition ſeveral Months together, and took many Things for a Cure, without any Effect; but hearing of the great Good that Tar-water had done in ſeveral Caſes, he drank it, and ſoon found Benefit from it, which encouraged him to continue the drinking of it, with ſuch good Succeſs, that he was ſoon perfectly recovered of his Ailment. His Diſcharge of Blood ceaſed, and he made his Water as clear as ever, without the leaſt Colour or Tincture of Blood, and without any Pain, all the Parts being healed, and in *February* 1745, he continues very well, and attributes his Cure wholly to Tar-water.

281. A Gentlewoman, who lives in the Country not far from *Dublin*, was for many Years afflicted with a Cancer in her Breaſt, which had been cut by Surgeon *Dobbs*, but it ſtill grew again, became hard, and was exceſſively painful; and notwithſtanding the great Danger and Torture that attends the Ope-

ration,

ration, ſhe reſolved to undergo another Cutting to get rid of her conſtant Pain, and came to Town for that Purpoſe; but the Surgeon finding that ſhe had got a freſh great Cold, and a violent Cough with it, he would not venture to cut her Breaſt till her Cough was removed, and adviſed her to go to the Country to be cured of her Cough. She was there perſuaded to drink Tar-water on that Account, which ſhe did with ſuch Effect, that ſhe ſoon got rid of her Cough; and finding that Tar-water agreed with her Stomach, and that it alſo made her Breaſt eaſier, ſhe continued the drinking of it for a conſiderable Time, by which Means her Breaſt grew eaſy and ſoft, and ſhe mended daily to her great Comfort and Surprize; and ſhe got ſo much Relief, that ſhe laid aſide the Water for ſome time. In what State ſhe now continues in, I am not informed.

282. *A Copy of a Letter from the Reverend Mr.* Thomas Dawſon, *of* Tallow, *in the County of* Waterford, *to* Thomas Prior, *Eſq*; *dated* February 25, 1745.

I take leave to ſend you the two following Caſes, wherein, among ſeveral others in my Neighbourhood, Tar-water has proved ſucceſsful; and as the Diſorders therein mentioned are common and often fatal, ſo a Publication of the Cure of them may be of Service to Mankind, whoſe general Good ſeems to be the Deſign and End of your Enquiries.

283. *The Caſe of Mrs.* Guinane, *Wife of* John Guinane, *of* Tallow, *in the County of* Waterford, *Merchant.*

The ſaid Mrs. *Guinane*, was violently ſeized with hyſteric Fits in the Year 1744, attended with Laughing, Crying, and frequent Swoonings, which continued for ſeveral Months, though Phyſicians, by various Medicines, endeavoured to cure her of them.

them. She went to the Salt-water, and bathed therein, pursuant to their Advice, for a considerable Time; but received very little Benefit thereby. At last, she betook herself to the drinking of Tar-water, pursuant to the Directions of the Author of *Siris*, and by regularly and constantly drinking the same for about the Space of three Months, she perfectly recovered her Health, and has been free from the said hysteric Fits ever since, though she despaired of being ever cured of them.

284. *The Case of Mr.* Thomas Lowris, *of* Tallow, *in the County of* Waterford.

The said Mr. *Lowris* was in a deep Consumption for four or five Years, and so greatly emaciated, and so yellow, that all who saw him, seemed to despair of his Life. About two Years ago, he began to drink Tar-water, and having in a few Months received great Benefit thereby, he continued ever since to drink the same regularly, and has perfectly recovered his Health and Complexion, to the great Surprize of all that knew him.

285. A Gentleman near *Caple-street*, informed me on the 22d of *February* 1745, that for several Years he used to be troubled with Fits, which gave him great Uneasiness in his Stomach, and were attended with a violent Pain, which ran along the Bottom of his Belly, and fixed itself in his left Hip, with a great Inclination to puking. These Pains continued for two or three Days, while the Fits lasted, He thought his Ailment was a windy Colic; and accordingly he took many Things, but without any Benefit. He found that he grew worse, and that his Fits returned upon him more frequently and with more Violence. He used also to have Fits of the Gout in his Feet, without any great Violence. But having read the Treatise on Tar-water in *April* 1744, he resolved to drink it, and he had not

not taken it above three Weeks, before he had a sensible Benefit, and, continuing to drink it, he in a little time after, to his great Surprize, discharged two Stones near as big as Peas, and then, and not till then, he discovered that his Disorder was the Stone and Gravel; upon which the Pain in the Bottom of his Belly went off, he got Ease in his Stomach, and recovered his Appetite and Rest. He has since voided Gravel at several Times, and of late, three smaller Stones, which gave him Pain in their Passage, and he does not doubt, but that he voided Gravel and small Stones formerly, without knowing it, when he had those violent Fits. But now that he knows what his Disorder is he can better guard against it. These Fits of the Gravel and Stone return now and then upon him, and are likely to do so, till they are all carried off; for which Purpose, he finds Tar-water to be very useful. He assured me, that, since he began to drink Tar-water, which he constantly doth, he has not been confined one Day with the Gout. He has had some Twitches of it now and then, but they go off soon without Pain; and as he has received so much Benefit by Tar-water, he often recommends the Use of it to others.

286. I am informed, that a Gentleman, who had gone through a Course of *Stephen*'s Medicines, took Tar-water, which he found more successful in the Gravel.

287. Some Gentlemen, who, on catching the least Cold, used to be troubled with sore chopp'd Lips, which they could not heal or cure by any of the Salves prescribed for them, were eased of that Disorder by bathing their Lips with Tar-water, which soon healed them; and they who had sore and running Nostrils received the same Benefit, by bathing them with the Water. These slight Instances are mentioned, only to shew the healing Quality of Tar-water: and it is also found by Ex-

perience that a Plaister of Tar is a safe and effectual Cure for Sores and Swellings in the Backs of Horses. And now I am upon this Topick, I shall beg Leave to mention what several Gentlemen informed me of, that they gave two or three Quarts of Tar-water a Day to some of their Horses which had great Colds and Disorders, and received no Benefit by the Drenches of Farriers, so that they were afraid of losing them, and the Effect was, that they soon recovered. And perhaps it may be advisable in all Distempers of Brute Creatures, where the Blood is corrupted, as in Glanders in Horses, and in Infections of the horned Cattle and Sheep, which are thought to be incurable, to give them Tar-water warm in plenty, as it is found by Experience in so many Instances to correct and sweeten the Blood and Juices of the Body, remove Obstructions, and invigorate the Spirits. At least it may be proper to make Tryal when the Case is desperate.

288. The Small-pox having proved very mortal last Season, some were advised to give their Children Tar-water warm, and the Effect was, that they who drank it before they were seized with the Small-pox, generally had it favourably; but they who took it during the Time of the Sickness also, came off still better, there was no Appearance of Danger, the Pock generally distinct, little or no Sickness, and no Marks left by it. These Accounts I had from several Persons of Credit, and in particular, that in and about *Clonmell*, the Small-pox was so very fatal last Summer, that above three Hundred dyed of it, for the most Part of the confluent Kind. Some were at last advised and prevailed upon to give their Children Tar-water warm, and in plenty, as Mr. *Gordon*, an eminent Brewer there, did to four or five of his Children, who all came off very well. This encouraged Mrs. *Powel* to give it to three of her Children, who had the like Success, and

had it so favourably, that they were hardly sick. Whereas others, who were treated in the common Way, were for the most part carried off by the Malignity of the Distemper; and I can't hear that any, who took Tar-water, miscarried. For which Reason, many now fall into the Use of it with great Benefit, and do not apprehend such Danger from that fatal Distemper as formerly they did. Such is the Power and Efficacy of Tar-water in asswaging and curing Fevers and inflammatory Disorders.

289. The Reverend Mr. *Skelton*, Minister of *Newry*, made his Son about thirteen Years old, drink Tar-water, before he had the Small-pox, and when he was lately seized with it, he gave him a full Wine-glass of it every two Hours, during the Time he was ill of the Disorder; by practising on him in this Manner, the Child was hardly sick, the Pock filled very well, and left no Marks. When Children are treated after this Manner in the Small-pox, and drink plentifully of the Water warm, they generally have it very favourably.

290. Several Instances have been communicated to me by Persons of Credit, of wonderful and unexpected Cures performed by Tar-water in Disorders peculiar to the Female Sex at the Times of their Delivery; and also in provoking the Menses in some where they were wanted, and in restraining them in others, when they become immoderate. But in these Cases, Names are not to be published.

291. There are several Gentlewomen in this Town, whose Names I shall forbear to mention, who, having been troubled with Rheumatic Pains, Oppression and Load in their Stomachs, Want of Appetite and Rest, Streightness in their Chests, Cough, and scorbutical Disorders, were cured or greatly relieved by the Use of Tar-water, though drank but in small Quantities. Several Gentlemen of my Acquaintance were affected the same Way, and

and received the like Benefit. But it would be endless to enumerate all of them, or to wait for more Cases, which come every Day to our Knowledge. If any new remarkable Instances should happen for the Future, of Cures performed by Tar-water, in any of the Disorders mentioned in this Narrative; or if any Discoveries should be made of it's Success in other Distempers; it is to be hoped that they, who shall receive the Benefit, will be so good and grateful, as to communicate the Particulars of their Cases, and that others will be found, who will give themselves the Trouble to collect and publish them for the good of Mankind, with or without the Names of the Patients, as the Patients themselves shall desire. And this Request is desired not only in the Case of Tar-water, but of every other Medicine, which may have the same good Effects.

292. Having now swelled this Narrative to a Size far beyond my first Intentions, I shall forbear troubling the Reader with any more Cases. A great Number of others have been mentioned to me from Time to Time; but the Want of Leisure, or Opportunity of getting a particular Account from the Patients themselves, who lived at a Distance, and were Strangers to me, and the Shyness of others in communicating their Ailments and Recoveries, lest their Names should be published, (though I always declared that when I should publish the Case of any one, I would forbear mentioning their Names if they desired it) for these Reasons, I neglected to make a Collection of more Cases; and indeed, there was the less Occasion for doing so, as every City and large Town in the Kingdom can furnish many Instances of great and unpexpected Cures performed by Tar-water alone, which every one may be satisfied of the Truth of, who will give himself the least Trouble of enquiring. Besides, as I was already furnished with a great Number of remark-

remarkable Cases and Cures in several Distempers, I had the less Reason to take Notice of others of the same Kind. But as the Power and Efficacy of Tar-water, in curing many Disorders, is happily experienced by great Numbers, and stands sufficiently confirmed by the many authentic Instances produced in this Narrative, which the World hath not been yet acquainted with, it would be a Prejudice to Mankind to defer any longer the Publication of them; it being reasonable to expect, that others, in the like Disorders, may receive equal Benefit by the same Means. It has often grieved me, to hear of several Persons dying of acute Disorders, which were suddenly and effectually cured by Tar-water alone, as appears from several Instances in this Narrative; and it is probable, they might have received the same Benefit, if the same Medicine had been made use of; at least, it was proper to try it, when the Case was desperate. For the Reasons aforesaid, it was high Time to publish this Narrative, that every one may be fully apprized of the Power of this Water, and make trial of it in parallel Cases.

293. The Gentlemen of the Faculty, who are Men of superior Skill and Abilities, can and will, without Doubt, apply and improve these Hints and Experiments. But though I am no Physician, yet I hope I may be allowed to relate Matters of Fact in this Narrative, and to give an historical Account of the Effects of Tar-water, as they were communicated to me by Letters from the Patients themselves, and in their own Words, or from other Gentlemen, who had their Informations from the Patients, at the same Time mentioning their Names and Places of Abode. I took from others the Particulars of their Cases from their own Mouths, and for greater Exactness, read them over to them, when they were written down. I have mentioned some Cases, where the Names of Persons and Places are omitted; but

these Cases I had from Gentlemen of Integrity and Credit, who assured me of the Truth of the Facts, in the Letters which they sent me, at the Times the Cases happened, and when every Circumstance was fresh in their Memories, which Letters are now in my Custody; they were not willing to mention the Names of Patients, particularly of the Female Sex, without their Consent, which could hardly be obtained. But I have not the least Reason to doubt of the Truth of the Facts, which are so well attested. But if any Person should be desirous to know the Names, or Places of Abode, of any of the Patients whose Names are omitted, I shall, for their private Satisfaction, gratify them in that Particular.

294. Having closed my Register of Cases, I shall beg Leave to make some Remarks, which occurred to me from Reading those Cases, and from the Observations of my Correspondents.

I. It must be Matter of Surprize, to find, that in the Space of one Year and an half, such a Number and Variety of Distempers have been cured, or greatly relieved by this one Medicine. Thousands have received Benefit, and daily do receive Benefit in *Ireland*, *England*, *Holland*, *France*, *Portugal*, and *Germany*, by the Use of Tar-water. The Letters sent to me signify the same; the least Enquiry may satisfy others of the Truth thereof; this Narrative shews it, and the *Index*, hereunto annexed, points out the various Sorts of Ailments, wherein it has proved successful. The Treatise on Tar-water, called *Siris*, has been translated into the *French*, *Low Dutch*, *German* and *Portugese* Languages, and Extracts thereof have been published in the *Magazines*. By so general a Publication, the Use of Tar-water, as a Medicine, came to be universally known, and being strongly recommended by the Author, from his own Experience, for the Cure of several Distempers, many were induced to make Trial of it, and found immediate Relief: This encouraged others to make Use of it also, and they received the same Benefit thereby. And such was the growing Credit of this Medicine, that several, who had been long afflicted with grievous Ailments, without receiving any Relief by the Prescriptions of Physicians, though they never heard that Tar-water was made use of in the like Disorders, yet were willing to try, and soon found a wonderful and unexpected Relief. Some who had taken Tar-water for one Disorder, were, at the same Time, affected with another, and both were removed by this powerful Medicine. Some of the Virtues of Tar-water were thus accidentally discovered, and by many subsequent Trials, on others, fully confirmed.

295. The happy Discovery of the Efficacy of Tar-water, in curing most Kinds of Fevers and Pleurisies, is a Thing of singular and most extensive Benefit to Mankind, and confirmed by so many Trials, that they who are acquainted with this Practice, think themselves in little Danger from Fevers; and it is found by Experience, that the larger the Quantity of Tar-water that is taken in Fevers by the Patient, the sooner he recovers. If he takes but two or three Quarts a Day, the Fever may last four or five Days; but if four, five, or six Quarts, or more, be drank warm in twenty four Hours, they often find the Fever quite carried off in a Day or two. And what is very remarkable, there is no Instance of Danger or Harm done by any Quantity taken; on the contrary, Patients in Fevers are in higher animal Spirits, the more they drink, the Water passing through their Bodies by Urine or Perspiration, as fast as it is taken in, and thereby carrying off the noxious Humours, and Venom of the Distemper the sooner. The Patients at the same Time get sound Sleep, and a better Appetite than

is usual in Fevers. My Correspondents farther assure me, that they never knew an Instance where warm Tar-water was given betimes in a Fever, and in due Quantity, that it failed of Success. It is judged, that the greater Part of grown People, who die in their Beds, die of some Kind of Fever or other: Therefore, if Respect were only had to this one Article of Fevers, wherein Tar-water is so successful, it would seem to follow, that nothing is more beneficial to the Life of Man, or that would save more Lives, than this Water duly prepared and taken.

296. II. The next Observation I shall make, is, on the Variety of Distempers cured by Tar-water, and even such as are opposite in their Natures. This has been judged to be impossible by some, who have decried the Use of Tar-water: Though Fact and Experience, the surest Guides for knowing the Force of any Medicine, are entirely against them; not only in the Case of Tar-water, but of several other Medicines, which frequently produce contrary Effects in different Constitutions, and sometimes different Effects in the same Constitution. Some who first wrote and spoke against Tar-water, at the same Time frankly owned, that they had never made any trial of it. How then could they form any Judgment of the good or bad Qualities of it, or expect that others should be swayed by their Opinions, when no Way supported by Experiment, the only sure Rule to go by? A Gentleman of the Faculty, one Day, asked me, if Tar-water was a Panacea or a Cure for all Distempers. I told him, that I thought no Body could answer that Question, but a Person who had tried it in all Distempers, and in Variety of Cases of every Distemper, which I had not done, and I believe no Body living had yet done; and that until Trial had been made, no Judgment could be formed in what Cases it was

good

good or not. I then desired leave to ask him the following Question, In what Disorder Tar-water was not good? This, I said, because I was amply furnished with many Instances of Cures performed by Tar-water in all the common Distempers in *Dublin*, to which I could refer him for his Satisfaction, if he should mention any of them: but after considering some time, he asked me, if it was good for the Stone? I answered, that I had not yet heard that it was made Use of for the Stone, but that I could give him many Instances, where it was of great Use in the Gravel, and I thought what was good for the Gravel, might also be good for the Stone. But that in all these Cases, nothing but Experience and undoubted Facts can or ought to determine our Opinions. Some who were offended to find Tar-water recommended for so many different Distempers, for that very Reason were for exploding it, as of no Use in any Case whatsoever; without considering that whatever corrects and sweetens the Blood, mends the Stomach and removes Obstructions, as Tar-water manifestly doth, must be of Use in all Distempers, and thereby assist Nature to make a perfect Cure. The universal Medicine as well as the Philosopher's-stone have been always treated as vain Attempts: But if the former be possible in Nature, no Medicine seems to bid so fair for that Character as Tar-water: but without making any Pretensions to such an extraordinary Prerogative, I shall only observe, that it is happy for the World to be possessed of a Medicine that has done, and daily doth great Service in so many different Maladies, without repining, that it cannot do the same in all.

297. III. The third Remark I shall make, is on the Safety of this Medicine. Some Physicians advise and prescribe it. Others say, that it is good in many Cases, and that they do not find it do Harm in any. Some say, that it is neither good nor bad,

while others suggest, that it is dangerous in inflammatory Cases, by an over-heating Quality: But the contrary thereof is manifest, from its curing Fevers, Pleurisies, Small-pox, and other inflammatory Disorders, in a short Space of Time; and it is so far from increasing Inflammations, that it wonderfully assuages them. Some Patients, on drinking Tar-water, were immediately seized with a Vomiting, which much alarmed them; but they soon found that Tar-water, by thus discharging a great deal of foul Stuff out of their Stomachs, gave them immediate Relief, and the Vomiting soon after stopped. Others had a Purging for a Day or two, on taking Tar-water, which they also did not like; but the Purging soon ceased, when it carried off the peccant Humours, and they received great Benefit by the Operation. Some Patients, who were troubled with violent scorbutical Disorders, Eruptions, Itch, Blotches, running Sores, found, on the drinking Tar-water a few Days, that their Sores, Itchings, and Eruptions grew more troublesome, and increased on the Surface of their Bodies, in greater Quantity and Violence, and then thought Tar-water did them Harm; some were so imprudent as to stop drinking the Water, when it was doing them all the Good imaginable, by driving from the Blood all the noxious Humours to the Surface of the Body; while others, who persisted in drinking it, soon found the Scurvy, Eruptions, and other Blotches on their Bodies, die away and heal, to their great Relief. Some, on whom Tar-water works by Perspiration, found that it made them Costive, and heated them; upon this, they laid it aside; others, who in the like Case persisted in drinking it, soon found, that, after the Tar-water had done its Work by Perspiration, they returned to their natural State, and got the Relief they expected. Nature does not work two different Ways at the same Time; if it works by Stool, Perspiration ceases

ceases for the Time; if by Perspiration, then the other stops. If both those Channels are stopped, there is no Way left for Nature to discharge the vitiated Humours, but by Urine: And this is the way that Tar-water generally operates. These are, for the most Part, the Cases wherein Tar-water has been imagined to do Harm. But it is hard, that Tar-water should be charged with doing Hurt in such Cases, when it was doing the greatest Service to the Patients. It is true, that very bad Tar, and Tar-water, have often been made use of, and as true, that several Persons, at the Time they drank Tar-water, indulged themselves in the Use of strong Liquors, and Spirits; and therefore, it is no Wonder, if they did not receive the Benefit that otherwise they might have got. On the whole, I do not find any Instance, where Tar-water ever did any real Harm, which cannot be said of any other Medicine.

298. IV. Chronical Disorders, wherein the whole Mass of Blood and Juices of the Body have been long vitiated, require a Length of Time and Patience to effect a Cure; and if they be very grievous, the Quantity of Tar-water to be taken in such Cases should be increased from a Pint to a Quart a Day, beginning with a Noggin or a Quarter of a Pint, to find how it agrees with the Stomach; and so continuing to drink it often in small Quantities; it being found by Experience, that the more the Patients drink in such Cases, the sooner they recover.

299. Scurvies make a great Part of the Ailments of People, in this Part of the World, and yet we find by the many Instances produced in this Narrative, that the worst Kinds of them, attended with running Sores, Blotches, Scruff, *&c.* were perfectly cured by Tar-water, which heals up all the Sores, and in some Measure, embalms scorbutic Bodies alive.

300. The ſame Succeſs has attended internal Ulcers in the Bladder, Lungs, urinary Paſſages, venereal Taints, and in Ulcers on the outward Parts of the Body, owing to the healing Quality of Tar-water. Even the King's Evil, and other ſcrophulous Diſorders, which are commonly reckoned incurable, have yielded to the Power of this Water, as may be ſeen by ſeveral Caſes in this Collection; inſomuch, that we have Reaſon to believe, that any King's Evil may be cured by Tar-water; having never heard that it failed of Succeſs, when regularly and plentifully taken, and eſpecially when at the ſame Time the Sores were anointed with the Oil ſkimmed from the Tar-water.

301. Scald Head, inveterate Itch, and even Cancers, have yielded to the healing Quality of Tar-water.

302. Though nervous Caſes require a long time to perfect a Cure, yet we find that Hyſterics, Fits, and Palſies have been cured by Tar-water alone. Mr. *Hanning*'s Daughter mentioned in the Collection, who was ſeized with a Palſy, ſo that ſhe could neither ſpeak nor move a Limb in *November* laſt, is now in *March* following, briſk and lively, and perfectly well, notwithſtanding the Severity of the Weather. And I am informed, that a Woman, who was troubled with Fits for above a Twelvemonth, which often returned, and cauſed her to lye ſpeechleſs and ſenſeleſs a long Time together, being adviſed to take Tar-water, a Quart a Day; on doing ſo, ſhe had but one Fit in three Weeks paſt, and that occaſioned by a Fright. I know of others, who having been long troubled with Fits, have had no Return of them ſince they began to drink Tar-water. It is adviſed in ſuch Caſes, to give it freely and boldly.

303. Many Inſtances are produced of Perſons who have been cured or greatly relieved of Diſor-

ders in the Bowels, Colics, Megrims, inveterate Head-achs, Agues, Rheumatiſms, exceſſive Thirſt, and fixed Pains in ſome Parts of the Body. Others, who were tortured with exceſſive Pains, on taking Tar-water, unexpectedly diſcovered that their Ailment was owing to the Stone and Gravel, in diſcharging which, they found Tar-water to be very uſeful.

304. Many who laboured under a lowneſs of Spirits, Diſorders in their Stomachs, want of Appetite and Sleep, found thoſe Diſorders carried of by the Uſe of Tar-water.

305. many are the Inſtances of thoſe who being long afflicted with Aſthmas, Shortneſs of Breath, and Difficulty of Breathing, violent Coughs, Wheezing, Stuffings and Decays, ſore Throats and Squincy, have been either entirely cured, or greatly relieved by Tar-water.

306. As to the Gout, the Diſeaſe of the Rich, we find that ſome, greatly afflicted with that Diſorder, by the conſtant and regular Uſe of Tar-water, have had no Return of their Fits ſince they began to drink the Water; occaſioned by a kindly Perſpiration in their Limbs, which they never had before, and which recovered the Uſe of them, and removed all their Pains. Others, on drinking the Water, found the ſame Benefit; but by laying aſide the Uſe of it too ſoon, their Fits returned upon them, though later than uſual, yet with this Advantage, that they were not ſo violent nor laſting. Others grown in Years and much enfeebled with the Gout, though they got Spirits, Appetite, and Reſt, and ſome Relaxation of their Pains by the Uſe of Tar-water, yet, as this Liquor was not to their Taſte, they either diſcontinued the Uſe of it, or took it in ſuch ſmall Quantities, that the Weakneſs in their Limbs ſtill continued, and their Fits returned on Change of Weather, or on catching Cold. And

now

now we find by Experience, that the surest Way of dealing with the Gout, is not only to drink the Water before and after the Fit, but during the whole Time of the Fit, and that in the Quantity of a Quart a Day, warm, which gives such a Discharge by Perspiration or Urine, as relieves Nature and removes the Pains. But if Gentlemen will continue in the Use of strong Liquors, and high Feeding, it must be presumed, that the same Cause will still produce the same Effects.

307. As to the Small-pox, with which nine Parts in ten of all People are seized in one Part or other of their Lives in this Part of the World, I shall only observe, that the great Number of Negroes cured on the Coast of *Guinea* of the Small-pox by Tar-water, as mentioned in this Narrative, and many others who have been cured in this Kingdom the latter End of last Season, when it was so rife and mortal, by the same Means, evidently shew, that Tar-water is a sovereign, safe, and efficacious Medicine for the Cure of this fatal Distemper, by giving it warm, and in Plenty, both before, and in the whole Time of the Illness. And I do not doubt, but that others, who will put it in Practice, will find the same surprizing Success.

308. But the greatest and most useful Discovery of this, or perhaps of any other Age, is that of Tar-water curing so suddenly and effectually, all Sorts of Fevers, Pleurisies, and inflammatory Distempers, whereby two Thirds of Mankind are carried off before their natural Time. These Maladies destroy more of the human Species, than all the Artillery great and small in the World can do, and yet are themselves easily subdued by Tar-water.

This late Discovery of the Virtues of Tar-water stands so confirmed by the Authentic Proofs mentioned in the Narrative, that nobody can doubt the Truth thereof, who doth not at the same Time deny ny Facts, which are so many, and so well attested. But this may be put on a short Issue, it is in the Power of any one, and every one is concerned in the Event, to make a fair Tryal of the Truth or Falshood of this Discovery, and see whether Tar-water taken in due Time and Quantity, before the Fever has utterly destroyed the Crasis and Constitution of the Blood, will not entirely subdue and carry off the Fever in a few Days, of any kind whatever.

309. But then to give Tar-water fair Play, the following Caution should be observed, which has been found necessary in many Instances, *viz.* That the Water be good in its kind, that it be administered to the Patient lying in Bed, in the Beginning of the Fever, and that warm, in the Quantity of half a Pint or more every half Hour, according to the Age and Strength of the Person, till the Patient takes six or eight Quarts in the Space of twenty four Hours; and that no other Medicine be taken with it; that Care be taken against catching Cold; that when the Fever abates, no Nourishment be given but what is very light and cooling; and that when the Fever is gone, the Patient keep his Bed a Day or two longer, free from Noise and People's talking, to prevent a Relapse. It is found by Experience in many Instances, that Patients in Fevers cannot drink too much Tar-water, there is no Danger from Excess, the more they drink the sooner they are cured; it hath been often observed, that the Heat and Thirst they have on such Occasions so reconciles the Water to them, that they can drink a great Quantity without disgust; they have generally a great flow of Spirits during the whole Time they drink, get Intervals of Sleep, and when the Fever abates, they have commonly keen Appetites, which ought not to be indulged too soon or too much. It is amazing to see with what Speed and

Success

Succefs Tar-water taken copioufly, as above-mentioned, cures the moft violent Pleurifies, without Blifters or Medicines, and without bleeding, which in the common Practice is exceffive. It is faid, the late Honourable Mr. *Hamilton*, Collector at *Cork*, had 150 Ounces taken from him in pleuretic Diftemper of which he died. It is proper to repeat and inculcate the Advantage of being cured by a Cordiel, rather than by Evacuations, which at beft often leave a Patient weak and languifhing for Years together. Nothing is fo dangerous as neglecting the Beginnings of Fevers. *Principiis obfta*, is a good Maxim with Refpect to the natural as well as political Body: Some People are apt to hold out as long as they can, and go abroad with Fevers upon them; By thus expofing themfelves, they inflame their Diforders, and render them very dangerous. The beft Courfe to take in fuch Cafes is to go to Bed and drink Tar-water. The Efficacy of Tar-water in curing Fevers, evidently fhews, that it is not of an inflaming or heating Nature. And yet fome have thought themfelves heated by Tar-water, who at the fame Time drank too freely of ftrong Liquors. And I am credibly informed, that fome noted Drinkers of Whifky complained that Tar-water gave them the Megrim, a Diforder which in others, it is known to have cured. If therefore any one complains of being heated by Tar-water, let it be enquired at the fame Time whether he doth not indulge himfelf in the Ufe of fermented or diftilled Liquors.

310. Some People cannot comprehend, that a Medicine, which in flow gradual Courfe removes chronical Difeafes, fhould be proper in acute Cafes which require Difpatch. But nothing hinders, why the fame Medicine, which drank daily in fmall Quantities proves a leifurely Cure for chronical Ills, may not alfo, if drank copioufly, and in very large Quantities,

Quantities prove a speedy Cure for acute Cases, such as all kinds of Fevers.

311. Having thus recapitulated several Maladies in which Tar-water has been found successful, I shall beg Leave to recommend the Use of it in a particular Manner to seafaring Men, who are so useful to every trading Nation, and whose Lives ought therefore to be preserved with the utmost Care. They are subject to many Distempers, besides those common to other Men at Land, which they contract at Sea, by the Change and Inclemency of the Weather in long Voyages, by the Heat or Cold of the Climate, by great Fatigues, salt Provisions, close suffocating Air in the Ships, *&c.* which produce Fevers, Calentures, Scurvies of several Kinds, Ulcers, running Sores, Looseness of their Teeth and many other Disorders, for which they commonly have little or no Provision of Medicines or Accommodation, or any Person on board of Skill to assist them, by which Means great Numbers of them perish miserably. Now as it is found by Experience, that Tar-water cures those Disorders, it is recommended, that in every Ship, Provision be made of several Barrels of good Tar, and that a Vessel of Tar-water be always prepared to be given in Plenty to such of the Crew, who happen to labour under any of those Distempers; by which Means, the Lives of Thousands may be saved. Spruce-Beer, which is a great Antiscorbutic, and a-kin to Tar-water, would also be very useful in Sea Voyages.

312. Since Tar-water is so safe and cheap a Medicine, and found by Experience to cure many chronical Distempers as well as slight Disorders, it is recommended to provide Tar and Tar-water in every Hospital, Infirmary, and Work-house; and that a Barrel of Tar-water be always at hand for every one to repair to, who may be afflicted with such Maladies, to drink thereof, as much, and as often

as

as there is Occasion. By these Means, the Lives of Numbers may be saved, and the Patients either cured or greatly relieved. From many Tryals of the good Effects of this Medicine, we find that the Use of Tar-water is introduced into the Hospitals at *Lisbon*, with great Advantage. We have many Instances in this Narrative of People, who were kept a long Time in the Infirmaries, in Order to be cured, and were afterwards turned out as Incurable, and yet those very People, were in some Time after perfectly recovered by Tar-water, to the Surprize of those who had them under their Care before. Besides, this Method would save great Sums to the Hospitals in the Expence for Medicines. And as all Hospitals and Infirmaries are supported at the Charge of the Public, or by private Donations and voluntary Contributions, it should be the Business of those concerned in the Government of them, to lessen the Expence as much as possible, consistent with the Health and Lives of the Patients. And I am inclined to believe, that many of those who are lodged in *Guy*'s and other Hospitals as Incurables, may be cured or greatly relieved by Tar-water, and so make room for others to be admitted. Whereas at present, little Care is taken of their Recovery, as being deemed incurable, and they stay there only to spend a wretched Life. Though it is believed that some of them would be sorry to be cured, and thereby be obliged to leave the Hospital, where they live in tolerable Ease, to get a Livelihood abroad by their own Labour. This deserves the Attention of the Public.

313. It is recommended to all Gentlemen who live in the Country and Market-towns, that in Compassion for their poor Tenants, Neighbours and Servants, they will be so good and humane, as to provide Quantities of Tar, and make Tar-water thereof, and distribute the same liberally to such as want

want it, and are destitute of all Means, which are proper to cure them of the Disorders they are frequently afflicted with.

314. The Use of Tar-water is also recommended to sedentary Persons, which by its diuretic Quality, greatly prevents Head-ach, Bloating, Dropsy, Stone and Gravel, which sedentary People are subject to from the want of Exercise.

315. V. In all odd and new Cases, where People are at a loss what to do, and even in desperate Cases where Patients are given over, and no Hopes left, it is recommended to try Tar-water, which has been found in several Instances to recover Patients from the Brink of Death.

316. I have an Account, that Tar-water is in great Vogue at *Paris*, notwithstanding the Endeavours of some interested Persons against it. An *Irish* Physician prescribes it to his *French* Patients with great Success, and has got into good Business thereby.

317. Since I have mentioned foreign Practice, it comes into my Thoughts to insert the Testimony or Attestation of two foreign Physicians, against the Notion of an inflaming Heat in Tar-water, entertained by some among us who would decry that Medicine. Doctor *De Linden*, a *German* Physician now in *London*, wrote a Letter about six Months ago, from which are taken the following Extracts. It seems that learned Foreigner had mistaken the Sense of *Siris*, as attributing such Heat to Tar-water, which Opinion both he and his foreign Correspondent, set themselves to refute. *I myself* (saith Doctor *De Linden*) *have drank about twenty five Gallons of Tar-water constantly every twenty-four Hours three Pints, and that of the Colour of* Spanish *Wine, and I never found any Effect that we may call a physical Heat in the Blood, notwithstanding that I am of a very sanguine Temperament, and the least Thing can occasion*

occasion in me an Inflamation. He adds, *I would not have taken the Freedom to acquaint you with this if I had not in this Point been attacked by the first Physician to a certain great crowned Head in* Germany, *and President of a most illustrious* Collegium Medicum. After which, Doctor *De Linden*, sets down Part of this Correspondent's Letter, containing the following Words: *I am glad we have got into our Faculty a Reverend Divine, but I am still more pleased with his Discovery; and I agree in every Thing with him, because I have experienced Tar-water myself; but there is one Error committed.* He then proceeds to refute the Error, supposed to be in *Siris*, viz. *that Tar-water is Heating.* After which, he subjoins these Words: *In Reality, Tar-water is of such a mild Nature, that it never can inflame, nor create an Inflamation in the Blood. I agree with every Thing else, and blessed Thanks be to the Bishop for his valuable Discovery.* It is probable, Foreigners might mistake *warming* for *heating*; and so conceive that when Tar-water was said in *Siris* to warm, it was understood to heat. But certain it is, that in many Parts of that Treatise, all inflaming Heat is expressly denied to be in Tar-water. Thus in the seventy-fourth Section it is said; *The Salts, the Spirits, the Heat of Tar-water, are of a Temperature congenial to the Nature of Man, which receives from it a kindly Warmth, but no inflaming Heat.* And in the following Section, Tar-water is affirmed to be *so far from increasing a feverish Inflammation, that it is on the contrary, a most ready Means to allay and extinguish it.* There are so many other Passages to the same Effect, throughout the whole Book of *Siris*, that it would be endless, as well as needless to enumerate them.

318. I should not omit to take Notice, that several Ladies, who had received great Benefit by Tar-water, at the same Time recovered their Com-

plexions

plexions and Bloom, and that others, who had ſqueamiſh Stomachs, and could not bear to take Tar-water in the Morning before Breakfaſt, yet found it to agree well with them an Hour or two after eating. An old Lady has been greatly relieved by drinking conſtantly every Day, no more than one Wine-glaſs in the Morning.

319. A great Deal depends on the Goodneſs of Tar-water. Tar being looked upon as a Naval Store, could not be imported without Riſque and Difficulty in time of War: Hence for ſome time no Tar could be got that was fit for making Tar-water; ſome was adulterated with the Mixture of other Stuff, and Retailers frequently ſold for freſh Tar, that which had been formerly uſed. By theſe Means ſeveral have been diſappointed and abuſed by bad Tar-water; ſuch Tar-water as is of a brown Colour or ſweetiſh flat Taſte, is bad, but they who have once drank good Tar-water, can eaſily diſtinguiſh the bad, which has no Spirit. Liquid Tar, which is the firſt running from the Billets, from whence the Tar flows by ſmothering Heat of Fire, is generally the beſt. And yet no certain Judgment can be formed of the Goodneſs of Tar, by the Colour or Conſiſtence, till Trial be made, by making Tar-water of it. When a Veſſel of Tar has ſtood long on an End, a Sediment often falls to the Bottom, which Sediment ſhould not be made Uſe of for Tar-water.

320. The adding artificial Helps to plain ſimple Remedies, often diſturbs their Operation, and render thoſe Medicines ineffectual: I have an Account of two Caſes, where Phyſicians preſcribed the Bark with Tar-water: But the Patients found not the Benefit, till they took Tar-water alone. Some have put a Drop of the Oil of Nutmegs to a Glaſs of Tar-water, which made it more palatable; others have added a ſmall Spoonful of Mead, White-wine,

or Cyder, which made the Draught more agreeable; but it were better no Spirits should be taken with it, or any Thing else that might weaken the Virtue of the Water, and it is therefore more adviseable to take it pure, and a little Use will reconcile it to the Palate.

Fir-trees grow naturally in most Parts of the World, in hot Countries as well as cold, but chiefly in the mountainous Parts of both. After this Manner, Providence furnishes in great Plenty, the Means, of preserving Health and Life by the simplest Medicines.

321. It is proper to warn those who expect the whole Benefit of Tar-water, to be very temperate in the Use of strong Liquors fermented or distilled. They weaken and frustrate the Powers of Tar-water, which of itself is a sufficient Cordial. It has a great Effect upon the Nerves and Spirits, animates the Heart without disordering the Brain, and is an Antidote against Cold, Fatigue, and Thirst. That is certainly the best Cordial which encreases the animal Spirits, without inflaming the Blood, or disturbing the Nerves, as all inebriating Liquors never fail to do: If this be the Effect of Tar-water, as I am assured it is, it may be of Use in our Armies and Fleets.

322. I have no View in giving myself this Trouble, but to promote the good of Mankind, without any Desire to incroach on the Province of Others. They who railed and argued against Tar-water on the first Publication of *Siris*, insisted that particular Cases, with all their Circumstances, should have been exhibited to the Publick, that they might examine into the Truth of the Cases, and be better able to judge of the Effects of this Water. The Names of Persons, who were alledged as Instances of the Virtues thereof, were not mentioned in *Siris*. On this Omission they triumphed, and treated the Whole with Ridicule. But this Narrative sufficiently

 ently

ently supplies that Defect, and is the best Answer to all their Objections. Such a Number of Cases so fully described and attested, must be the best Refutation of all their Railleries and Reasonings, which are directly against Matter of Fact, the only safe Rule to judge by.

323. It is very probable, that I shall be judged, and even condemned by some, for being so sanguine, and so greatly prepossessed in Favour of Tar-water. I own I am, but it is for the best Reason in the World. I am fully convinced of the Efficacy of Tar-water in curing a great Number of Distempers of the most grievous and dangerous Kinds, by the many Instances, Cases, and Matters of Fact, produced in this Narrative, and communicated to me from time to time, by a great Number of Gentlemen and others of good Credit and Integrity from all Parts; who had no other View in so doing, than that others might receive the same Benefit they had obtained themselves. And all this so well attested, that I have not the least doubt of the Truth thereof. If there are any, who have any Doubts, they may repair to the Patients themselves, whose Names and Places of Abode, are herein mentioned for that very Purpose, and be fully satisfied of the Truth of all, or any of the Cases herein related. I have recommended Tar-water myself to many; several of them were perfectly cured of their Disorders; hardly one that did not receive Benefit, and none that got Harm by it. What greater Proof can be given of the Truth or Certainty of any Matter of Fact? Or what better Criterion or Rule can be chosen for determining the Use of Power of any Medicine, than many and frequent Trials and Experiments, well attested and vouched, and open to all the World? Such Proofs and Evidences are produced in behalf of Tar-water. Some few Instances of Cures wrought by Tar-water, being communi-

cated to me in the Beginning, induced me to make farther Inquiries into the Effects of it; the more I enquired, the more I was satisfied of the extraordinary Virtues of Tar-water: And found many as ready to communicate their Cases, as I was to receive them. From these Informations, this Narrative has been formed, and has swelled to the Size the Reader sees it in. I had promised to publish such Cases as occurred to me; they who sent them, as well as others, expected it from me, and it would have been very wrong, and even criminal in me, to have stifled or suppressed them.

324. The Variety of Examples in the Collection will direct any Persons, where to find their Cures in particular Cases for which they might not otherwise think of Tar-water. And for this Purpose, an alphabetical Index or Table is annexed to this Narrative, which points out the several Distempers mentioned in this Collection, wherein Tar-water has proved successful, with a Reference to the Sections, where those Distempers are taken Notice of.

325. After the foregoing Sheets were printed off, the following Instances of curing the King's-evil by Tar-water came to my Knowledge, and are therefore inserted in this Place.

A particular Gentleman having informed me of three Persons cured of the King's-evil, he brought to my House, at my Desire, on the 12th of *March* 1745, two of the Patients, and a Gentlewoman, who is a near Relation of the Third, who gave me the following Account of their Cases.

326. *Martha Quarle*, about eleven Years old, late of *Glasnevin*, and now living in *Dolphins-barn-lane*, near the Rose and Crown, soon after the hard Frost was afflicted with running Sores, and Holes in one of her Hands and Arms, and under one of her Eyes, which continued to increase, insomuch that it infected her upper Jaw; in this Condition she was

was ſent to *Mercers* Hoſpital, where ſhe ſtayed three Weeks, in which time the Sore under her Eye was a little healed, and ſtopped running; but in a Fortnight after ſhe left the Hoſpital, it broke out again, and a Splinter of a Bone came off from her Hand. But in 1744 her Parents were adviſed to give her Tar-water, half a Pint a Day, and to apply a Plaiſter of Tar to all the Sores, and a large Tent covered with the Plaiſter to the Hole under her Eye: In a little time, a large Piece of her Jaw-bone, with ſome of her Teeth, came off, and by drinking the Water, and applying the Plaiſters for near three Months, all her Sores healed, and ſhe perfectly recovered, and has continued well this Year and half paſt.

327. *William Murray*, about twelve Years old, Son of *Matthew Murray*, in *Black-horſe-lane*, had running Sores in his Hands and Legs ſoon after the great Froſt, ſo that he was not able to ſtir a Foot, and had great Pains in his Head for a Year. The Boy drank Tar-water, which in a Fortnight's Time carried off the Pains in his Head and then applied the Tar-Plaiſter to the Sores a little before laſt *Chriſtmas*, whereby all the Sores are healed up, leaving a great many Marks in his Arm. And the Boy ſtill continues to drink Tar-water, and finds himſelf very hearty.

328. A young Gentlewoman, aged 21 Years, from the Time ſhe was three Years old had a running Evil in one of her Hands, and her Jaws, and ſhe continued in this State many Years without Relief: She was at the Waters of *Loughleah*, in the County of *Cavan*, and was long under the Care of Surgeons without Benefit. Splinters of Bone came from her Hands. But in 1744 ſhe drank Tar-water in ſmall Quantities, and applied the Plaiſter of Tar, which in four Months Time healed them up, and ſhe is now perfectly well.

329. And on the 13th of *March* 1745, *James Moony*, Shoe-maker, Son of *Arthur Moony*, who lives at the *Bull's-head* in *Stafford Street*, came to me at the Desire of a Gentleman to give me his Case which is as follows: In the Winter after the great Frost, he was afflicted with running Sores, which broke out in many Parts of his Left-hand, and in his Back, and quite disabled him from following his Trade, and for which he tried many Things without any Benefit. He attended at the Infirmary on the *Inns-quay*, for two Months, where many Surgeons practised upon him; but he got no Relief by any Things they did, and was at last told by them, that there was no other Remedy than to cut off his Hand above the Wrist: Upon which, he attended no more at the Infirmary. But in *August* 1745, he was advised to drink Tar-water; which he did for two Months, about a Pint a Day, and washed the Sores with the same Liquor, and the Effect was, that he found the Sores begin to heal in the second Month, and most of them were healed up in the End of that Month, and he recovered his Appetite and Spirits, which he had lost before, and then laid aside Tar-water, before he was perfectly cured, having two small Sores not quite healed; but he has began to drink the Water again, and finds himself much better already, and hopes to perfect his Cure in a little Time.

330. It is very probable that these Patients, would have been sooner cured, if they had taken Tar-water in great Plenty; half a Pint a Day was too small a Quantity to effect a Cure in a short time: In such grievous Cases a Quart a Day should have been taken, which might have recovered the Patients in less than half the Time, as we find to have happened in other Instances; and the Water should not be laid aside, till they were perfectly cured.

331. In some Hospitals and Infirmaries, where Patients

Patients have had their Hands, Arms, or Legs, ſwollen and inflamed with terrible running Sores, which ate into, and rotted the Bones, and which could not be cured by any of their Medicines, the Surgeons in ſuch Caſes, for fear of a Gangrene or Mortification, ſometimes cut off the Limb; which, if it doth not end with the Death of the Patient, reduces him at leaſt to Want and Beggary. Such Operations ſhould not be attempted, but in the laſt Extremity. And we have Reaſon to ſuſpect, that it is ſometimes done without ſuch Neceſſity; in Regard we find ſeveral Patients mentioned in this Narrative, who were condemned to be ſerved the ſame Way, as the only Means to ſave their Lives; and being told ſo much, and terrified, ran away, or quitted the Hoſpital; yet thoſe very Patients were afterwards recovered by the Uſe of Tar-water, and perfectly reſtored to the Uſe of their Limbs, without any ſuch Mutilations. It is to be hoped that for the future, we ſhall hear but little of ſuch Amputations, ſo ſhocking to Nature, ſince we find that Tar-water not only prevents thoſe Ailments from coming to a dangerous Height, but cures them when they do, and when all other Hopes are loſt. And indeed, it is reaſonable to believe, when the whole Maſs of Blood is corrupted, that the cutting off a Limb will not cure the Corruption, which will be apt to break out in ſome other Part.

332. The Murrain, which has lately raged in many Parts of *Europe*, among the horned Cattle, and now prevails in ſome Parts of *England*, ſhould engage our Attention to prevent the ſpreading of ſo deſtructive a Malady. And as this Diſtemper appears by its Symptoms to be a Kind of Fever, it is recommended that Tar-water be tried in the following Manner: Let the ſick Beaſt have poured down its Throat a Quart of warm Tar-water, made ſtronger than uſual, by ſtirring each Gallon eight or

ten Minutes, and this to be repeated every Hour or two for the firſt Day, while the Beaſt is awake. On the ſecond, let one Half of the former Quantity be given, and on the third Day, half of that which was given on the ſecond: Which laſt Quantity is to be continued till the Cure is perfected; during which time, the Beaſt ſhould be houſed and lie warm. I have no Experience of the Succeſs of this Method, as there is no Infection of that Kind in this Kingdom, but recommend it from the analogous Effects that Tar-water hath in curing Fevers and Infections. It is worth while to try it for the good of the Publick, the Expence being but a Trifle. It may be adviſeable alſo to dawb the Noſtrils, Ears, *&c.* of all the Cattle, whether infected or not, to prevent catching or communicating the Infection by the Air. And alſo to make the Beaſt ſwallow one Egg-ſhell full or two of crude Tar.

333. I ſhall add no more, but only ſubjoin to this Treatiſe two Letters from the Author of *Siris*; the firſt addreſſed to me, containing ſome farther Remarks on the Virtues of Tar-water, and the Methods for preparing and uſing of it, which was firſt publiſhed in the Year 1744; and the ſecond, lately ſent to me from the ſame Author, containing ſome farther Diſcoveries, Obſervations and Reflections on the Virtues and Effects of Tar-water.

A LET-

A LETTER TO *Thomas Prior*, Esq; FROM THE AUTHOR of *SIRIS*,

Containing some farther Remarks on the Virtues of TAR-WATER, and the Methods for preparing and using it.

Non sibi, sed toti.

Nothing is more difficult and disagreeable, than to argue Men out of their Prejudices; I shall not, therefore, enter into Controversies on this Subject, but if Men dispute and object, shall leave the Decision to Time and Trial. SIRIS, Sect. 68.

1. AMONG the great Numbers who drink Tar-water in *Dublin*, your Letter informs me, there are some that make or use it in an undue Manner. To obviate these Inconveniences, and render this Water as generally useful as possible, you desire I would draw up some general Rules and Remarks in a small Compass, which accordingly I here send you.

2. Pour a Gallon of cold Water on a Quart of liquid Tar, in a glazed Earthen Vessel; stir, mix and work them thoroughly together, with a wooden Ladle, or flat Stick, for the Space of five or six Minutes. Then let the Vessel stand close covered three Days and Nights, that the Tar may have full Time to subside. After which, having first carefully skimmed it, without moving

ing the Veſſel, pour off the clear Water, and keep it in Bottles, well corked, for Uſe. This Method will produce a Liquor ſtronger than that firſt publiſh'd in *Siris*, but not offenſive if carefully ſkimmed. It is a good general Rule, but as Stomachs and Conſtitutions are various, it may admit of ſome Latitude. Leſs Water or more ſtirring, makes it ſtronger, as more Water, or leſs ſtirring, makes it weaker. It is to be noted, that if ſeveral Gallons are made at once in the ſame Veſſel, you muſt add five or ſix Minutes ſtirring for every Gallon. Thus two Gallons of Water, and two Quarts of Tar, require ten or twelve Minutes ſtirring.

3. The ſame Tar will not do ſo well a ſecond Time, but may ſerve for other common Uſes: The putting off Tar that hath been uſed, for freſh Tar, would be a bad Fraud. To prevent which, it is to be noted, that Tar already uſed is of a lighter Brown than other Tar. The only Tar that I have uſed, is that from our Northern Colonies in *America*, and that from *Norway*; the latter being thinner, mixeth eaſier with Water, and ſeems to have more Spirit. If the former be made uſe of (as I have known it with good Succeſs) the Tar-water will require longer ſtirring to make it.

4. Tar-water, when right, is not paler than *French*, nor deeper coloured than *Spaniſh* White-wine, and full as clear; if there be not a Spirit very ſenſibly perceived in drinking, you may conclude the Tar-water is not good; if you would have it good, ſee it made yourſelf. Thoſe who begin with it, little and weak, may, by Habit, come to drink more and ſtronger. According to the Seaſon, or the Humour of the Patient, it may be drank either cold or warm: In Colics I take it to be beſt warm. If it diſguſts a Patient warm, let him try it cold, and *vice verſa*. If at firſt it creates, to ſome ſqueamiſh Perſons, a little Sickneſs at Stomach, or Nauſeating, it may be reduced both in Quality and Quantity. In general, ſmall Inconveniences are either removed, or borne with ſmall Trouble; it lays under no Reſtraint, as to Air, Exerciſe, Cloaths, or Diet, and may be taken at all Times of the Year.

5. As to the Quantity in common chronical Indiſpoſitions, one Pint of Tar-water a Day may ſuffice, taken on an empty Stomach, at two or four Times, to wit, Night, and

and Morning, and about two Hours after Dinner and Breakfast; more may be taken by strong Stomachs. Alteratives in general, taken in small Doses, and often, mix best with the Blood; how oft, or how strong each Stomach can bear, Experience will shew. But those who labour under great and inveterate Maladies, must drink a greater Quantity, at least one Quart every twenty-four Hours, taken at four, six, or eight Glasses, as best suits the Circumstances and Case of the Drinker. All of this Class must have much Patience and Perseverance in the Use of this, as well as of all other Medicines, which, if sure and safe, must yet, from the Nature of Things, be slow in the Cure of inveterate chronical Disorders. In acute Cases, Fevers of all Kinds, it must be drank in Bed warm, and in great Quantity, (the Fever still enabling the Patient to drink) perhaps a Pint every Hour, which I have known to work surprising Cures. But it works so quick, and gives such Spirits, that the Patients often think themselves cured before the Fever hath quite left them. Such therefore should not be impatient to rise, or apply themselves too soon to Business, or their usual Diet.

6. To some, perhaps, it may seem, that a slow Alterative in chronical Cases, cannot be depended on in Fevers and acute Distempers, which demand immediate Relief. But I affirm, that this same Medicine, which is a slow Alterative in chronical Cases, I have found to be also a most immediate Remedy, when copiously taken, in acute and inflammatory Cases. It might indeed be thought rash to have tried it in the most threatening Fevers and Pleurisies without Bleeding, which in the common Practice would have been held necessary. But for this I can say, that I have Patients who would not be bled, and this obliged me to make Trials of Tar-water without Bleeding, which Trials I never knew unsuccessful. The same Tar-water I found a slow Alterative, and a sudden Febrifuge. If the Reader is surprized, I own myself to be so too. But Truth is Truth, and from whatever Hand it comes, should be candidly received. If Physicians think they have a Right to treat of religious Matters, I think I have an equal Right to treat of Medicine.

7. Au-

7. Authority I have no Pretence to; but Reaſon is the common Birth-right of all: My Reaſons I have given in *Siris*: My Motives every one will interpret from his own Breaſt: But he muſt own himſelf a very bad Man, who, in my Caſe, (that is, after long Experience, and under full Conviction of the Virtues and Innocence of Tar-water) would not have done as much. All Men are, I will not ſay allowed, but obliged to promote the common Benefit; and for this End, what I could not in Conſcience conceal, that I do, and ſhall publickly declare, maugre all the Spleen and Raillery of a World, which cannot treat me worſe than it hath done my Betters.

8. As the Morning's Draught is moſt difficult to nice Stomachs, ſuch may leſſen, or even omit it, at the Beginning, or rather poſtpone it till after Breakfaſt, and take a larger Doſe at Night. The Diſtance from Meal-time need not be more than one Hour, for common Stomachs, when the Liquor is well clarified and ſkimmed. The Oil that floats on the Top, and was ſkimmed off, ſhould be carefully laid by, and kept for outward Sores. In the Variety of Caſes and Conſtitutions, it is not amiſs that there ſhould be different Manners of preparing and taking Tar-water: Trial will direct to the beſt. Whether there be any Difference between old Tar, or new Tar, or which of all the various Tars, produced from different Trees, or in different Parts of the World, is moſt medicinal, future Trials muſt determine.

9. I have made a ſecond Sort of Tar-water, to be uſed externally, as a Waſh or Lotion, for the Itch, Scabs, Ulcers, Evil, Leproſy, and all ſuch foul Caſes, which I have tried with very good Succeſs, and recommend it to the Trial of others. For inveterate Caſes of that Kind, Tar-water ſhould be drank, a Quart every twenty-four Hours, at four, ſix, or eight Glaſſes; and after this hath been done, at leaſt for a Fortnight, the Lotion is to be applied outwardly, and warm, by bathing, fomenting, and ſteeping, and this ſeveral times in the twenty-four Hours, to heal and dry up the Sores, the Drinking being ſtill continued. This Water, for external Uſe, is made in the following Manner: Pour two Quarts of hot boiling Water on a Quart of Tar, ſtir and work it ſtrongly, with a flat Stick, or Ladle, for a full Quarter of an Hour; let it

ſtand ſix Hours, then pour it off, and keep it cloſe covered for Uſe. It may be made weaker or ſtronger, as there is Occaſion.

10. From what I have obſerved of the Lotion, I am inclined to think, it may be worth while, in obſtinate and cutaneous Ailments, Leproſy, and Weakneſs of Limbs, to try a Bath of Tar-water; allowing a Gallon of Tar to every ten Gallons of boiling hot Water; ſtirring the Ingredients a full half Hour; ſuffering the Veſſel to ſtand eight or ten Hours, before the Water is poured off, and uſing the Bath a little more than Milk-warm. This Experiment may be made in different Proportions of Tar and Water. In *Dublin* many Caſes occur for Trial, which are not to be met with in the Country.

11. My Experiments have been made in various Caſes, and on many Perſons; and I make no Doubt its Virtues will ſoon be more fully diſcovered, as Tar-water is now growing into general Uſe, though not without that Oppoſition which uſually attends upon Novelty. The great Objection I find made to this Medicine is, that it promiſes too much. What! ſay the Objectors, do you pretend to a Panacea? a Thing ſtrange, chimerical, and contrary to the Opinion and Experience of all Mankind. Now, to ſpeak out, and give this Objection, or Queſtion, a direct Anſwer, I freely own, that I ſuſpect Tar-water is *a* Panacea. I may be miſtaken, but it is worth Trial; for the Chance of ſo great and general a Benefit, I am willing to ſtand the Ridicule of propoſing it. And as the old Philoſopher cried aloud, from the Houſe-tops, to his Fellow Citizens, *Educate your Children*; ſo, I confeſs, if I had a Situation high enough, and a Voice loud enough, I would cry out to all the Valetudinarians upon Earth, *Drink Tar-water*.

12. Having thus frankly owned the Charge, I muſt explain to you, that by a Panacea is not meant a Medicine which cures all Individuals, (this conſiſts not with Mortality) but a Medicine that cures or relieves all thedifferent Species of Diſtempers: And if God hath given us ſo great a Bleſſing, and made a Medicine ſo cheap and plenty as Tar, to be withal ſo univerſal in its Effects, to eaſe the Miſeries of human Life, ſhall Men be ridiculed or bantered out of its Uſe, eſpecially when they run no Riſque in the Trial? For I can truly affirm, that I never knew

knew any Harm attend it, more than ſometimes a little Nauſea, which if the Liquor be well cleared, ſkimmed and bottled, need not, I think, be apprehended.

13. It muſt be owned I have not had Opportunities of trying it myſelf in all Caſes, neither will I undertake to demonſtrate *a priori*, that Tar-water is a Panacea. But yet, methinks, I am not quite deſtitute of probable Reaſons, which, joined to what Facts I have obſerved, induced me to entertain ſuch a Suſpicion.

14. I knew Tar was uſed to preſerve Cattle from Contagion; and this may be ſuppoſed to have given Riſe to that Practice of drinking Tar-water for a Preſervative againſt the Small-pox. But as the Tar-water uſed for that Purpoſe was made by mixing equal Quantities of Tar and Water, it proved a moſt offenſive Potion; beſides, as a freſh Glaſs of Water was put in for each Glaſs that was taken out, and this, for many Days, on the ſame Tar, it followed that the Water was not equally impregnated with the fine volatile Spirit, though all alike ſtrongly ſaturated with groſs Particles.

15. Having found this nauſeous Draught very uſeful againſt the Small-pox, to as many as could be prevailed on to take it, I began to conſider the Nature of Tar. I reflected that Tar is a Balſam flowing from the Trunks of aged Ever-greens; that it reſiſts Putrefaction; that it hath the Virtues of Turpentine, which, in Medicine, are known to be very great and manifold; but I obſerved withal, that Turpentines, or Balſams, are very offenſive in the taking: I therefore conſidered diſtinctly the ſeveral conſtituent Parts of Balſams; which were thoſe, wherein the medicinal Virtues reſided, and which were to be regarded rather as a viſcous Matrix, to receive, arreſt, and retain the more volatile and active Particles; and if theſe laſt could be ſo ſeparated and diſengaged from the groſſer Parts, as to impregnate a clear and potable Liquor, I concluded, that ſuch Liquor muſt prove a Medicine of great Force, and general Uſe. I conſidered, that Nature was the beſt Chemiſt and Preparer of Medicines, and that the Fragrance and Flavour of Tar argued very active Qualities and Virtues.

16. I had, of a long Time, entertained an Opinion agreeable to the Sentiments of many antient Philoſophers,

That

That Fire may be regarded as the animal Spirit of this visible World. And it seemed to me, that the attracting and secreting of this Fire in the various Pores, Tubes, and Ducts of Vegetables, did impart their specifick Virtues to each Kind; that this same Light, or Fire, was the immediate instrumental or physical Cause of Sense and Motion, and consequently of Life and Health to Animals; that on Account of this Solar Light, or Fire, *Phœbus* was, in the antient Mythology, reputed the God of Medicine: Which Light, as it is leisurely introduced, and fixed in the viscid Juice of old Firs and Pines, so the setting it free in part, that is, the changing its viscid for a volatile Vehicle, which may mix with Water, and convey it throughout the Habit copiously and inoffensively, would be of infinite Use in Physick, extending to all Cases whatsoever, inasmuch as all Distempers are, in effect, a Struggle between the *Vis vitæ* and the peculiar Miasma, or *Fomes morbi*; and nothing strengthens Nature, or lends such Aid and Vigour to Life, as a Cordial which doth not heat.

17. The solar Light, in great Quantity, during the Space of many successive Years, being attracted and detained in the Juice of antient Ever-greens, doth form and lodge itself in an Oil so fine and volatile, as shall mix well with Water, and lightly pass the *Primæ viæ*, and penetrate every Part and Capillary of the organical System, when once exempt and freed from the grosser nauseous Resin. It will not therefore seem unreasonable, to whoever is acquainted with the medicinal Virtues of Turpentine in so many different Distempers, for which it hath been celebrated both by ancient and modern Physicians, and withal reflects on the Nausea, or Clog, that prevents their full Operation and Effect on the human Body; it will not, I say, seem unreasonable to such a one to suppose, that, if this same Clog were removed, numberless Cures might be wrought in a great Variety of Cases.

18. The *Desideratum* was, how to separate the active Particles from the heavy viscid Substance, which served to attract and retain them, and so to order Matters, that the Vehicle of the Spirit should not, on the one hand, be volatile enough to escape, nor on the other, gross enough to offend. For the performing of this, I have found a most easy, simple, and effectual Method, which furnished

a poa potable inoffensive Liquor, clear and fine as the best White-wine, cordial and stomachic, to be kept bottled, as being endued with a very sensible Spirit, though not fermented.

19. I tried many Experiments as to the Quantity of Water, and the Time of stirring and standing, in order to impregnate and clarify it, and, after all, fixed on the forementioned Receipt, as the most generally useful for making this salutiferous Liquor well impregnated, and not offensive to common Stomachs, and even drank with Pleasure by many: In which the most medicinal and active Particles, that is, the native Salts and volatile Oil of the Balsam, being disentangled and separated from its gross Oil and viscous Resin, do, combined together, form a fine balsamic and vegetable Soap, which not only can pass the Stomach and *Primæ viæ*, but also insinuate itself into the minutest Capillaries, and freely pervade the whole animal System; and that in such full Proportion and Measure, as suiteth every Case and Constitution.

20. The foregoing general Considerations put me upon making Experiments in many various and unlike Cases, which otherwise I should never have thought of doing, and the Success answered my Hopes. Philosophical Principles led me to make safe Trials, and on those Trials is founded my Opinion of the salutary Virtues of Tar-water; which Virtues are recommended from, and depend on, Experiments and Matters of Fact, and neither stand nor fall with any Theories or speculative Principles whatever. Howbeit, those Theories, as I said, enlarged my Views of this Medicine, led me to a greater Variety of Trials, and thereby engendered and nourished my Suspicion, that it is a Panacea. I have been the more prolix in these Particulars, hoping that, to as many as shall candidly weigh and consider them, the high Opinion I conceive of this Medicine, will not seem altogether an Effect of vain Prepossession, or blind empiric Rashness, but rather the Result of free Thought and Enquiry, and grounded on my best Reason, Judgment, and Experience.

21. Those who have only the Good of Mankind at Heart, will give this Medicine fair play; if there be any who act from other Motives, the Publick will look sharp and beware. To do Justice to Tar-water, as well as

ſo thoſe who drink it, regard muſt be had to the particular Strength and Caſe of the Patients. Grievous or inveterate Maladies muſt not be treated as common Caſes. I cured a horrible Caſe, a Gangrene in the Blood, which had broke out in ſeveral Sores, and threatened ſpeedy Death, by obliging the Perſon to drink nothing but this Liquor for ſeveral Weeks, as much and as often as his Stomach would bear. Common Senſe will direct a proportionable Conduct in the other Caſes. But this muſt be left to the Conſcience and Diſcretion of the Givers and Takers.

22. After all that can be ſaid, it is moſt certain, that a Panacea ſounds odd, and conveys ſomewhat ſhocking to the Ear and Senſe of moſt Men, who are wont to rank the univerſal Medicine with the Philoſophers Stone, and the Squaring of the Circle; whereof the chief, if not ſole Reaſon, I take to be, that it is thought incredible, the ſame Thing ſhould produce contrary Effects, as it muſt do, if it cures oppoſite Diſtempers. And yet this is no more than every Day's Experience verifies. Milk, for Inſtance, makes ſome coſtive, and others laxative: This regards the Poſſibility of a Panacea in general; as for Tar-water in particular, I do not ſay it is a Panacea, I only ſuſpect it to be ſo. Time and Tryal will ſhew.

23. But I am moſt ſincerely perſuaded, from what I have already ſeen and tried, that Tar-water may be drank with great Safety and Succeſs, for the Cure or Relief of moſt, if not all Diſeaſes; of Ulcers, Itch, Scald-heads, Leproſy, Kings-Evil, Cancers, the foul Diſeaſe, and all foul Caſes; Scurvies of all Kinds, Diſorders of the Lungs, Stomach, and Bowels, in Rheumatic, Gouty and Nephritic Ailments, Megrims, inveterate Head-achs, Epilepſies, Pleuriſies, Peripneumonies, Eryſipelas, Small-pox, all Kinds of Fevers, Colics, Hyſteric and all nervous Caſes; Obſtructions, Dropſies, Decays, and other Maladies. Note that for Agues it ſhould be drank warm, and often, in ſmall Glaſſes, both in and out of the Fit, and continued for ſeveral Days to prevent a Relapſe. Nor is it of Uſe only in the Cure of Sickneſs, it is alſo uſeful to preſerve Health, and guard againſt Infection, and in ſome Meaſure even againſt old Age, as it gives laſting Spirits, and invi-

gorates the Blood. I am even induced, by the Nature and Analogy of Things, and its wonderful Succefs in Fevers of all Kinds, to think that Tar-water may be very ufeful againft the Plague, both as a Prefervative and a Cure.

24. But I doubt no Medicine can withftand that execrable Plague of diftilled Spirits, which do all, without Exception, (there being a cauftic and coagulating Quality in all diftilled Spirits, whatever the Subject or Ingredients, may be) operate as a flow Poifon, preying on the Vitals, and wafting the Health and Strength of Body and Soul; which Peft of human Kind is, I am told, gaining Ground in this Country, already too thin of Inhabitants.

I am, &c.

A SE-

A SECOND LETTER FROM THE AUTHOR of *SIRIS*, TO *Thomas Prior*, Esq;

1. YOUR Attention to whatever promotes the publick Good of your Country, or the common Benefit of Mankind, having engaged you in a particular Enquiry concerning the Virtues and Effects of Tar-water, you are entitled to know what farther Discoveries, Observations and Reflections I have made on that Subject.

2. Tar-water, in the several Editions of *Siris*, hath been directed to be made by stirring three, four, five, or six Minutes, for a Gallon of Water, and a Quart of Tar. But although it seem best made, for general Use, within those Limits, yet the Stomach of the Patient is the best Rule, whereby, to direct the Strength of the Water; with a little more stirring, six Quarts of good Tar-water may be made from one of Tar; and with eight Minutes stirring, I have known a Gallon of Tar-water produced from second-hand Tar, which proved a good Remedy in a very bad Fever, when better Tar could not be had. For the Use of Travellers, a Tar-water may be made very strong, for Instance, with one Quart of Water, and a Quart of Tar, stirred together for the Space of Twenty Minutes. A Bottle of this may serve long on a Road, a little being put to each Glass of common Water, more or less, as you would have it stronger or weaker. Near ten

Years ago, a Quart of about this Strength was given to an old Woman, to be taken at one Draught by Direction of a young Lady, who had consulted one in my Family, about the Method of preparing and giving Tar-water, which yet she happened to mistake. But even thus, it did Service in the Main, though it wrought the Patient violently all manner of Ways. Which shews, that Errors and Excesses in Tar-water, are not so dangerous, as in other Medicines.

3. The best Tar, I take to be that, which is most Liquid, or first running from the Billets of Fir or Pine, which grew on the Mountains: It hath a greater Share of those antiscorbutic vegetable Juices, which are contained not only in the Leaves and tender Tops, but in all Parts of the Wood; and these, together with the Salts of Wood-soot, being in the Composition of Tar superadded to Turpentine, render Tar-water a Medicine, if I am not mistaken, much more extensive and efficacious, than any that can be obtained from Turpentine alone.

4. The Virtues of the Wood-Juices shew themselves in Spruce-Beer, made of Melasses, and the black Spruce-Fir in the northern Parts of *America*; and the young Shoots of our common Spruce-Fir, have been put to Malt-Liquor in my own Family, and make a very wholsome Drink.

5. Tar-water seldom fails to cure, or relieve, when rightly made of good Tar, and duly taken. I say, of good Tar, because the vile Practice of adulterating Tar, or of selling the Dregs of Tar, or used Tar for fresh, is grown frequent, to the great Wrong of those who take it. Whoever hath been used to good Tar-water, can readily discern the bad by its flat Taste, void of that warm cordial Quality found in the former; it may also be expedient for knowing fresh Tar, to observe, whether a fat oily Scum floats on the Top of the Water, which is found to be much less, if any at all, on the second making of Tar-water. This Scum was directed to be taken off, not from its being apt to do Harm when drank, but to render the Tar-water more palatable to nice Stomachs. Great Quantities of Tar are produced in *Germany*, *Italy*, and other Parts of the Wolrd. The different Qualities or Virtues of these, it may be worth while to try, and I wish the Tryal were made principally

by

by observing, which giveth most Sense of a lively cordial Spirit upon drinking the Water.

6. This Medicine of Tar-water worketh various Ways, by Urine, by Perspiration, as a sudorific, carminative, cardiac, astringent, detergent, restorative, alterative, and sometimes as a gentle purgative or emetic, according to the Case or Constitution of the Patient, or to the Quantity that is taken; and its Operation should not be disturbed. I knew two Brothers ill of a Fever about the same Time; it wrought on the one by copious Sweating, on the other altogether by Urine; and I have known it to act at different Times differently, even on the same Person, and in the same Disorder; one while as a Diaphoretic, or Sudorific, another as a Diuretic. Its general Character is Diuretic, which shews, that it cleanseth the urinary Passages, preventing thereby both Stone and Gravel, against which it hath been found very useful, and much safer than mineral Waters, by reason of its balsamic healing Quality.

7. Tar-water doth recover and impart vital Heat, but imparts no inflaming Heat. I have seen a wonderful Cure wrought on a Child about eight Years old, and past all Hopes, by pouring several Spoonfuls of Tar-water down his Throat, as he lay quite subdued by a most violent Fever, without any Appearance of Sense or Motion, the Nostrils drawn back, the Eyes fixed, the Complexion deadly wan. And yet Tar-water, forced down by Spoonfuls, seem'd to kindle up Life a-new; and this, after Sage-tea, Saffron, Milk-water, Venice-treacle, *&c.* had been used without any Success.

8. This is of itself a sufficient Cordial, friendly and congenial to the vital Heat and Spirits of a Man. If therefore strong Liquors are in the accustomed Quantity superadded, the Blood being already, by Tar-water, sufficiently warmed for vital Heat, the strong Liquors superadded will be apt to over-heat it, which over-heating is not to be imputed to the Tar-water, since, taken alone, I could never observe it attended with that Symptom.

9. And tho' it may be no easy Matter to persuade such as have long indulged themselves in the free Use of strong fermented Liquors and distilled Spirits, to forsake their pernicious Habits, yet I am myself thoroughly persuaded, that in Weakness or Fatigue of Body, or in low Spirits, Tar-

water alone doth far ſurpaſs all thoſe vulgarly-eſteemed Cordials, which heat and intoxicate, and which coagulate the Fluids, and, by their cauſtic Force, dry up, ſtiffen, and deſtroy the fine Veſſels and Fibres of the unhappy Drinkers, obſtructing the Secretions, impairing the animal Functions, producing various Diſorders, and bringing on the untimely Symptoms of old Age. Nothing doth ſo much obſtruct the good Effects of Tar-water, as the Abuſe of ſtrong Liquors. Where this is avoided, it ſeems no chronical Malady can keep its Ground, or ſtand before Tar-water conſtantly and regularly taken, not even hereditary Diſtempers, as the moſt inveterate King's-Evil, nor even the moſt confirmed Gout; provided it be drank a Quart a Day, at ſix or eight Glaſſes, and at all Seaſons, both in and out of the Fit, and that for a great Length of Time, the longer the better. It is to be noted, that in Fits of the Gout, Colic, or Fever, it ſhould be always drank warm. On other Occaſions, warm or cold, as the Patient likes.

10. The Inference I make is, that thoſe who expect Health from Tar-water, have leſs Need of any other Cordial, and would do well to ſacrifice ſome Part of their Pleaſure to their Health. At the ſame Time I will venture to affirm, that a Fever produced either from hard Drinking, or any other Cauſe, is moſt effectually and ſpeedily ſubdued, by abſtaining from all other Cordials, and plentifully drinking of Tar-water: For it warms the Cold, and cools the Hot: Simple Water may cool, but this, at the ſame Time that it cools, gives Life and Spirit. It is, in Truth, a Specific for all Kinds of Fevers; the ſame Medicine, which is a leiſurely Alterative in chronical Diſorders, being taken in larger Quantities, is a ſpeedy Cure in acute ones.

11. Thoſe who, without Knowledge or Experience of Tar-water, have been ſo active and earneſt to diſcredit its Virtues, have much to anſwer for, eſpecially with Regard to acute inflammatory Diſtempers, in which it doth Wonders. It is in thoſe Diſorders, ſo fatal and frequent, that I have had moſt Opportunities of obſerving its Virtues, nor can the World ever know the juſt Value of this Medicine, but by trying it in the like Caſes.

12. When Patients are given over, and all known Methods fail, it is allowed to try new Remedies. If Tar-

water

water was tried in ſuch Caſes, I do verily believe, that many Patients might thereby be reſcued from the Jaws of Death: Particularly, I would recommend the Tryal of it in the moſt malignant and deſperate Fevers, or Small-pox, attended with purple, livid, or black Spots. It is my ſincere Opinion, that warm Tar-water, drank copiouſly, may often prove ſalutary, even in thoſe deplorable Caſes.

13. My Opinion is grounded on its ſingular Virtues in correcting, ſweetening, and invigorating the Blood, and in curing Cancers and Gangrenes, or beginning Mortifications, ſuch as thoſe Spots do indicate. I have lately known it drunk with good Succeſs in a very painful and unpromiſing Wound; and am perſuaded, that if it were drank plentifully, during the Dreſſing of all Sorts of dangerous Wounds, it might aſſwage the Anguiſh, and forward the Cure; as it abates feveriſh Symptoms, and by rendering the Blood balſamic, and diſpoſing the Parts to heal, prevents a Gangrene.

14. Tar *itſelf is* an excellent Medicine, being ſpread on a Cloth, and applied warm to an Ulcer or Wound. I have known the ſame applied to a very large and painful Tumour, cauſed by a Sprain or Bruiſe, ſpeedily aſſwage the Pain, and reduce the Swelling. I may add, that Tar (mixed with Honey to make it leſs offenſive, and) taken inwardly, is an admirable Balſam for the Lungs; and a little of this, taken together with Tar-water, haſtens its Effect in curing the moſt obſtinate and waſting Coughs; and an Egg-ſhell full of Tar, ſwallowed and waſhed down with a Quart of Tar-water, Night and Morning, hath been found very uſeful for the ſame Diſorder in Horſes.

15. Sitting over the Vapour of the heated Lotion, deſcribed in my former Letter, is excellent in the Caſe of Piles or Fiſtula; eſpecially if fomenting with the ſaid Lotion be added, as alſo anointing with the Oil ſcummed from the Top of Tar-water Tar-water hath been ſnuffed up the Noſtrils with good Succeſs, for a great Heavineſs of the Head, and Drowſineſs. It is a very uſeful Waſh for weak, dr , or itching Eyes; an excellent Preſervative for the Teeth and Gums; alſo a good Drink and Gargle for a ſore Throat: I may add, that I have known it ſucceed in Caſes where it has been tried without Hopes of Succeſs, particularly in Deafneſs. I have known Life ſuſtained

ſtained many Days together, only by drinking of Tar-water, without any other Nouriſhment, and without any remarkable Diminution of Strength or Spirits; it may therefore be of ſingular Uſe, and ſave many Lives in the Diſtreſs of Famine at Sea, or in Sieges, and in Seaſons of great Scarcity. The Virtue of Tar-water flowing like the *Nile* *, from a Secret and occult Source, brancheth into innumerable Channels, conveying Health and Relief, wherever it is applied; nor is it more eaſy and various in its Uſe, than copious in Quantity. How great Havock, nevertheleſs, is made by the Small-pox, raging like a Plague, in *New England*, and other Parts of *America*, which yet abound with Tar! and how many thouſand Sailors, in all Parts of the World, are rotting by the Scurvy with their Remedy at Hand!

16. Many in this Town of *Cloyne* have, by the copious drinking of Tar-water alone, been recovered of the moſt violent Fevers, attended with the moſt threatning Symptoms, and much heightened by Relapſes from Miſmanagement. It would be tedious to enumerate all the Caſes of this Kind, which have happened at *Cloyne*, and in my own Family; where many Fevers, pleuretic, as well as others, attended with violent Stitches, Difficulty of Breathing, and Spitting of Blood, have been cured by Tar-water; and this I can with Truth affirm, that I never knew it regularly tried, in any inflammatory Caſe, without Succeſs: But then it muſt be given in Bed, warm and very copiouſly, with all due Caution againſt Cold, Noiſe, and improper Diet.

17. I have often obſerved, when a Patient, on the firſt Attack of a Fever, hath betaken himſelf to his Bed, and drank Tar-water regularly and conſtantly, that he hath had ſuch favourable Symptoms, ſo good Appetite, and ſo ſound Sleep, that the Fever paſſed almoſt as nothing; nor was to be diſtinguiſhed otherwiſe, than by a quickneſs of Pulſe, a little feveriſh Heat, and Thirſt. The more that Patients in a Fever drink, the better they find themſelves; and their liking to Tar-water grows with their want of it, by a certain Inſtinct or Dictate of Nature; inſomuch that I have known Children in very high

* The *Nile* was by the antient *Ægyptians* called *Siris*, which Word alſo ſignifies, in *Greek*, a Chain, though not ſo commonly uſed as *Sira*.

Fevers

Fevers, who, at other Times, could hardly be prevailed on to drink a single Glaſs, drink ſix or eight in an Hour.

18. I can truly affirm that for the Caſes within my own Obſervation, inflammatory acute Diſtempers cured by Tar-water, have been, at leaſt, ten Times the Number of any other. Theſe indeed ofteneſt occur, as cauſing the chief Deſtruction and general Ravage of Mankind; who are conſequently debarred from the principal Uſe and Benefit of this Medicine ſo long, as they give Ear to the Suggeſtions of thoſe, who, without any Experience thereof, would perſuade them, it is of an heating or enflaming Nature; which Suggeſtion, as I am convinced myſelf, by long and manifold Experience, that it is abſolutely falſe, ſo may all others alſo be ſufficiently convinced of its Falſhood, by the wonderful Fact atteſted by a ſolemn * Affidavit of Captain *Drape*, at *Liverpool*; whereby it appears, that of 170 Negroes ſeized at once by the Small-pox on the Coaſt of *Guinea*, one only died, who refuſed to drink Tar-water; and the remaining 169, all recovered by drinking it, without any other Medicine, notwithſtanding the Heat of the Climate, and the Incommodities of the Veſſel. A Fact ſo well vouched muſt, with all unbyaſſed Men, outweigh the poſitive Aſſertions of thoſe who have declared themſelves Adverſaries of Tar-water, on the Score of its pretended heating or inflaming Quality.

19. The Skill and Learning of thoſe Gentlemen in their Profeſſion, I ſhall not diſpute; but yet it ſeems ſtrange, that they ſhould without Experience pronounce at once, concerning the Virtues of Tar-water, and aſcribe to it pernicious Qualities, which I, who had watched its Workings and Effects for Years together, could never diſcover. Theſe three laſt Years, I have taken it myſelf without one Day's Intermiſſion; others in my Family have taken it near the ſame Time, and thoſe of different Ages and Sexes; ſeveral in the Neighbourhood have done as much, all without any Injury, and with much Benefit.

20. It is to be noted, the Skin and the Belly are Antagoniſts; that is, the more paſſeth by Perſpiration, the leſs will paſs another Way. Medicines therefore, which cauſe the

* See Captain *Drape*'s Affidavit in page 19, 20.

Patient

Patient to perſpire, will be apt to make him coſtive. Therefore, when Tar-water worketh much by Perſpiration, the Body may chance to be bound. But ſuch Symptom, though it ſhould be attended with a little more than ordinary Warmth, need not be dreaded by the Patient; it being only a Sign, that his Cure is carried on by driving out the peccant Matter through the Skin; which is one of the Ways whereby Tar-water worketh its Effect. And when this Effect or Cure is wrought, the Body of itſelf returneth to its former natural State; and if ſome have been bound in their Bodies, I have known others affected in a contrary Manner upon drinking Tar-water, as it hath happened to operate either in the Shape of a Diaphoretic, or of a gentle opening Medicine. I have even known a coſtive Habit more than once removed by it, and that, when the Caſe was inveterate, and other Methods had failed.

21. I mentioned the foregoing Article, upon calling to mind, that two or three Patients had, for a Time, complained of a binding Quality in Tar-water. I likewiſe remember that one in a high degree of the Scurvy was diſcouraged from the Uſe of Tar-water, by its having cauſed an uneaſy Itching all over his Body. But this was a good Symptom, which ſhewed the peccant Humours to be put in Motion, and in a fair Way of being diſcharged through the Skin.

22. An Humor or Flatus put in Motion, and diſlodged from one Part, often produceth new Pains in ſome other Part; and an efficacious Medicine, as it produceth a Change in the Oeconomy, may be attended with ſome Uneaſineſs, which yet is not to be accounted a Diſtemper, but only an Effect or Symptom of the Cure.

23. The Salts of Tar-water have nothing of the firey and corroſive Nature of lixivial Salts produced by the Incineration of the Subject; they not being fixed Salts, made by the extreme Force of Fire, but volatile Salts, ſuch as pre-exiſted in the Vegetable, and would have aſcended in Smoak, if not prevented by the Sods or Covering of the Billet Piles. This though already hinted in *Siris*, and plain from the Manner of making Tar, I have thought fit to repeat and inculcate, becauſe, if duly attended

tended to, it may obviate Suſpicions about Tar-water, proceeding only from an Ignorance of its Nature.

24. Every Step that I advanced in diſcovering the Virtues of Tar-water, my own Wonder and Surprize increaſed, as much as theirs to whom I mentioned them: Nor could I, without great Variety and Evidence of Facts, ever have been induced to ſuſpect, that, in all Sorts of Ailments whatſoever, it might relieve or cure, which at firſt Sight may ſeem incredible and unaccountable; but on maturer Thought, will perhaps appear to agree with, and follow from the Nature of Things. For it is to be noted, that the general Notion of a Diſeaſe ſeemeth to conſiſt in this: That what is taken in, is not duly aſſimilated by the Force of the Animal Oeconomy; therefore it ſhould ſeem whatever aſſiſts the *Vis Vitæ* may be of general Uſe in all Diſeaſes, enabling Nature either to aſſimilate, or diſcharge all unſubdued Humours or Particles whatſoever. But the Light or Æther detained in the volatile Oil, which impregnates Tar-water, being of the ſame Nature with the Animal Spirit, is an Acceſſion of ſo much Strength to the Conſtitution, which it aſſiſts to aſſimilate or expel whatever is alien or noxious.

FINIS.

An ALPHABETICAL

INDEX or TABLE

Of the ſeveral Diſtempers mentioned in the foregoing

NARRATIVE;

Wherein TAR-WATER hath been found ſucceſsful with References to the Sections, where thoſe Diſtempers are taken Notice of.

Note, The Figures refer to the Sections, and not to the Pages.

A.

AGUE, *Section*, 46. 208. 214. 247.
Aſthma, 33. 69. 71. 89. 90. 99. 108. 112. 130. 145. 146. 152. 153. 154. 155. 181. 188. 196. 221.

B.

Barrenneſs, 241.
Bileous Fever, 274.
Bloody-flux, 102.
Bloody-urine, 280.
Blood from the Lungs, 83.
Boiles, 95.
Bruiſe, 244.

C.

Cancer, 51. 271. 281. 240.
Canker in the Mouth, 98.
Colic, 29. 62. 134. 135. 144. 204.
Cold, 151. 287.
Conſumption, 186. 284.
Contraction of the Bowels, 222.
Coſtiveneſs, 96. 238. 239.
Cramps, 85. 96. 172. 190.
Coughs, 40. 47. 66. 70. 79. 80. 83. 84. 92. 93. 101. 112. 120. 122. 123. 124. 125. 139. 145. 151. 153. 206. 219. 220. 221. 232. 270.

D.

Deafneſs, 96. 201. 223. 237. 276.
Dead Ague, 217.
Decay, 64. 70. 89. 92. 111.

111. 133. 139. 150. 203. 224.
Diabetes, 236. 279.
Difficulty of Breathing, 112. 120. 124. 133. 152. 159. 224.
Disorders of Women in Lying-in, 278. 290.
Dizziness, 50. 110. 129. 273.
Dropsy, 57. 103. 188.
Dry Cough, 105.

E.

Erysipelas, 106. 192.
Excrescence on the Head, 229.

F.

Facies Hippocratica, 99.
Fever, 96. 101. 121. 127. 161. 210. 213. 214. 233. 251. 252. 253. 254. 255. 256.
Fits, 234. 285. 302.
Fluor Albus, 115.
Foul Disorder, 202.

G.

Giddiness, 86.
Gonorrhœa, 112.
Gout, 85. 88. 107. 109. 129. 134. 135. 156. 157. 214. 215. 216. 218. 231. 232. 257. 258. 285.
Gravel, 29. 87. 110. 134. 223. 232. 285. 286.
Green Sickness, 48.

H.

Hardness of the Belly, 157.
Heaving, 86.
Head-ach, 96. 232. 242. 273.
Heart-burn, 98. 172.
Hectic, 83. 99.
Hoarseness, 172. 197.
Hysterics, 94. 97. 147. 283.

I.

Jaundice, 149.
Ill Habit of Body, 207.
Imposthume in the Head, 272.
Incurables, 83. 279.
Inflammation in the Head, 192.
——— in the Leg, 180. 275.
——— in the Lungs, 151. 252.
Inflammatory Disorders, 45. 80.
Itch, 113. 117. 129.

K.

Kings-evil, 136. 137. 177. 178. 179. 211. 225. 326. 327. 328. 329.

L.

Lameness in the Limbs, 191.
Loathing in the Stomach of all Sustenance, 73. 86.
Looseness, 121. 239.
Looseness of the Teeth, 110.
Loss of the Use of the Limbs, 78.
Loss of Complection, 93.
Lowness of Spirits, 46. 84. 100. 129. 149. 150. 228.
Lumbago, 76.
Lumps in the Head, 228.
——— under the Jaws, 127.

M.

Megrim, 96. 142. 273.

Menses, 290.

N.

Nervous Disorders, 62. 87. 94. 115.

Numbness, or tingling in the Legs, 184.

O.

Oppression in the Stomach, 64. 79. 176. 291. 232.

——in the Chest and Heart, 159.

P.

Pains in the Arm, 154.

——in the Back, 134. 172.

——in the Back-sinews, 195.

——in the lower Parts of the Back, 212. 279. 110.

——in the Belly and Hip, 285.

——in the Chest and Body, 224.

——in the Bowels, 104. 135. 147.

——in the inward Parts, 203. 212.

——in the Legs, 189. 227.

——in the Head, 81.

——in the Side, 77. 80. 176. 187. 246. 256. 277. 279.

——in the Stomach, 104. 126.

——in the Limbs, 73. 144.

Palsy, 29. 160.

Paralytic Disorder, 97. 230.

Palpitation of the Heart, 62. 77. 81. 94. 96. 131.

Piles, 29. 212.

Peripneumony, 252.

Pleurisy, 101. 309.

Pleuritic Disorders, 99. 133. 138. 230.

Prolapsus Uteri, 267.

R.

Rheumatism, 29. 100. 118. 143. 222. 226.

Rheumatic Pains, 63. 76. 96. 107. 158. 291.

S.

Shortness of Breath, 77. 120. 122. 123. 221.

Scald Heads, 199.

Sciatica, 107.

Scurff, 185. 235.

Scurvy, and scorbutic Disorders, 29. 40. 63. 67. 73. 82. 91. 95. 96. 97. 103. 113. 140. 159. 175. 181. 185. 204. 205. 219. 235.

Small-pox, 42. 52. 127. 209. 259. 260. 288. 289.

St. *Antony's* Fire, 106.

Spitting of Blood, 80. 111. 145. 200. 269.

Great Spitting, 169. 220.

Spots black, 234.

Sickness in the Stomach, 62. 86.

Spasms, 62. 81.

Sores, outward running, 235.

Sore Leg, 250. 275.

Sore chopped Lips and Nostrils, 287.

Sore Throat, 172. 182. 248.

Sores and Swellings in the Back of Horses, 287.

Sleepiness, 110. 142.

Stiffness in the Limbs, 107.

Stitches, 101. 122. 133. 251. 261.
Strangury, 236.
Streightneſs in the Breaſt, 120. 291.
Stone, 134. 285.
Stupidity, 270.
Sweats, 80. 99.
Sweats in the Night, 83. 111. 129. 133.
Swellings in the Bowels, &c. 47. 68. 103. 153. 157. 158. 189.
Swellings in the Legs, Thighs, &c. 206. 221. 229. 256.
Swooning, 283.

T.

Tenderneſs in the Feet, 85.
Teeth looſe, 98. 110.
Tetter, 245.
Great Thirſt, 119.

U.

Ulcer in the Bladder, 93. 279.
Ulcer in the Lungs, 99.
Ulcer in the Throat, 210.
Ulcers, 103. 179. 183. 186. 193. 194. 202. 211. 212. 225. 243. 250.
Urinary Paſſage in Pain, 280.
Vapours, 228.
Vomiting, 62.

W.

A large Wen, 208.
Wind in the Stomach, 232.
Want of Perſpiration in the Feet, 85.
Want of Appetite, 40. 64. 68. 73. 77. 79. 80. 84. 93. 110. 122. 126. 133. 134. 135. 150. 153. 158. 169. 217. 224. 228. 232.
Want of Sleep, 73. 80. 120. 122. 133. 134. 135. 217. 224. 228.
Want of Complexion, 318.
Tar-water particularly recommended to Seafaring Men, 311.
——to Hoſpitals, Infirmaries, Poor-houſes, &c. 312.
——to Gentlemen in the Country, for the Relief of the Poor, 313.
——to ſedentary Perſons, 314.
——in new and deſperate Caſes, 315.
——for the Murrain among Cattle, 332.
The Opinion of ſome foreign Phyſicians, that Tar-water is not inflaming, 317.

The firſt LETTER *of the Author of* Siris.

Gangrene in the Blood, *Section*, 21.
In what Diſtempers Tar-water is ſucceſful, 23.

The Second LETTER.

Tar-water for Travellers, how made, 2.
The beſt Tar, 3.
Tar-water worketh ſeveral Ways, 6.
Tar-water ſucceſsful in a deſperate Fever, 7.

Tar-

Tar-water a sufficient Cordial, 8.
Strong Spirits destructive, 9.
Tar-water recommended in the most malignant Fevers, 12.
——in dangerous Wounds. 13.
Tar good for Ulcers, Wounds, Tumors, and Coughs, 14.
Tar-water good for Piles, and Fistula, Heaviness in the Head, and Drowsiness, for weak, dry, and itching Eyes, for the Teeth, Gums, sore Throat, and Deafness, and to supply the Want of Nourishment, 15.
Tar-water successful in many Instances in Fevers, 16.
——always gives great Spirits, 17.
Inflammatory acute Disorders, cured by Tar-water, ten Times the Number of any other. No inflaming, or heating Quality in Tar-water, 18.
Tar-water taken for Years, without any Injury, and with much Benefit, 19.
Tar-water sometimes binds, but this is no bad Symptom, but a Sign of Cure; and sometimes removes a costive Habit, 20.
A Humor dislodged from one Part, sometimes produceth an Uneasiness in another, this a Symptom of Cure, 22.
Salts of Tar-water, have nothing of the fiery or corrosive Nature of lixivial Salts, 23.
Tar-water may be of Use in all Ailments by assisting the *Vis Vitæ*, and enabling Nature to assimilate or remove all noxious Humours, 24.